Benjamin Gregory

The holy catholic church, the communion of saints

a discourse delivered at Brunswick Chapel, Newcastle, July 29th, 1873

Benjamin Gregory

The holy catholic church, the communion of saints
a discourse delivered at Brunswick Chapel, Newcastle, July 29th, 1873

ISBN/EAN: 9783744735858

Printed in Europe, USA, Canada, Australia, Japan

Cover: Foto ©Lupo / pixelio.de

More available books at **www.hansebooks.com**

THE HOLY CATHOLIC CHURCH, THE COMMUNION OF SAINTS.

A Discourse,

DELIVERED AT BRUNSWICK CHAPEL, NEWCASTLE,

July 29*th*, 1873,

IN CONNECTION WITH THE ASSEMBLING OF THE

WESLEYAN-METHODIST CONFERENCE.

BEING

THE FOURTH LECTURE ON THE FOUNDATION OF THE

LATE JOHN FERNLEY, ESQ.

WITH NOTES, AND SUPPLEMENTARY ESSAYS ON THE HISTORY OF CHRISTIAN FELLOWSHIP, AND THE ORIGIN OF THE " HIGH CHURCH " AND " BROAD CHURCH " THEORIES.

BY THE REV. BENJAMIN GREGORY.

LONDON:
WESLEYAN CONFERENCE OFFICE,
2, CASTLE-STREET, CITY-ROAD;
SOLD AT 66, PATERNOSTER-ROW.

1873.

PREFACE.

My aim in these pages is to present, clearly and convincingly, the true idea of the Christian Church. I have neither evolved it out of my own consciousness, nor constructed it according to the systems of uninspired men, but have betaken myself directly, and confined myself exclusively, to the only authoritative and trustworthy instructors— Christ and His Apostles; referring to other teachers for confirmation only, as they simply elicit the meaning of the sacred text, or in refutation of unwarrantable interpretations, or exposure of polemical interpolations or manipulations of Holy Writ. This latter part of the work has been the only unpleasant part. If in clearing away arbitrary theories, which have long overlain the yet perfect outline of the Temple of God, I have sometimes shown too much directness and incisiveness, it must be remembered that the task of the excavator is rough work, and that the Divine idea of the Church has lain for ages like some grand temple in the desert, entombed in the sand-drifts of centuries.

A great weight was taken from my mind by a mild complaint in the current *London Quarterly Review*, that the Lecture, as delivered, did not "present more directly the specific Methodist idea of the Church." The one thing which, above all others I dreaded, deprecated and watched against, was the very thing which, it seems, I was expected to do, namely, to give a specific Denominational idea of the Church. This presentation of the specific idea of some particular Denomination has been the fatal flaw of all the ablest books upon the Church, from Belarmine, Hooker, and Field, to M'Neile and Goulburn. If I had understood that to be my duty, I should have declined the task without a moment's hesitation. If my dread of the temptation to handle "the Word of God deceitfully" had not rescued me from perplexing a great subject by one more sectional book upon the Church, my sense of the ludicrous, no doubt abnormally developed, would have stood me, for once, in good stead, by rendering it impossible for me to present the *specific Methodist* idea of the *Catholic* Church!

Whatever coincidence, then, may strike the readers of this book between Methodism and the Divine idea of the Church must be wholly credited to Methodism, and not at all to any special pleading of mine.

I fear that a certain want of artistic compactness may be detected in some parts of the Lecture. This results from the blending of Lecture with exposition; my text presenting, in my judgment, the full Divine idea of the Church. But I hope that the Analysis will lay bare the thread of continuity.

I send forth the Volume with a painful sense of its incompleteness: but I think I have a claim on the clemency of critics as to the literary demerits of my Book (as to any divergences from Scripture I hope no mercy may be shown). The task was laid upon me in a way which to my *feeling* was imperative. The subject was chosen for me, not by me; that subject being the most difficult, the most tampered with, of any in the whole range of theology; and having a vaster vicinage than any other: and it was only by working *overtime* that the order could be met by the date fixed. Methodism has no Canonries; and the office which I have the honour to hold has strained the strength of stronger men than I. It is but fair to add that the incompleteness of the Book is due also to the dread of increasing its bulk. Two supplemetary Essays which I have written I am obliged to suppress for want of room—the one on *Heresy and Schism*, the other on *The Power of Binding and Loosing*. I have also spent much thought on, and collected some material for, an Essay on *Baptism and the Lord's Supper*. If, however, I have been enabled to do anything towards helping any one to say more intelligently and more devoutly, "I believe in the Holy Catholic Church, the Communion of Saints," my toil will be well repaid.

It is right to add, that a fear of presuming too much on the patience of my audience, combined with a sudden attack of indisposition, induced me in the delivery of the Lecture to pass over considerable portions, which in its permanent form it seems right to retain. I regret, however, that I have not thrown into the notes much of what is left in the text.

Stoke Newington,   BENJAMIN GREGORY.
December 16, 1873.

ANALYSIS.

	PAGE
Grandeur of the Divine Idea of the Church	1
Arbitrary human Church-Ideals	2
Fragmentary Truth in All	3
Source of the true Church-Idea	5

SCRIPTURAL CHURCH PRINCIPLES.

I. The Church not a thing of rigid Definition . . . 5
   (1.) Not defined by Christ 6
   (2.) Not formulated by the Apostles 7
   (3.) Simplicity of the conception of the Church . . 8
   (4.) Etymology and original meaning of the word . 9
II. The Church a Definite Community 10
III. The two principles not Incompatible 13
   (1.) The Church at once visible and invisible 13
   (2.) The Mission of the Church 15
IV. The Church, the Body, and the Bride of Christ. . . 17
   (1.) The Spirit of Christ the Soul of the Church . . 21
   (2.) The Church a Family and a City 22
V. The Church a Living and Organic Unity: not a mere Corporation 22
VI. The Church is Shaped by its inherent Life . . . 24
   (1.) Its protoplasm and formative Life-force . . 25
   (2.) Principles and process of organization 26
      (a.) The Advent of the Spirit, the Inauguration of the Church 27
      (b.) The Christian supersedes the Jewish Church 27
VII. The Church is the Organ of the Spirit . . 28
VIII. Differentiation of Function : the Apostolate 29

	PAGE
IX. The Divine Right of Common Sense and Charity: No particular form of Organization prescribed: This Principle Illustrated by "The Acts"	31
(1.) Elasticity of the Framework	33
(2.) The Diaconate called for by an emergency	34
(3.) Officers of Finance must be Spiritual	37
(4.) Spontaneous action of private members	37
(5.) Scriptural Quakerism	39
(6.) Unition of the Churches	41
(7.) Peter no slave of Legality	43
(8.) Incidental initiation of Gentile Churches	44
(9.) Principles rather than Prescriptions	45
(10.) Origin of the Eldership	46
(11.) Apostolic Noninterference	49
(12.) Local Organization	51
X. The Church nevertheless a Law-abiding Society	53
(1.) The Council at Jerusalem	55
(a.) The true Basis of Church Recognition	57
(b.) Unanimity, how attained	59
(c.) Order, Oversight, Subordination essential	60
XI. The Church a Self-edifying Organism	61
(1.) Every Member of the Church a Joint of the Spiritual Supply	61
(2.) "The Effectual Working in the measure of every part"	65
(3.) The Universal Mutual Ministry	67
(4.) Every Member has a Special Gift	71
XII. Hence, the Communion of Saints an Essential of the Church	73
(1.) Fellowship, What is it?	75
(2.) The Four Elements of Church-Life	77
(3.) Obligatoriness of Mutual Edification	79
(4.) Classification of Converts	83
(5.) Close Church-fellowship essential to Compact Church-order	85
(6.) Communication of Faith	87
(7.) Acknowledgment of Good	91
(8.) Mutual Vigilance	93

ANALYSIS.

	PAGE
(9.) The Primitive Lovefeast and its Objects .	94
XIII. The Special Functions of the Ministry	99
(1.) Bishops and Deacons . .	. 99
(2.) The Divine Call	. 101
XIV. Legitimate Constituency of the Church .	. 102
(1.) Terms of Admission	103
(2.) The Church an Association for Moral, Spiritual, and Heavenly purposes	105
(3.) The holiness of the Church not merely hypothetical or corporate, but individual	. 106
(4.) Discipline Essential to the Church	107
(5.) Ministerial and Personal Responsibility for the maintenance of Church-purity	. 107
(6.) Proven Wickedness not to be tolerated	107
(7.) Excommunication and the relation to the Church of the excommunicated	107
(8.) The Church the responsible Guardian of its own morals and reputation . .	. 107
(9.) Binding and Loosing	. 108
(10.) Rights and responsibilities of local churches . . .	108
(11.) Secondary Excommunication	. 109
(12.) Christ-like Intolerance	. 110
(13.) Converse directions examined and weighed . . .	111
(a.) Parable of the Tares: Distinction between the Church and the Kingdom .	. 112
(b.) Servants must not sow Darnel .	. 113
(c.) Ananias and Sapphira .	. 119
(d.) Parable of the Draw-Net .	. 121
(e.) The Final Scrutiny . . .	. 123
(f.) Similitude of the Great House . . .	. 125
(g.) When is Church Secession Guiltless ? .	. 129
(h.) Broad Church theory false	. 131
(i.) Renders the Church "a servant unto tribute" .	133
(j.) Restoration of the Fallen . . .	. 135
(k.) Excommunication a terrible act .	. 137
XV. The Unity of the Church	. 141
(1.) Elements of Unity	. 141

	PAGE
(2.) Where is the Catholic Church?	143
(3.) The Visibility of the Church	145
(4.) The one Spirit makes the one body	149
(5.) Unity, how manifested and maintained	151
(6.) Unity of the Primitive Church	155
(7.) Church Feeling	157
(8.) There is still one body	159
(9.) Sentiment of Historical Continuity	165
(10.) Wherein Historical Continuity consists	167
(11.) Irritability a property of life	169
(12.) "One Lord, one faith"	171
(a.) Doctrinal Basis of the Church	173
(b.) Unitarians not Members of the Church	175
(c.) The Rule of Inclusiveness	177
(13.) "One Baptism"	179
(14.) "One God—in you all"	181
(15.) The Church a Supernatural Society	183
XVI. Relation of the Church to the World	183
(1.) Who are the "Other Gentiles?" Contrast and Antagonism	185
(2.) The Church a Sympathizer	189
(3.) The Church the great Agent of Civilization	191
XVII. The Future of the Church	192
(1.) Unity of the Faith attainable	193
(2.) Manhood of the Church attainable	195
(3.) Impediments to Unity	197
(4.) Winds of Doctrine	199
(5.) Unification not to be effected by Absorption	201
(6.) Denominationalism not Sectarianism	203
(7.) Successionists obstructive to Union	205
(8.) Hopeful Signs	207
Conclusion	210

THE HOLY CATHOLIC CHURCH, THE COMMUNION OF SAINTS.

"THERE is one body, and one Spirit, even as ye are called in one hope of your calling; one Lord, one faith, one baptism, one God and Father of all, who is above all, and through all, and in you all. But unto every one of us is given grace according to the measure of the gift of Christ. Wherefore He saith, When He ascended up on high, He led captivity captive, and gave gifts unto men. . . . . And He gave some, apostles; and some, prophets; and some, evangelists; and some, pastors and teachers; for the perfecting of the saints, for the work of the ministry, for the edifying of the body of Christ: till we all come in the unity of the faith, and of the knowledge of the Son of God, unto a perfect man, unto the measure of the stature of the fulness of Christ: That we henceforth be no more children, tossed to and fro, and carried about with every wind of doctrine, by the sleight of men, and cunning craftiness, whereby they lie in wait to deceive; but speaking the truth in love, may grow up into Him in all things, which is the head, even Christ: from Whom the whole body fitly joined together and compacted by that which every joint supplieth, according to the effectual working in the measure of every part, maketh increase of the body unto the edifying of itself in love. This I say therefore, and testify in the Lord, that ye henceforth walk not as other Gentiles walk, in the vanity of their mind."—Ephesians iv. 4—8, 11—17.

THE Apostle, gazing entranced on the boundlessness of God's love to man, yearns for an ascription of praise which may, at least in infinity of duration, correspond to that illimitable love: " Now unto Him that is able to do exceedingly abundantly above all that we ask or think, according to the power that worketh in us, to Him be glory in the *Church*, by Christ Jesus, world without end." A magnificent conception rises before his mind of a vast association, never to be disbanded, but to stretch in unbroken continuity through the centuries of time and the cycles of eternity; a countless priestly temple-choir which has struck up the anthem of praise to God, never to be ended, never to be intermitted: "Unto Him be glory in the Church, by Christ Jesus, throughout all ages, world without end." *What is this grand association called the Church?* The passage which I have read brings it before us fully; places us in front of the Divine ideal of the Christian Church. But it does more than this, it lays down the working-plan on which the Church is to be constructed. Let us ask, What is the true idea of the Church, and where that true idea is to be sought?

Where must we seek for the true idea of the Church? The question, What is the true idea of the Church? cannot be answered until this preliminary question has received a satisfactory reply. The necessity that the question, *Where* is that true idea to be sought? should take temporary precedence is apparent, inasmuch as many conflicting theories and ideals of the Church are abroad in the world; many unwarrantable theories and arbitrary, fanciful ideals. In glancing at these theories and ideals we must remember that, at present, we are not criticising theories themselves, but the methods by which they are reached. As to the conclusions, all we just now find fault with is, their extreme precariousness, being arrived at by such unsafe processes.

These theories are either adjusted to existing institutions, framed to fit those institutions as they are, not to modify or regulate them; doctrines not moulding institutions, but moulded on institutions, which institutions had been shaped by the endless interaction of human thinkings, fancies, passions, and mundane vicissitudes; dogmas made to prop up overgrown and hollow assumptions, or to lend the semblance of reality to illusive imaginings,—such as the Roman Catholic theory of the Church, which is historically later by many centuries than the Church itself; or hypotheses elaborately constructed to justify and glorify the present actual position of some ecclesiastical corporation, such as the Anglican High Church theory, framed so as to be most advantageous to the pretensions of the existing English Establishment, and least advantageous to all other Christian communities; or theories made to meet the case of a professedly Christian, but in reality, to an awful extent, heathen and infidel people, such as the Broad Church theory, according to which the only heresy is a firm and consistent belief, and the only schism the coming out from the world and being separate; or theories like that of the Society of Friends, originating in a vehement recoil from ecclesiastical exaggerations, affectations, usurpations and restrictions; or theories generated by a hasty dissatisfaction with the actual condition of the Church, such as Novatianism in the early history of the Church, and Plymouth-Brethrenism in our own day; or theories which assume that it is possible by force of external arrangements to recall the past and forestall the future, such as current Irvingism; or political and secular theories, which thrust into the foreground the secondary objects of the Church, subjecting its spiritual to its social mission, its effectiveness as the real civilizer and pacifier; or last of all, theories which captivate the imagination by their poetic or æsthetic charm, but do not command the conscience by Divine authority, — sentimental, antiquarian, philosophic ideals of the Church.

Amidst this seething chaos of opinion where shall we look? To whom shall we go for the true idea of the Church? "Go!" some reply, " Why, go to the Church herself; who so competent as she to tell you what she is?" Now, we will not say that this is a preposterous reply, inasmuch as it is palpably no reply at all: for how can we betake ourselves to the Church to solve any difficulty whatsoever, until we be first certified as to what or which the Church is? For anything that a free-minded inquirer can at the outset allow himself to know, that which most loudly and threateningly announces itself as *the* Church may be a colossal cheat. Where then shall we go for an answer to the question, What is the Church? Surely, to the Divine Founder of the Church Himself, and those whom He expressly commissioned to sketch the working plan, and to lay the first and pattern course of living masonry in this great temple?

Yet, if we should find that not one of the current theories of the Church is altogether false, however wrong the mental methods by which they were arrived at, let us not start or stumble at the discovery. If reverence for Revelation should lead us to re-affirm certain principles embodied or presupposed in various adverse systems, let us not forthwith reject those principles with disgust or dismay. If we should find after all that the Church is an institution, and not a mere ideal; that there is a real historic continuity of the Church, a veritable visibility, an indestructible unity, an infallible infallibility; let us not cry, *That is Popery!* and shake it off as Paul shook off the viper into the fire. If we should find in the Church of Revelation, a spacious, an eager inclusiveness, whether as to the states and stages of the spiritual life, the clearness and comprehensiveness of doctrinal teaching, and the free play of individual tastes and tendencies; a motherly tenderness, a hatred of putting away, a genuine humanitarian element; let us not cry, *That is latitudinarianism!* and flee from it as from the face of a serpent. If we should find withal a sensitive exclusiveness and a simplicity and sociality of sacramental observance; let us not exclaim, *That is Plymouth-Brethrenism!* and dismiss it with a sneer. If we should come upon a lofty, and, to some eyes, a quaint postponement of the form and letter to the power and spirit; let us not say *That is Quakerism!* and pass it on as a thing to be indulged, not recognised. What is there to sadden or alarm, if it should turn out that the true ideal of the Church is not the present speciality of any one particular Christian community or school of theological thought, but that "broken lights" have fallen on us all from the Father of lights; that we have all much to learn from each other, and that there is not one of us but has somewhat to teach. Let us betake ourselves at once to Christ and His Apostles to ascertain the true idea of the Church, free from all the morbid incrustations which have through the ages gathered round it. And having ascertained, and whilst ascertaining, the true idea of the Church from the lips of its Founder and Head, and the pens and the practice of His Apostles, we must resolutely and religiously hold to that idea, not permitting any intellectual pre-occupation or imaginative predilection, or the authority of any post-apostolic teacher, to modify that idea in the slightest, or meddle with it at all; nor must we permit any apprehension of the direction in which any clear Scriptural principle is leading us deter us from pursuing it; for if we allow ourselves to falter in our inquiry, or any merely human figure to come between us and the light, to us the Divine ideal of the Church will be blurred and distorted, and our Church action will be blundering and obstructive at best.

I. We find that the Church is not a thing of rigid definition, and yet is nevertheless a definite community, with a distinct object and reason of existence, with a corporate and confidential fellowship upon plain, precise and peremptory conditions.

In vain we search amongst the sayings of Christ for any definition of His Church. He clearly and decisively foreannounced His Church. He spoke of " My Church," " The Church." He proclaimed Himself the Builder of the Church, and its all-pervading Occupant; He foreshadowed its assailants and its struggles; He guaranteed its invincibility and permanence; He endowed it with inviolable autonomy ; a constitutional, *not arbitrary*, authority over its members, and that on the express ground of His own perpetual presence in its assemblies, whether for worship, fellowship, social prayer, or *discipline* (for He decreed it discipline),—the preservation of its own purity and concord, by the correction of faulty and the exclusion of incorrigible members. He declared, "*I* will build *My* Church, and the gates of hell shall not prevail against it." " If he neglect to hear the Church, let him be unto thee as an heathen man and a publican. Verily I say unto you, Whatsoever ye shall bind on earth shall be bound in heaven; and whatsoever ye shall loose on earth shall be loosed in heaven. . . . *For* where two or three are gathered together in My name, there am I in the midst of them." But nowhere does Christ tell us, in direct, definite terms, what the Church is. The Church was never verbally formulated, either by Christ or His Apostles. The only approach to or substitute for a definition of the Church to be found in the New Testament, is the employment of interchangeable, though not absolutely equivalent expressions. For all practical purposes,—those of charity, mutual recognition and intercommunion, Church purity, distinctiveness, and self-preservation, the synonymous phrases used by St. Paul are amply sufficient. We have from the

Spirit, through him, descriptive designations of the constituent elements of the Church, though not one definition of the Church. These are the following:—"All that in every place call upon the name of Jesus Christ our Lord, both their's and our's." (1 Cor. i. 2.) Is not this an indication of the bounds of the Catholic, the all-comprising Church? "All them that love our Lord Jesus Christ in sincerity" (Eph. vi. 24); "As many as walk according to this rule," namely the rule of living, the habits or habitudes of the "new creature." (Galatians vi. 15, 16.) We have here an indication clear enough for all practical purposes of the rightful and real constituency of the Catholic Church, in plain English, the Church which excludes none that have a right to be included. No Christian community can, without the most egregious violation of the sanctity of language, call itself Catholic, which shuts out any one, much more any company, bearing these Divinely-indicated and Divinely-impressed marks of the true Church. All the other marks or signs of the true Church which have been insisted upon are human after-thoughts, ingeniously invented to suit the invidious claims of some particular form of ecclesiasticism.

And, this absence of express definition of the Church is full of authoritative significance. The reason of this reserve is to be found, not only in the fact that the Bible is not a dictionary, but also in the certainty that the Divinest definition would have been misused, even by the Church itself: and therefore Christ has built His Church,

> "With crystal walls too lucent to behold;
> That none may take the measure of the place."

This, then, is the first Church principle:—*The Church is not a thing of rigid definition.*

But is it not noteworthy that the disciples never asked the Master for an explanation of the meaning of the word *Church*, much less for an authoritative definition of it? To their minds the word carried with it its own meaning; it was luminous with its own significance. All the obscurity and confusion which have gathered about this word result from human efforts to make the Church something else than its Divine Founder and living Head designed, or *will allow* it to be. To the disciples the Church was " no parable." They never said, " Declare unto us this." With them the word seemed to involve as little practical embarrassment as theoretical vagueness. It was plainer than *how to pray*, or else not so necessary to be known. They said eagerly, " Lord, teach us to pray ?" but never, *Lord, show us how to go about the formation of Thy Church?* They understood the Master too well to put such a question. Had He not said, "*I* will build *My* Church"? This was no " hard saying," like the foretelling of His death, which " they understood not, and were afraid to ask Him." It was not even the subject of discussion amongst themselves. We find them " questioning among themselves, what the rising from the dead should mean," but never, *what the Church should mean*. Depend upon it, this much-vexed word *Church* stands for a very simple idea after all—*if our minds were but as simple as the idea !*

How had the word *Church* become to the disciples such an unmistakable household word? *From the Old Testament Scriptures.* The Greek word by which the Evangelists render that which our Lord would employ in speaking the vernacular of His native land is the same which, in the Greek translation of the Old Testament, is given as the equivalent of the Hebrew words which our English Bible renders " congregation." And the Hebrew word most frequently used is singularly equivalent with the Greek word in its root-idea, which is that of a *call*, or summons. The Hebrew word is never used to denote a promiscuous or incidental assemblage, a *crowd* or *concourse*. It always indicates a regular *body*,* and usually a summoned or stated assembly of such individuals *only* as hold the right and privilege thus to assemble, "*whose names are written*" in the public register as the legal constituents of that assembly. So thoroughly was this the case, that "the congregation" *was* the congregation, whether actually congregated or not, inasmuch as initiation and enrolment constituted membership. And in the Greek word, the idea of privilege and consequent *exclusiveness* is the prominent, the essential conception. The Greek ἐκκλησία, which the Christian *Church* chose as its namesake, was a parliament of the free and enrolled citizens, of which the membership, rights, immunities and dignities were most jealously guarded. The mere fact of birth or residence in a city, for however long a time, did not invest a man with membership in the *ecclesia*—the civil church of that city—however rich, learned, influential, *virtuous*, the man might be. Privilege, franchise, distinction, qualification, circumscription, *exclusiveness*, in so far as privilege and distinction necessarily imply exclusion as their counterpart, are of the very essence of

---

* No less an authority than Gesenius gives as a secondary meaning of the word קָהָל " any *assembly* or *multitude*." But the instances which he cites disprove his statement. In all of them but two our translators rightly render the word, " company," " assembly," or " congregation ;" and their arbitrary divergence in those two instances into the translation " multitude " (in the parallel passages they have " company "), lowers and impairs the sense of the original. Gusetius, however (a lexicographer now too much overlooked), says, *ad voc*,—All the various uses and derivatives of this word have respect to *a calling together*—" *Quidquid ad eam pertinet, etc.*"

the Old Testament congregation and the New Testament Church.*

II. This, then, is the second principle at which we have arrived. *The Church is a definite community, with a distinct object and reason of existence; a corporate, confidential fellowship upon plain, precise, peremptory conditions.*

* Etymological and classical meaning of the word ἐκκλησία, as bearing upon its use in the New Testament:

The most frequent sense of the word is the general assembly of the citizens of Athens for purposes of discussion, and in later and better known times, for legislation. The power of the *ecclesia* dates from the Constitution of Solon, but he does not seem to have been its originator. It is probable that every Greek state had its popular assembly, like the *agora* described in Homer.

The term is not, however, confined to the Athenian Assembly. Herodotus (Bk. iii., ch. 142) uses it of a Samian gathering—whether a legal body or a mere public meeting is uncertain. Μαιάνδριος . . . ἐκκλησίην συναγείρας πάντων τῶν ἀστῶν. . . . Cf. Acts xix. 39. ἐν τῇ ἐννόμῳ ἐκκλησίᾳ.

N.B.—Athens, Samos, and Ephesus were all Ionic cities. The name of the similar assembly at Sparta was ἀπέλλα. Cf. Hesychius *ad voc.*

The word itself is connected with the verb καλέω, to call; ἐκκαλέω, to call out, to summon.

ἔκκλησις is used by Polybius (Fr. 44) in the sense of our duelling phrase, "calling out," *i. e.*, challenging. It is also employed for magical evocation. ἐκκλησία is therefore a *summoned* assembly, like the Latin comitia, *calata*, from *calare*. The Latin phrase, *e. g. com. curiata, centuriata,* or *tributa,* means a regular, duly constituted meeting.

ἐκκαλέω simply means to call out, *e.g.* Eurip. Bacchæ, 170. Κάδμον ἐκκάλει δόμων, *evocare*, not *cliere*.

The meaning of the word ἐκκλησία, at Athens was the citizens *assembled by summons*.

ἐκκλησία in the New Testament, being the equivalent for the words translated "congregation" in the Old Testament, doubtless possesses the associations of those words.

The word κλητός is closely connected with ἐκκλησία; wherever it is used in the New Testament, the notion of summoning is prominent, *e. g.* Rom. i. 1. κλητὸς ἀπόστολος. 1 Cor. i. 1. τῇ ἐκκλησίᾳ τοῦ Θεοῦ . . . κλητοῖς ἁγίοις.

It is a primary, and must be a fixed idea with reference to the Church. It is in possession, and must never be dislodged by any process of ejectment or eviction, however plausible or positive. When Christ first made to His disciples the grand announcement, "I will build My *Church*," they never could have understood the word (with which they were perfectly familiar) in any other sense than that of a gloriously privileged community, membership in which must presuppose solemn individual admission after strict scrutiny of claim, to the sensitive exclusion of all who would not submit to the terms of admission; an enrolled order, the members of which have a character to maintain and obligations to fulfil, the wilful or reckless non-fulfilment of which must entail forfeiture of its honours and advantages. No man, Jew or Greek, reading the book of the Acts, and coming upon the word *Church*, given, as it always is, without explanation, could possibly conceive of it otherwise than as a distinct privileged community, corporation, society, fellowship, brotherhood. A promiscuous Church! an indiscriminately inclusive Church! a Church to which any man may challenge admission by virtue of his general respectability, is a flat contradiction in terms, an utterly unthinkable thing.

It may be asked with perfect fairness, Is it not possible to press an etymology too far? Certainly. If the original constitution of the Church, or if the shape it took at the period of its formation, could be proved to be out of keeping with the strict meaning of the word, and out of accordance and analogy with the sense which it confessedly bore at the time when it was adopted as the designation of the Christian brotherhood, then it would be mere muddling pedantry to insist upon its etymology, or even its simple, primary sense.*

* Many ancient writers, however, do insist upon the etymology of the

But is it so? First of all, Christ must have had the highest reason for choosing that word as the sacred and perpetual designation of the new community which He was about to found. *Perpetual* designation, for who could think, who has ever thought of superseding the title which He had chosen? Moreover, if He were using the familiar and already sacred word *Church* in a totally new and arbitrary sense, He would assuredly have appended an explanation. But the disciples, whom He knew too well to be very slow in grasping a new idea, believed that they understood it. He allowed them so to think. Moreover, when St. Luke, moved by the Holy Ghost, records the most salient and significant events in the first period of the Church's history, he too uses the word Church without any direct explanation, simply saying, "The Lord added to the Church." And the indirect explanation supplied by the phrase for which he makes the word *Church* the compendious designation is in exact accordance with the common acceptation of the term, as implying a definite, privileged association around a common centre (that centre being the doctrine of the Apostles), with terms of membership and a recognised basis of union, that basis being *doctrinal.* "They continued steadfast in the Apostles' doctrine and *fellowship.*"

And yet this Gentile word *Ecclesia—Church*, was stamped with a new significance, so expansive and lofty that it became "a new name" for the people of God, "which the mouth of the Lord" did "name." (Isaiah lxii. 2.)

But how are these two primary Church principles to be correlated and reconciled?—I. *The Church is not a thing of*

word as indicative of its meaning: not only the Latin Father, Augustine (Exp. ad Rom.), but the Greek, Clement of Alexandria (Circ A.D. 255, Strom vii. 5, and elsewhere), also Methodius.

rigid definition. II. *The Church is a definite community with a distinct object and reason of existence ; a corporate and confidential fellowship, upon plain, precise, peremptory conditions.*

The seeming incompatibility of these positions will disappear if we bear in mind that the Church is first of all *a spiritual community*, that is, a society of souls, having the profoundest and most vital relations with the invisible and eternal world; and yet is, at the same time an institution, existing in the present world and acting on the present world—the grandest institution of human history. And the members of the Church as a mundane institution are not always numerically and individually identical with the members of the Church as a spiritual community, a society of souls, which is in living communication with the invisible and eternal world. This distinction, between the Church as a spiritual community and the Church as a mundane institution, results from the following facts which will appear in the course of our inquiry.

(1.) From the sovereign prerogatives of the Holy Spirit, the " free Spirit," whose office it is (as we shall presently see) to collect and animate this spiritual community; Who *bloweth where* He *listeth*, and will not be shut in by or shut up to any outward forms or officiations whatsoever.

(2.) From the universality of the Church's mission and the beneficent boundlessness of its invitation, and the authoritative urgency of its summons, so that every form and extreme of moral compulsion is brought to bear upon them that are without, (Parable of the Marriage Feast,) and from the searching sweep of the Church's appliances. (Parable of Draw Net.)

(3.) From the fallibility of the human officials whose function it is to admit into the external fellowship of the Church, upon strict and faithful, yet most delicate and hopeful scrutiny; here and there "one" having a moral attire so like the Wedding Garment that none but "the King" can detect the specious intruder. (Parable of the Wedding Garment.)

(4.) From the stealthy action of the devil, to whose empire the Church is aggressively opposed, who contrives to induce into the Church members of his own party so like the true children of the Church, in some states and stages of their growth, that the eye of the faithful overseers cannot be trusted to discriminate between them. (Parable of the Tares.)

(5.) From the mysterious freedom of the human will and the consequent incalculable developments of human character; so that the good seed which has a promising spring and even a vigourous summer, may yet fail of a fruitful autumn (Parable of the Sower); and through the weakness and unfaithfulness of Church officials, such as the angel of the Church in Pergamos, the holders of corrupt and corrupting doctrine are allowed to remain in the Church (Rev. ii. 14, 15), and the ruling representative of a Church may himself lose the life of God, like the angel of the Church in Sardis. (Rev. iii. 1.)

(6.) The Church, being the administratrix or stewardess of a divine system of healing and help—not the sole consignee of grace, must needs be tender and maternal in its discipline, giving to all its questionable members the benefit of a doubt. (Parable of the Tares.)

(7.) Because the individual believer holds directly on Christ and through Him on the spiritual community,—so that even if separated from the external institution by his own innocent mistake, or by the erring or unjust decisions of the Church authorities, he is still a member of the body of Christ.

We must now look at the Church as a historical institution, a distinct association, a corporate fellowship; and ask

What is the object or what the objects of its existence? These are plainly stated in the New Testament.

(1.) The Church is to be the continuator on earth of Christ's work of invitation, teaching, restoration, sympathy, and consolation;—not of atonement, that He "finished" "by one offering of Himself once for all." With that express exception, it is to be the conscious and subservient instrument in carrying on the work which Christ initiated, "all that Jesus began both to do and teach." (Acts i. 1.) It is to be the organ of His highest action upon the world, and that not only by authorization, but, still more, by the derivation of life from Him, and by the fact that His Spirit is its animating principle. In this, as in other, respects, "the Church is His body." This Christ Himself said, "As My Father hath sent Me, even so send I you." (John xx. 21.) To which announcement correspond the words of the beloved disciples, "As He is, so are we in this world." (1 John iv. 17.) And to this agree the words of the prophet where after speaking in the person of Christ, "The Spirit of the Lord God is upon Me; because the Lord hath anointed Me to preach good tidings unto the meek; He hath sent Me to bind up the brokenhearted, to proclaim liberty to the captives, and the opening of the prison to them that are bound; . . . to comfort all that mourn:" he adds that the comforted mourners in Zion shall in turn take up and carry forward His gracious work on a large scale; "They shall build the old wastes, they shall raise up the former desolations, and they shall repair the waste cities, the desolations of many generations." (Isaiah lxi. 1, 2, 4.) Yes, this work of universal restoration is to be not only the enterprise of the collective Church, but to each living member a personal "work of faith and labour of love," as Christ Himself asserts, "Verily, verily, I say unto you,

He that believeth on Me, the works that I do shall he do also; and greater works than these shall he do; because I go unto My Father." Thus the Church is to be like Him, the great Burden-Bearer and Blessing-Bringer.

Another object of the Church is—to be " the pillar and ground of the truth,"—that is, to give a massive, permanent, stately, graceful, impressive and attractive visibility to the teaching of Christ, to be a living and most lovely embodiment and presentation of His religion, even in its lowliest members—domestic servants, "that they may adorn the doctrine of God our Saviour in all things." (Titus ii. 10.)

The object of the Church, again, is to form a glorious society composed of individuals rescued from the alienation, corruption, and hopelessness of the world, and in process of training for, and assimilation to, the society of heaven, of which society they already form an integral portion.

Another leading object of the Church is to be Christ's embodied host set in array against the marshalled forces of evil, "the gates of hell" which "shall not prevail against it."

And, in the beginning, thus we find it to have been, in fact.

The new-born Church was the organ of Christ. It is impossible to read with one's heart open that blessed book misnamed the Acts of the Apostles (it should be called the Acts of Christ) without incessantly exclaiming, " Lo, Christ is with them always!" Is there anything done of which He is not the Doer? If daily accessions crowd into the Church— Who brings them? "The Lord added to the Church daily." If miracles are wrought—Who works them? The Lord wrought special miracles by the hands of this or that Apostle. If through the preaching of the disciples scattered abroad by persecution, "a great number believed and turned unto the Lord," it was because "the hand of the Lord was with them." And thus it is throughout.* There have been many and very able Lives of Christ written in our time, both by believers and by unbelievers, but they have all in common this one great defect—they terminate with His Ascension; which is, as if any one professing to write the Life of a great King, should suddenly break off at his accession to the throne. The fact is that the history of the Church, or indeed of the World, from the Ascension to the Second Advent, can only be intelligently written as the Life and Times of King Jesus. And this St. Luke clearly intimates at the very opening of the Acts, when he says that in his former treatise,—his Gospel,—his purpose was to give a compendium of "all that Jesus *began*, both to do and teach," implying that in his later treatise, the *Acts*, he proceeds to give an outline of what Jesus went on to do and teach by the agency of His Church.

Although no strict definition of the Church is given in Holy Writ, yet a clear and complete ideal is set forth; and that organization is the best which tends most strongly and securely to the realization of that ideal. The ideal of the Church was not fully realized in the Apostolic times, but is to be realized before the completion of the Church's history. All the church arrangements made by the Holy Spirit, through the Apostles, were made with direct reference to the ultimate attainment of this perfection, "for the perfecting of the saints, for the work of the ministry, for the edifying of the body of Christ: *till* we all come," etc. Let us glance at this ideal of the Church in the various aspects presented to us in the New Testament.

1. "The Church, which is His body, the fulness of Him that

* Baumgarten (Apostolic History), and Wordsworth (Commentary), see this fact clearly and state it forcibly.

filleth all in all." This implies a most real and realizable, sensitive, intimate, living union of Christ with His Church. Each is the complement of the other: they have a mutual consciousness. Christ and His Church are not only mutually related, but also mutually affected. Christ is not the Head of a dead body, but of a living one. The Church is in such wise the body of Christ, that she is also His "fulness." Not only is He her fulness, but she is His fulness. The Church is in a special and most true sense necessary to Christ. A Churchless Christ would be a bodiless Head, even as a Christless Church would be a headless corpse. "This is a great mystery . . . concerning Christ and the Church;" but it is none the less a fact. The Church is the final cause of all Christ's action as Monarch of the universe. He is "Head over all things to the Church." She is to wear the crown matrimonial of heaven, and when He presents her to Himself, His universe shall be her dower, and He will present it to her. Dear as is His creation to His loving heart, His Church is infinitely dearer still. The vital union of Christ with His Church rests on the unity of the individual members of the Church with Christ, as the Source and Sustainer of their spiritual life. This vital union is expressed by Christ Himself as a mutual indwelling and abiding: "Abide in Me and I in you." "He that eateth My flesh, and drinketh My blood, dwelleth in Me, and I in him." He presents this truth to us, not only as a matter of faith, but also of experience: "Ye shall *know* that I am in My Father, and *ye* in *Me* and *I* in *you*."

The Church, in becoming the receptacle of Christ, becomes the fulness of Christ, after the same manner that His "strength is made perfect in weakness." Christ's strength is not only all-sufficing, but in its rich excess, its redundant overflow, would run to waste, unless it could find the helpless to support. It is strength treasured up for His Church, and held in trust for His Church. Thus the Church, as receptive of His Spirit, His peace, His holiness and moral power, becomes His fulness. In it He sees of the travail of His soul and is *satisfied*. He says of His Church, "This is My rest for ever; here will I dwell, for I have desired it." The Church is the Spouse of Christ; His "other self," without whom the Second Man would be, like the first man before the creation of Eve, perfect in himself, but alone, having none to bless, "with kindred consciousness endued." As Eve was of Adam's flesh and bone, so "we are members of" Christ's "body, of His flesh, and of His bones." (Eph. v. 30.) As Eve sprung from Adam's side, so sprung the Church from the side of Christ crucified. Her very substance, her spiritual body, the new, the heaven-born nature of her individual members, is derived from Him and dependent upon Him. The Church is to Christ the realization and the embodiment of His own full idea of spiritual beauty and perfection. The Church is His fulness of restful, blissful, consummate satisfaction, in loving and being loved again. He will present it to Himself in its final completeness, both numerical and spiritual; "not having spot or wrinkle, or any such thing."

To have a Church which He can call His own is His highest conception of bliss, and the reciprocal devotedness of Himself to His Church and of His Church to Himself its profoundest realization. Herein is love! To woo the guilty to reconciliation, the unlovely and unloving, the hateful and the hating to the most sacred, sensitive endearment, to indissoluble oneness; to win the reluctant, the averse, the repellent, by an all-subduing warmth, energy, and persistence of persuasion; and then with nothing but sheer and slow consent, with no dower but debt, to betroth the long-resisting one; and then to educate the untamed and untaught, to beautify the unsightly, to attach the changeful, froward, and perverse; to raise to such a height of loveliness, nobleness and devotedness as shall at last richly repay all the infinite foregoing outlay of sacrifice and sorrow;—*this is love*, which, had it not been revealed from heaven, could never have been dreamed of on earth. What else has history to compare with this? Could philosophy in its proudest moods, could poetry in its boldest flights, attain to this? Nay, what wonder has science that may compete with this? Well may the strongest human intellects eagerly penetrate the mysteries of nature; but "*these* things the angels desire to look into."

"As the bridegroom rejoiceth over the bride, so shall thy God rejoice over thee;" "He will rest in His love, He will joy over thee with singing." In the construction of His own unutterable love, His Church is indispensable to Him, so that the Head cannot say to the body, "I have no need of thee." Every increase of light, love, and holiness which living members of the Church attain is at once a part of Christ's communicated fulness, and an accession to His own complacency and loving delight. His fulness is, as it were, redoubled when His Church is "filled with all the fulness of God." He Whose fulness fills, floods, feasts creation is Himself filled, flooded, feasted with the lovingness and loveworthiness of His Church. It is this boundless ever-expanding receptivity of the Church, corresponding to His own exhaustless and unintermitted communicativeness, which constitutes the Church " the fulness of Him that filleth all in all."

For Christ's Headship of the Church, as the God-man, is not a mere honorary or even a mere official Headship, as the supreme authority in a merely human corporation; it includes the actual communication from Christ to His members of strength, peace, blessedness and purity, in fact, of His own "nature," and a reciprocal consciousness between Him and them.

And not only is the Church the body by whose membership He acts upon the world, and carries on to completion His mission among men, but it is the medium whereby His perfections become most gloriously manifest to the highest order of His creatures—"That *now* unto the principalities and powers in heavenly places might be known by the Church the manifold wisdom of God," and "He *shall* come to be glorified in His saints, and to be admired in all them that believe."

We are also taught *how* Christ animates His body the Church,—even by the communication of His Spirit. And it is this fellowship,—this common participation—of the Spirit (Philippians ii. 1) which constitutes the real, essential oneness of the Church. "There is one body," because there is "one Spirit." It is one body by virtue of that one all-pervading, all-animating Spirit. The *real* Church is the aggregate of human beings who are animated by the Spirit of Christ. It is He who effects their aggregation, He is the Gatherer as well as the Garnisher of the living stones of the temple, and it is He who fills them with life.

The Church, then, is not a mere social organization, institution, or corporation, such as may legally hold property, dependent for its continuous existence on official succession. The body of Christ is far from being absolutely identical with the church which has hitherto been too exclusively the theme of Church-historians. It is a unique social phenomenon, which rests on supernatural facts. No wonder that it is misconceived by the acutest of unspiritual men, especially when so deplorably misrepresented by its unspiritual *attachés*, and hid from view by the poisonous, parasitical growths which have fastened and fattened on its externals.

2. The Church is a *family*, it is "the *household* of faith" (Gal. vi. 10), "the household of God." (Eph. ii. 19.) Its central rite is a family meal: its worship is family worship: family converse is an essential element of its life.

3. The Church is a *city* (Eph. ii. 19), "compact together," "at unity with itself." But this unity by no means necessitates uniformity. What advantage were it to St. Petersburgh that its streets are built at right angles, if that only gave a clear *rake* to the artillery of civil conflict?

4. The Church is represented as a most intimate association of individuals, who, in obedience to the call of God, have *come out from among* those who remain heedless of that call, and who continue *separate* from them. We see that the *internal* relations of a church are of the closest and most endearing character: its members are "yoked together;" they have "fellowship," "communion," "concord," "agreement;" they have "part with" each other; they form "the temple of the living God;" and they are His family by individual reception as the "sons and daughters" of "the Lord Almighty." The utmost capability of language is strained to set forth the living oneness of a Church of the one living God.*

5. Last of all we find the Church to be *an organic unity*, a mutual incorporation so living and intimate as to form, in union with Christ, so to speak, one corporate personality, a new and nobler type of human nature, "one new man." (Eph. ii. 15.) The Apostle, in his glowing descriptions of

---

* See on this subject a paper by the author of this Lecture, entitled, "Personal Holiness *the Great Object of Creed and Church Membership*," in the Wesleyan Methodist Sixpenny Magazine, October, 1870.

the Church as a "commonwealth" (Eph. ii. 12), a "household," a "city," and "one body," had before his view a visible confraternity, an institution of which the world without could take knowledge. And this, by a marvellous anticipation of the discoveries of modern physiological science, he compares to the human body, which he regards as an analogue of Church life, Church structure, and Church function :—" May grow up into Him in all things which is the Head, even Christ: from Whom the whole body fitly joined together and compacted by that which every joint supplieth, according to the effectual working in the measure of every part, maketh increase of the body unto the edifying of itself in love." And let us never forget that this is no mere ideal, but *the working plan on which the Church as an institution is to be formed.*

The first principle implied in this analogy is, that as the self-constructive force of the human body—that by which it *makes increase of itself*—flows from the head; the head being the focus of feeling and force, of sensation and vital energy, to the whole body, every particle being sensitively and effectively connected with it,—so in like manner *Christ is the living Head of the Church,* "from Whom the whole body maketh increase." Christ's Headship of His Church is not a merely titular Headship, any more than the human brain is the merely titular sensorium of the human body. Christ is as actually (and far more actively) the *sensorium* of His Church as the brain is the sensorium of the body. And this, as we have seen, was recognised and realized in the first age of the Church; *as it is this day* in all living churches.

The Church no more needs, can no more do with, a visible, vicarious head, than the body needs, or could bear the encumberance of a visible, vicarious brain.

And Christ is in such wise the Head of His Church, that He is the direct Head of every living member of the Church, even the lowliest and most unofficial, "the weakest believer that hangs upon Him." Hence the Church may not assume to intervene between Him and the individual believer, as the Roman Catholic and High Church theories most unscripturally, preposterously, and irreverently make out. Each individual believer is consciously united with Him, and in immediate and continuous correspondence with Him. "The head of every man is Christ." (1 Cor. xi. 3.) And as "Christ loved the Church, and gave Himself for it," so He "loved *me*, and gave Himself for *me*." Christ is the door to His own sheepfold (John x. 7, 8). Whosoever presumes to *come before* Him, and therefore between Him and His sheep, "the same is a thief and a robber." How often has the self-styled Catholic Church played the part of the fierce harlot in the famous judgment of Solomon, whose "*child died in the night, because she overlaid it!*" (1 Kings iii. 19—26.) How often has she, as if in the stupor of debauch, crushed out by her own pampered weight the young life to which she had given birth? And the murderous eagerness with which she has then invoked the secular sword to cut to pieces the living little ones which were not her own offspring, was the cruelty of vexation and envy, and the ferocious instinct of bereaved maternity.

The second Church principle implied in this similitude is, that *the Church*, like the human body, *is shaped by the life that is in it*. It is an established fact in physiology that the body is fashioned by the life within its embryonic mass—its substance, as the Psalmist terms it (Psa. cxxxix. 15, 16), and that according to a certain type as definite, and an aim as specific, as the ideal form which an artist has before his mind when he works up his material to whatever he may wish to make of it, so that it is "curiously wrought," and its members are "in continuance fashioned" by an inherent life-force, as if copied out of God's "book." The life-force which gives form to a human body works according to a plan quite as directly and steadily as does an architect or a ship-builder. The man-type, which could have no existence but in the mind of God until a man was made, is the programme on which the hidden life-force works. The life-force is an aim-force : and thus it is with Christ's body—the Church.

What, then, is the substance, the protoplasm out of which the Church is formed? and what the life-force that forms it? The formative life-force of the Church is the Spirit of God. The Church is animated, *ensouled*, shaped, actuated by the Spirit. On His advent at the day of Pentecost it started into being. And the substance out of which the Church organism *builds itself up*, by the Divine life within it, is nothing else but a seeking, beseeching, trusting, expecting, receptive soul. You can never make sound, vitalized Church-tissue or Church-fibrine out of anything else. What was the Church of Pentecost but an aggregation of souls pulsing with incipient life? And one of the most striking facts which reveal themselves to the student of the Acts of the Apostles is the close connection everywhere apparent between the spiritual life of the Church and the organization into which it shaped itself. The life must needs manifest itself in some organization, and the organization it actually took was assuredly not accidental, but according to a *law*. But that law was clearly not an outward, but an inward law. The organization of the primitive Church was, like the Priesthood of its Head, "not after the law of a *carnal commandment*, but after the *power* of an *endless life*;" the "*perfect* law of liberty," "the law of faith," "the law of the *Spirit of life* in Christ Jesus." The

Church, being a distinct society, must needs assume some organization: regulation, co-ordination, control, and diversity of office, differentiation of function, are essential not only to the permanence and growth of a society, but to its very existence. But what a wonderful spontaneousness, instinctiveness, extemporaneousness, there was in the shaping of its organization! The Spirit of the Lord was there, and "where the Spirit of the Lord is, there is liberty."

At the time when Christ appropriated to the new community which He was about to found the name which had heretofore belonged to the Jewish people, He implied that His community was to succeed and supersede the ancient Israelitish congregation. But whilst His bodily presence was yet with His disciples, He spoke of His Church as a future erection. He said, "I *will* build My Church." At the time of His ascension the Christian Church was not yet fully constituted. Its chief corner-stone was laid in Zion by the crucifixion and resurrection of Christ; but the structure had not yet commenced. It is true that its nucleus had been formed. In speaking of His Church, Christ addressed those who were already His disciples as the future Church, saying, "Whatsoever *ye shall* bind on earth shall be bound in heaven." He had spoken of it as rudimentally existing, even then, in the little gatherings of His followers, saying, "Wherever two or three *are* met together in My name, there am I in the midst of them." Shortly before His ascension He had given His disciples a universal commission, on the strength of His perpetual presence with them, saying, "Go, teach all nations, baptizing them, etc."; but they had not yet received the endowment which was to make them equal to their work. Hence, after His ascension, when the stupendous undertaking lay before them, their first step was to return; their first duty was to wait—to return to Jerusalem, and to tarry there until their endowment and equipment should arrive. What was that endowment? Whence was it to come? The endowment was " power ;" the source and direction from which it was to come was " from on high." That power was to be a Divine Presence, a Divine Personality—*the Holy Ghost.* Christ's parting direction had been, " Tarry ye in the city of Jerusalem until ye be endued with power from on high :" His parting promise, " Ye shall receive *power after that the Holy Ghost is come upon* you : and ye shall be witnesses unto Me, . . . unto the uttermost part of the earth."

We see, then, how justly the most ancient of the creeds immediately connects the Holy Ghost with the holy Church. The advent of the Comforter was the inauguration of the Church. The Christian Church dates, strictly speaking, from the day of Pentecost. When the Spirit came upon the hundred and twenty disciples, the religious centre was at once transferred from the temple on Mount Moriah to the upper room on Mount Zion. The glory of the Lord which Ezekiel had seen leaving the temple and hovering on " the mountain on the east side of Jerusalem," the Mount of Olives, the Mount of the Ascension, returned to the city, but found a new resting-place ; not now or henceforth on the temple-crowned height of Moriah, but on the upper room in Zion ; most likely the " large upper room " where Christ had eaten His last Passover with His disciples. The three thousand temple-worshippers who were converted on that day were added to the hundred and twenty in the upper room, who, with their three or four hundred brethren and sisters in Galilee, now formed " the Church." And the " great company of the priests " that soon afterwards " were obedient to the faith," exulted to find themselves merged in that royal priesthood whose anointing was the Holy Ghost, whose sacerdotal vestments were ordinary "garments," kept "unspotted from the world," whose liturgical processions were individuals with no distinctive garb, scattered wide over the city, visiting the fatherless and the widows in their affliction, and whose simple ritual was "breaking bread from house to house;" whose dignitaries were the sick poor and " widows indeed."

And when the little Church had received its all-sufficient endowment and equipment, what did they proceed to do? Did they forthwith resolve their prayer-meeting and waiting-meeting into a constituent assembly, and form the upper-room into a council-chamber, and draw up a paper constitution, or sketch a programme or plan of operations? No! nothing of the kind. No pattern had been showed them on the mount. They could not say, like David, when he sketched for Solomon the outline of the temple, "All this the Lord made me understand in writing by His hand upon me, even all the works of this pattern." Such a thought never occurred to them. It would have seemed to them, had it ever been suggested, an act of arrogant unbelief. Had not Christ said, " I will *build My* Church"? Had He not said, "When He, the Spirit of Truth, is come, He shall guide you"? What, then did they begin to do? Begin to *do?* "They began to *speak;*" *every one of them, man or woman, Apostle or private disciple,*—began to praise and to preach. How did they preach? and what? "As the Spirit gave them utterance."

Here then, we have gained another fundamental Church principle, namely, *the Church is the organ of the Spirit,* and that in its *individual members;* that *the Church is a living organism,* called into existence, *created,* shaped, animated, ensouled, actuated, by *the Spirit.* On His advent it starts into being; at His impulse it starts upon its feet! it speaks, with what power!—*as the Spirit gives it utterance.* Before the Spirit came, there was no organization, excepting the most rudimental and embryonic. True, there was the *protoplasm* out of which Church organism builds itself up, or rather is built up by the mysterious, the Divine life within it, communicated and sustained by the Spirit of God. And what, on analysis, do we find that protoplasm to be? We have seen that it is nothing else but a seeking, trusting, beseeching, expecting soul; a voluntary and cordial aggregation of such souls is a Church. Before the Spirit came, the Church was not a clay-Adam, shapely, perfect; coldly and unconsciously awaiting inspiration. It was an embryo, struggling with incipient life. In God's book all its "members were written," which, by the true law of spiritual evolution, in continuance "were fashioned," but "as yet there was none of them."

It is true, again, that the embryo was not altogether formless or featureless. Though the whole substance was homogeneous, there was a very notable differentiation of its component parts. All were disciples, believers; this was a common dignity, compared with which any distinction, however glorious, was very faint. But were "all Apostles?" That this distinction was of the highest importance is plain, inasmuch as the incidental, instinctive, natural filling up of the number of the Twelve was the only step the little body ventured on between the Ascension and the Day of Pentecost. And this distinction was to be perpetual, eternal. They were to have no partners, no successors, but through the ages sit on thrones judging the tribes of Israel. Thus, although the body was perfectly homogeneous,—" they were *all filled* with the Holy Ghost"—and although this individual and universal repleteness with the Spirit was the most significant and vital phenomenon of Pentecost; —establishing the importance and authority of the individual as well as of the collective body,—yet the Church was not a *non-nucleated* mass.

But the Apostolic authority did not check the free development of the Church's life. That which Samuel announced to the newly-anointed Saul was fulfilled in the newly-anointed Church and in each of its members: "The Spirit of the Lord will come upon thee, and thou shalt prophesy, . . . and shalt be turned into another man. And let it be, when these signs are come unto thee, that thou do as occasion serve thee; for God is with thee." And the structural type which the little Church assumed was in exquisite accordance with the personal life of each believer. The disciples, in shaping and settling themselves into an aggregate community, formed, as it were, one compact discipleship. The law of Faith and Grace, in this respect also, corresponded with the law of Nature. As the character of the separate molecules which make up a mass of matter determines the form of crystallization which that mass shall assume, and its mode of crystallizing, so the spiritual instincts and proclivities of the individual members of the little Christian Church in Jerusalem determined the shape which it took as an institution, and the very process by which it was shaped. And this spontaneity, freedom, improvisation, extemporaneousness of organization, did not issue in an amorphous Church, but, in the contrary, in an exquisitely symmetrical Church. For although the individual members, by virtue of their very individuality could not be without angles (as was seen in the dispute about the widows of the Grecians, in which the office of deacon originated), yet the life that was glowing and pulsing in each bosom was the self-same life, "and the multitude of the believers were of *one* heart and one soul;" literally, *to the multitude of the believers there was one heart and soul.*

Moreover from the difference between the mode of address in the Epistles, and that employed in the Revelation of St. John; that of St. John being to the angel of the respective churches, that of St. Paul being either " to the saints," or " to the saints with the bishops and deacons,"—it is plain that the Church-tissue had not, during the lifetime of the majority of the Apostles, assumed a structure which was regarded as too perfect to admit of readjustment.

How great a mistake it is to contend for a Divine right of any particular form of Church-organization or Church-government,—such as the Divine right of Episcopacy, of Presbyterianism, of Independency, or the absolute wrongness of any one or all of them, as the Plymouth Brethren and the Society of Friends would seem to maintain,—becomes more apparent on recognition of the fact, that the original structure of the Church was greatly modified by circumstances and emergencies. Hence no Divine right can be claimed for any particular form of Church-organization or government which does not include the Divine right of readjustment, according to circumstances and emergencies. A Divine right for government in the Church is clear from Scripture (and so it is indeed for government in the State, in fact, it is hard to see how there can be either Church or State without government); but no special form of government, either in State or Church, can challenge any special Divine right. It would be no more absurd to say that because in the days of St. Peter and St. Paul the civilized world was governed by the Emperor of Rome, therefore, a universal empire is the only legitimate form of government, than to assert that, because in the time of the Apostles the organization of the Church took such and such a shape, therefore no other form of Church-government is admissible The only Church-government which can justly claim a

Divine right is the government by sound, practical good sense, mutual compliance, and loving co-operation.

Another cognate fact must never be lost sight of, namely, That no form of organization whatsoever can constitute a community a Christian Church; inasmuch as it is impossible, by any arrangement of particles or persons, to give to the aggregate, or the community, any other character than that of the units, the individuals who go to make up that aggregate. You cannot make people Christians by bare baptism, or by giving them the Lord's Supper, or persuading them to join a Class, or placing them under the authority of a bishop or a presbytery.

Still further, To force upon a Church a perfect organization to which it had not yet grown would not promote its vitality, but, on the contrary, check and ultimately crush its vitality; would not speed its growth, but stunt and stop its growth. Whatever organization does not grow out of and grow with the Church's growth, and spring out of the Church's strength, and strengthen with its strength, must arrest its growth, and compress and cripple its strength. It is a well-known physiological fact, that with living creatures of the highest type, perfection, and so to speak, finality of organism, is inconsistent with rapidity of growth. The details of structure are never completed until growth is at an end. In like manner the framework of the primitive Church in its days of youthful vigour was compliant and expansive. And so of every church. Finality of organization is fatal to growth. The appliances of the early Church were the product of its exigencies and its aptitudes, and these were gradually unfolded. And as the Church multiplied its converts and enlarged its Geographical boundaries, so as to include various nationalities, it modified its forms whilst adhering strictly to original principles and proclivities.

The Lovefeast at Corinth was not made to conform rigidly to the Lovefeast at Jerusalem. And whilst in Christ Jesus there was neither Jew nor Greek, Barbarian nor Scythian, yet nationality was allowed to assert itself against a dead uniformity. Premature ossification dwarfs a man, and cramps a church.

Up to a certain point, structure is not only favourable but necessary to growth, beyond that point it hinders growth. We must not cut away cartilage because it is not yet bone, nor must we in Church-arrangements and appliances reject everything that is rudimental and provisional. To forbid readjustment by decreeing the finality of Church-arrangements, is to repress vitality by retarding growth.

In the State, that is the best Constitution which has grown with the growth of civilization, or rather is itself the growth of civilization; and correspondingly that is the best Church organization which has grown with the expanding life of the Church, which is itself, in fact, the outgrowth of the Church's life. "It is the Spirit that giveth life," God's "free Spirit" must uphold the Church as an institution, as well as the individual believer. All external realization of the Kindom of God must rest on, and result from the inward Kingdom—"righteousness, peace, and joy in the Holy Ghost."

The early Church, having no worldly wants required no worldly wisdom for its guidance. How calmly it awaited, how closely it followed the leadings of the Spirit and of Providence! It was in no haste to cut itself off from the past, nor to obtrude upon the public gaze the transference of the religious centre from the temple to the dwellings of Zion, where the Christians broke bread together, from house to house. The temple was their "daily" teaching-place. They "were all with one accord in Solomon's Porch:" "Peter and John" still "went up together to the temple at the hour of prayer." There was never a formal secession from the Jewish Church. The Apostles were very slow in abandoning the hope of the conversion of the great body of their fellow-countrymen, who had formerly been their fellow-churchmen. When they saw "many thousands" of the dwellers in Jerusalem alone, and among them "a great company of the priests," flocking into the Church of Christ, they might well be hopeful that no chronological chasm should completely break up the historical continuity of the Church of God in the two dispensations. They might well indulge the expectation that the Church of the Old Dispensation would be merged in the Church of the New.*

Hence the essential traits in the self-shaping of the primitive Church are phenomena of evolution. Those very usages which were derivative,—moulded on the model of the synagogue,—were not adopted on deliberation, but taken up, or rather stept into, without conscious imitation.

The like absence of any eager external constructiveness in the Church is evidenced by the mode in which the institution of the office of deacon occurred. At first the distribution of the Church-funds was under the absolute control of the Apostles. But even this was by the voluntary, instinctive act and deed of the members of the new Society. They "*brought* the money and *laid it* at the Apostles' feet,"— that is to say, spontaneously placed their donations under the absolute control of the Apostles, who, for a time, did not decline the responsibility and labour of superintending its

---

* It is impossible not to be reminded here of the bearing of early Methodism towards that church within which it was born. Nor is this a fanciful or delusive historical parallel, but an instance of the working of the same law of the Spirit.

disbursement. But "when the number of the disciples was multiplied," there arose a murmuring of the Grecians against the Hebrews, because their widows were neglected "in the daily ministration." There is nothing in the narrative to awake the suspicion that the Grecians were the victims of anything like intentional neglect. The original word gives the gentlest possible intimation of a slight preference,* and an unconscious partiality towards the Hebrews. The fibres of this root of bitterness grew out of the old Jewish life of the new converts. The Grecians formed a numerous class in Jerusalem, being either the children of an intermarriage between a Jew and a Greek (like Timothy), or (like St. Paul), of Jewish parents settled in a Greek-speaking city, wearing a Greek name, and receiving a Greek as well as a Hebrew education, or else proselytes of heathen parentage. Some jealousy had long existed between the pure Hebrews and these foreign brethren whose minds had been enlarged and enriched by Greek cultivation. The Hebrews proper were apt to look down upon the latter, and called them Grecianists (not Grecians, as in our version), as if they were but half-bred religionists; and these Grecianists, on their part, showed a suspicious sensitiveness to any slight, real or apparent, from their brethren of the Hebrew synagogues. These ancient heart-burnings, though in the newborn Church quenched by the glorious flood-tide of Divine love, were beginning to give forth a smouldering smoke from a little spark struck out from some unwitting preference shown to the Hebrew widows in the daily distribution of Church-monies to the needy members. Doubtless, the misunderstanding arose from the want of due consideration on the one side, and an over-sensitiveness on the other. After all, it was but an undertone of discord, "a murmur-

* παρεθεωρούντο.

ing," not an outcry. The Apostles at once called together the body of the disciples, and requested them to look out from among themselves seven well-spoken men, "full of the Holy Ghost and of wisdom," whom they—the Apostles—might appoint over the distribution of the Church-funds.

What are the principles evolved by this most significant occurrence, besides that spontaneity which we have already noted?

1. Do we not at once recognise the fact, that *there is in the Church no absolutism, but that of a sympathetic and practical good sense, under the guidance of the Holy Ghost?*

The Apostles, as was right and natural, took the initiative. The seven men *looked out by the whole community* were, as their names indicate, all taken from the aggrieved party. This showed that the gangrene of mutual dissatisfaction was only skin deep, and that the community were not unworthy of the confidence which the Apostles placed in them.

2. The Apostles avowedly acted on the principle of a pure and generous expediency, and a sanctified good taste. They simply said, "*It is not reason,*" literally, it is not pleasing, agreeable, grateful, fitting, "that we should leave the word of God and serve tables."

3. Still further, the proposal of the Apostles,—for that it was a *proposal,* and not an *injunction,* is plain from the statement that its adoption by the multitude of the disciples followed on the fact that it "*pleased*" them "all,"—the proposal not only divested the Apostles themselves of a large amount of official power, but also implied that the endowment of the Church with practical wisdom for the management of its temporal affairs, and with grace to use that wisdom in perfect charity, was not confined to the Apostles, but was shared with them by the body of the Church.

We see further, that the Apostolate was the source of

all office in the Church, for they not only took the initiative and devolved the responsibility of nomination and election on the believing multitude, but they reserved the actual appointment in their own hands. *"Look you out men whom we may appoint."* And not only so, but they ordained the nominees of the multitude with their own hands. And surely the right of ratification implies the right of rejection.

4. We also gain another most important and precious principle, namely, that the primal qualification for even a secular function in the Church is to be "full of the Holy Ghost;" and that in Apostolic times officers of finance were inducted by the most solemn ordination, the imposition of the Apostle's hands; so that a portion of the Apostolic authority was communicated to the deacons or stewards of the Church. Moreover, this specialization of labour by the impromptu creation of a new office, to meet a newly discovered want, arising out of the rapid numerical growth of the Community, and its inclusion of elements formerly antagonistic, was a development as natural as it was gracious.

A further notable instance of the dependence of the Church's movements on the indications of Providence, appears in the fact that the evangelization of Judea and Samaria was not the result of an organized aggression, but of a great breaking up, occasioned by persecution. These scattered refugees become at once a band of missionaries. *With no commission from the Apostles or the collective Church,* with no concert; without any authorization whatsoever, but that of the Spirit; they went everywhere preaching the word. The constraint was the commission. What right had these private disciples to preach? "They were all filled with the Holy Ghost." Had affairs been managed according to a well-rounded theory, that could never have happened.

Had the Book of the Acts been written after ecclesiasticism began to develop itself, like a hard cancerous substance, in the bosom of the Church, that would never have been written. For be it remembered, they baptized as well as preached. And how did the Apostles treat these uncommissioned preachers? They were content to follow in their wake. They sent down to Samaria the two foremost of the twelve, Peter and John, to complete the work which Philip, the poor-steward, had begun, by conferring on them miraculous gifts, which Philip, though he possessed them, was not able to communicate.

This was a wonderful step to be taken by private disciples without authorization, without rebuke from the Apostles. For this was something more than prophesying, that is, discoursing loftily under intense spiritual influence, on the wonderful works of God, as the hundred and twenty had done at Pentecost; something more than discussing incidentally with gainsayers, as Stephen had done in Jerusalem. It was preaching, as Peter had done. Is not this unconcerted and humanly uncommissioned assumption of the preaching function by private disciples, at the call of Providence and of the Spirit, a signal instance of the free spontaneous development of the Church? For who but the Spirit, and what but the Providence of God, made Philip the poor-steward Philip the Evangelist?

Unquestionably, on the other hand, there was a something, and that of very high importance, wanting to the churches founded by the unofficial refugees, until the two Apostles came down from Jerusalem to meet that want. And there was some power, which Philip the deacon possessed in a wonderful degree, which he nevertheless was not competent to communicate. What that power was the context enables us to determine with sufficient accuracy. First, it could not be forgiveness, salvation, for that the converts had before the arrival of the Apostles. They had believed, and were baptized, and therefore were saved. Second, that which they received through the Apostolic prayer and imposition of hands was immediately and vividly perceived, even by the most unspiritual observer. It was obviously some striking external effect, some brilliant and influential endowment, such as the shrewd, hard-headed, wrong-hearted, calculating, selfish Simon Magus thought it worth his while to bid for as a means of self-glorification. It was a miracle, which struck the mere natural man at once. Was not this a repetition, in part, of the phenomenon of Pentecost?—a supernatural command of other tongues, and a burning, high-toned, heavenly eloquence of praise, so that men spake with the tongues of angels? We know that this is what occurred at Cæsarea, under Peter's ministration; and so little is God's free Spirit bound by a rigid regularity, that these gifts came upon the first Gentile congregation before baptism.

The importance and necessity of this lesson is shown by the daring and dogged polemical disregard of the striking diversities in the Spirit's operation in these two critical and crucial events. Baronius and the Romanists insist upon the one instance, and Calvin and his partisans insist upon the other, and both alike refuse not only to correlate, but even to allow, any real significance to the complementary event which does not favour, but forbids and rebukes their respective theories.

But some man will say, *This has a very suspicious look of Quakerism.* Very well. Did we not agree at the outset not to distress ourselves—however we might feel momentarily disconcerted—at the discovery that this or that Christian community was not altogether in the wrong? How shocking that such saints as George Fox, William Penn, John

Woolman, Stephen Grellet, Elizabeth Fry, Buxton, Backhouse, George Washington Walker, etc., etc., should after all be found to be partly in the right! The error (I had almost said the heresy) of the Society of Friends, *in the matter of Church-organization* ("If shape that may be called which shape hath none"), is, that they presume to *restrict the freedom of the Spirit*, inasmuch as they will not allow Him to organize if He please, but will insist upon His always acting in an incalculable and inconsequent manner.* Hence the most impassioned rejection of forms has become the baldest, stiffest formalism.

The significance of this Apostolic visit and effective officiation and magnificent display of the "signs of an Apostle," is surely not far to seek. It gave solemn, formal, hearty recognition of the work, and it established a direct connection between these outlying churches in Judea and Samaria, and the mother Church at Jerusalem, and with the Apostles as the centre of the Church. It preserved the unity of the Church, and prevented its becoming a number of isolated, self-centred communities. Does not this prove that in the eyes of the Apostles and the first believers *the avowed practical recognition of the oneness and indivisibility of Christ's Church* is of the highest importance and necessity? The Church had now become a plurality. We forthwith read of "the *churches* throughout all Judea, and Galilee, and Samaria." But it had not thereby ceased to be a unity. These many churches made up one Church.

And the fact that the next stage in the extension of the Church was committed directly by the Spirit to the Deacon-Evangelist Philip is very noteworthy. It is he, not an

* Nevertheless no Christian community is more ready to acknowledge the Spirit's work on the character and in the labours of members of other Denominations.

Apostle, who is commissioned to send the Gospel to the uttermost parts of the earth by converting the Ethiopian treasurer to Christ; who, on his part, waited not for Apostolic officiation, but, believing and being baptized, "went on his way rejoicing," to bear the Gospel to his black-skinned and dark-minded fellow-countrymen, the curse-redeemed children of Ham. This shows that direct Apostolic recognition was not necessary in each individual case. The Deacon-Evangelist proceeds at once to preach the Gospel in the land of the old Philistines.

Beautiful is the picture which is given of the churches of the Holy Land. They "were edified"—built like a house —churches. There was a steady progression in knowledge and force of character, along with a compact unity; for it was *as churches* that they were built up,—"built upon the foundation of the prophets and apostles, Jesus Christ Himself being the chief corner-stone; in Whom all the building, fitly framed together," was *growing unto an holy temple in the Lord: in Whom also* they were "builded together for an habitation of God through the Spirit,"—" and walking in the fear of the Lord, and in the comfort of the Holy Ghost," they "were multiplied." Their being built up as churches is put in the forefront, and their numerical multiplication and local extension is represented as the sequence of their mutual coherence and united progression in knowledge and in love.

The unity of the Palestinian churches with each other and with the Mother-Church at Jerusalem, and the Apostles as its centre, was realized and strengthened by the itinerant superintendency of Peter, who, we are told, "passed through all;" the Apostle, treading in the steps of the Deacon-Evangelist and the preaching refugees, and building on the foundation which they had laid.

The next great advance made—the formation of the first Gentile church—is most markedly under the immediate direction of the Head of the Church Himself. The step which was to initiate such a magnificent series of events, constituting a new epoch in the history of the Church, did not originate in a solemn conclave of the Apostles; it was not the result of deliberation, nor was it the product of the daring enthusiasm of him who had thus far for the most part taken the lead, although always willing to follow. Whilst Peter is on his tour of superintendency, he receives direct instructions from the Master to use his golden key, and "open the door of faith unto the Gentiles." At the summons of a Roman officer he is to sacrifice all his national and religious caste-distinctions and antipathies; and this Jew, who had been called to hold the closest and most confidential "dealings with the Samaritans," is now to enter into the most intimate and endearing relations with the Gentiles. This work is assigned to Peter, not Philip, who must have been in the neighbourhood at the time; to Peter, that it might be fulfilled which was spoken by Christ Himself, "I will give unto thee the keys of the kingdom of heaven."

Yet in the continuous evolution of the Church we cannot but recognise the essential oneness of the work, attesting the Oneness of the Worker, amidst the most beautiful and instructive diversities of adaptation to varying characters and circumstances. An unbroken uniformity of sequence, in the developmental processes by which the Church is extended, testifies to the ever-active superintendence of an intelligent Power, a Divine Personality, Whose energy is throughout the motive force. We see purpose, plan, prevision; but the purpose, plan, prevision is not man's, but God's.

Another exquisite proof that the Church is the empire of Charity and Common Sense, not of overbearing human authority and unelastic routine, occurs on the return of Peter to Jerusalem, after he had laid the foundations of the Gentile Church. He who, on receiving his Lord's command to admit Gentile inquirers into the all-equal fellowship of the Gospel, did not wait to confer even with his brother Apostles; yet when confronted, challenged, and criticised by a certain narrow school of Christian thought within the Church at Jerusalem,—when "they of the circumcision contended with him," as if he had taken an unwarrantable step,— he simply "rehearsed the matter from the beginning, and expounded it unto them" at large, finishing with this appeal, "Inasmuch as God gave unto them the like gifts as unto us who believed on the Lord Jesus Christ, what was I, that I could withstand God?" This utterance at once transformed prejudice into praise. "When they heard these things they held their peace, and glorified God."

The free movement of the Spirit is also clearly seen in the next stage of the Church's progress. Our old friends the fugitives from persecution, had been steadily pushing forward the outposts of the Lord's hosts into heathen lands; into Phœnicia, Syria, and Cyprus, preaching at first, however, only to Jews. But now some of them who by language and education had strong sympathies with the heathen Greeks, begin to preach to them, without any other authorization than that of Peter's example. But the supreme authorization forthwith followed: "The hand of the Lord was with them, and a great number believed and turned to the Lord."

Yet no time is lost in establishing a vital sympathy between these Gentile churches and the Mother Church at Jerusalem, which is still the centre of the Church. Barnabas, not one of the Twelve, is deputed to visit these Gentile churches. He was selected on account of the fact that he too was a man of Cyprus, and was distinguished by benevolence and intense spirituality, qualities which pre-eminently fitted him to form a true estimate of the soundness of the work and the mode in which it should be carried on: " For he was a good (a benevolent) man, full of faith and of the Holy Ghost." He at once recognises in these communities of converted heathens brought to Christ by the uncommissioned and anonymous instrumentality of obscure disciples,—sprung from a Mediterranean island and the coast of Africa—" the grace of God." That was enough for him. He " was glad." He exhorts the new-born souls to steadfast loyalty, joins the band of unofficial preachers in proclaiming Christ to the Gentiles, and then, perceiving that the work of teaching must advance side by side with that of conversion, bethinks him that Saul's native city is not far off, hastens in search of him, brings him to Antioch, where the two devote a year to the building up and extension of a church of Gentile converts.

What a signal and significant instance of *the incidental initiation* of a mighty Church development,—*the first formation of churches of heathen converts who had not passed through the intermediate stage of Judaism.* This bold overleaping, or quiet ignoring, of the whole Old Testament organization, must have seemed to contemporaries not so much an evolution as a revolution, involving a sudden and immense expansion of the mind and heart of the Church, an expansion like that caused by the sudden ignition of a pent-up gas; for it broke down at once the huge and massive middle wall of partition between the Gentile and the Jew. The change was so marked as to arouse the attention of the heathen society around, who saw that this newly-formed community was not merely the latest school of Jewish thought, the most modern of the synagogues, but a new community requiring a new name; an association without a precedent, the Head of which was no human High Priest or Apostle, but *Christ*, for "the disciples were called *Christians* first at Antioch."

Yet the mode in which these Gentile churches showed their sense of oneness with the Mother Church at Jerusalem is very beautiful and touching. Some members of the Church in Jerusalem, endowed with the gift of prophecy, visited Antioch. One of them foretold an approaching universal famine. This calamity was to affect Syria as well as Palestine; themselves as well as their brethren in Judea. But their brethren in the Holy Land would be in greater straits than themselves, by reason of the rage of persecution. The Gentile Christians therefore resolved to make a collection, "every man" giving "according to his ability," and to send relief unto their Judean brethren. Thus the Pentecostal Spirit was at work in Antioch as well as in Jerusalem; amongst the converted heathen as well as the converted Jews.

Here, again, we must pause to note that *the early Churches acted less from prescriptions than from principles, and less from articulated principles than from intuitions.* What a contrast this presents to the capital error of the Church in after ages!

The self-abnegation of the twelve Apostles who were well-content to be left further and further in the background, to "decrease" so long as Christ should "increase," was in accordance with the utter absence of self-conscious egotism in the Church, which sees in its own accessions multitudes added to the *Lord*, and thus records its own conquests: "So mightily grew *the Word of God* and prevailed." Ecclesiasticism was not yet born; for Christianity was not yet carnalized.

Through the journey of Barnabas and Saul to convey the contributions of the Syrian Christians to Jerusalem, we incidentally become aware of a new office, or, at least, a new designation, that of the *Elders*. The contribution is " sent to the *elders*." This indicates some change in the economics of the Church. How this originated, whether by the suggestion of the Holy Spirit, or by the adjustments of experience, we are not told, because it is not necessary for us to know; inasmuch as we have already perceived that the framework of the primitive Church was not rigid and fixed, but compliant and expansive. *The wisdom which is from above* is ingeniously and cautiously constructive, it *dwells with prudence and finds out knowledge of witty inventions*. It is absurd to assume, as some Church-theorists do, that there was nothing preparatory or provisional, or permissive in the structure of the early Church.

Doubtless, the word Elder, like the word Church, was derived from the Hebrew vocabulary; but to what extent and in what respects the eldership of the Christian Church was moulded on the model of, or corresponded with the functions of the eldership of the synagogue, is quite another question. The Church was still Jerusalem, but it was *the New* Jerusalem,—Jerusalem from above, which is "*free*." But the constitution of the synagogue itself was not drawn out by the Divine draughtsman; it was the creation of devout and earnest common sense.*

---

* The fact must not be lost sight of, that the elders, on their first appearance, are represented as invested with a function of the diaconate—the trustee-ship, if not the administration of the Church-funds. Yet the diaconate was not superseded, as we learn from the Epistles. Perhaps the word *elders*, in this stage, simply means authorities, and includes the Apostles and the deacons. We know that the Apostles were also elders. So Peter styles himself "an elder;" we also know that the Apostles were not deacons.

The next great era in the history of the Church—the ordination of Paul and Barnabas by the prophets and teachers of Antioch to carry on missionary operations amongst the heathen, supplies another instance of freedom of Church-action, in supplying another proof that the Apostles did not assume the exclusive right to initiate great movements in the Church. If any of them had formed the preconception that thus it behoved to be, they were soon and very willingly undeceived. They well knew that the Sovereignty in the Church rested not with them, but with the Lord, acting by His Spirit. And if they had for a moment supposed that the Spirit would never originate great Church enterprises, but through them, they quickly found it otherwise. True, they held, and do still, by their writings and example, a veritable and substantive authority in the Church. Spiritually they sat on thrones, judging the tribes of Israel. That is to say, their authority was that of tribe-rulers, and not that of kings. Christ was King, resplendently visible to the eye of faith, though hid from that of flesh. His throne was the central throne, high, and lifted up—and they sat some on His right hand, others on His left hand in His kingdom. Then was brought to pass the saying that is written, "The Lord of Hosts shall reign . . . in Jerusalem, and before His ancients gloriously." (Isaiah xxiv. 23.)

Whensoever, wheresoever, by whomsoever, the Spirit prompted Church-action, and gave it His imprimatur of spiritural success, they at once recognised, reverenced, and rejoiced in His work. By Peter's own confession and appeal an Apostle was nobody, was nothing to countervail the action of the Spirit blowing as He listed. "What was I," he exclaims in the presence of the working Spirit, "that I could withstand God?"

The Apostles, conjointly with the elders of Jerusalem,

formed an appellate court for the settlement of doctrinal disputes, and matters of grave, practical difficulty arising amongst the Jewish or the Gentile churches; by individual letters to the churches the Apostles corrected abuses, denounced error, made authoritative and irreversible pronouncements on all matters of doctrine and morals; insisted upon order, purity, and harmony throughout the churches; exercised visitorial superintendence; broke up partisanship; commanded the exercise of Church-discipline in cases of scandal; and delivered to Satan for the destruction of the flesh, incorrigible offenders. What they preach is Gospel; what they write is law. Their Gospel is never inconsistent, never "yea and nay;" their letters are read to the churches as binding or loosing effectively for ever; and through their letters, which *remain*, their authority in the Church is permanent, stretching through the ages. They have no successors, they can have none, for they still reign. Moreover, they undertook the task of giving form and consistence to infant Christian communities, by deputing extraordinary Church-officers, such as Titus, *to ordain elders and set in order the things that* were *wanting;* and whether in session at Jerusalem, or on circuit among the churches, they formed the bond of Church-unity, and the magnetic pole of Church-sympathy.

But for all this one cannot but be struck by the conspicuous absence of all intermeddling officiality on the part of the Apostles. They were tender of the young life of the churches, as a nursing mother of her first-born. How careful they were not to interfere with the Spirit's action, and not to cramp or chill the rich excess of the Church's life!

Was there, then, in the Apostolic Church no authority, no regulation; no appellate jurisdiction to end all strife; no

Church to "*hear.*" There was all this. There was authority, both local and central;—regulation: all things were to be "done decently," *in fair form*—εὐσχημόνως—"and in order." Wherever there was a church at all, there was "the Church" to hear. But that authority was not a cramping authority, peevishly jealous of its rights; that "fair form" was not stereotyped; it had all the gracefulness of freedom. Authority and regulation formed but a background and base of operations for spontaneity of enterprise and a principle of cohesion for individual adventure and success. We must neither "loose the bands" of spiritual order, nor "bind the sweet influences" of spiritual freedom. What the Apostles did with the results of spontaneous evangelistic action was to lose no time in recognising it and *connecting* it.*

What maternal forbearance and indulgence they showed towards the generous, though sometimes troublesome, vivacity of the Church's childhood! They did not suppress the Corinthian Lovefeasts because of their abuses, or close the meetings for mutual edification because of their irregularities. "A judicious letting alone" formed a large element of their administration. They merely charged themselves with setting in order *the things that were wanting.*

A striking instance of this Apostolic non-interference was the movement to which we have just alluded. A significant mode of expression adopted by St. Luke is lost sight of in our authorized version. He writes, "Now there were in Antioch," *in the church as then existing*, κατὰ τὴν οὖσαν ἐκκλησίαν "certain prophets and teachers" (Acts xiii. 1): that is to say, men whose official duty consisted in the public exercise of these gifts of prophesying and teaching with which they were

* Methodists should be the last to stagger at this, for, on the principle of rigid ecclesiastical routine, how could such a movement as Methodism have originated?

E

endowed, — not elders or deacons, — but prophets and teachers, — *prophets* who under a special afflatus of the Holy Spirit reached a strain of supernatural eloquence in discoursing of the things of God, and were sometimes enabled and moved to foretell future events, and *teachers* who in a quieter and less extraordinary way, expounded and enforced the truth. Whilst these were "ministering," literally, doing public and sacred work, λειτουργόυντων—. officiating as prophets and teachers (not as priests) " ministering to the Lord " by the excitation and instruction of His Church, there came to them an injunction immediately from the Holy Spirit, to separate to an especial service under the Spirit's own direction and empowerment two of their number, Barnabas and Saul. This service was a mission to the Gentiles. Accordingly, the rest of the prophets and teachers, after fasting and prayer, solemnly ordained their two brethren, and bade them God speed.

How instructive is the difference between the course pursued by order of the Spirit and that which a rigid externality would have prescribed! Here the Apostles Barnabas and Saul are ordained by unordained men, and sent forth on a grand Christian enterprise; the eleven surviving Apostles not being consulted in the matter! The outward call and consecration of the Apostle Paul to begin his Apostolical labours amongst the heathen, and the connecting the results of those labours with existing Christianity, were given by neither Apostles, nor elders, not even by deacons or evangelists, but by " prophets and teachers." The Holy Spirit chooses His own instruments, and He chooses them in His own way.*

---

* George Piercy was wise in first offering himself to the Conference and Wesleyan Missionary Committee ; but had they declined his services, he would have had a right to go to China and carry out his commission there as best he could.

But whilst there was such wise and generous care not to check the free growth of the Church, or cramp the young lustihood of its members, or chain down its muscular energy, or repress its spirit of daring enterprise, or restrict the self-unfolding of its resources, yet the necessity of order, government, and authority in the Church, was recognised and acted upon. Paul and Barnabas took care not to leave the new converts in the various cities which they had evangelized during their missionary tour as a mere incoherent and inorganic social aggregation, without internal structure or external symmetry, without any established subordination or centre of control. Christian liberty is not an unregulated liberty; Christian equality is not anarchy, but has its co-ordinating and its co-ordinated portions; its regulative and its operative members. Christian fraternity has its elders and officials. The best instructed among the new converts had been drawn from the synagogue, and had been trained to its orderly but free arrangements. Now they needed support against its persecutions. Most of them had been drawn from heathen communities, and they too had been accustomed to a well-articulated social constitution. They would want a stay against the adverse pressure of the unholy usages and institutions in which they had been brought up. The two Apostles therefore could not leave these believing companies without laying a foundation of Church order and initiating some stable organization. Hence they did not content themselves with "confirming the souls of the disciples, and exhorting them to continue in the faith." They also "ordained for them elders in every church." Without some governmental provision of this kind the bands of disciples could have no solidity or permanence; and without solidity and permanence how could they have growth? The Christian Church is a household, but it presents the picture of a well-managed household, "governed by *system*, because regulated by principle." Lofty as was the dignity and venerable as was the sanctity of the individual, there must be subordination in the community; so *on the summit of Christian equality the Apostles fixed firmly the banner of Christian authority.*

But that the two Apostles made these appointments without the concurrent action of the communities is inconceivable. Had they done so they would have put themselves in opposition to Apostolical precedent, and inverted the procedure of the Twelve at Jerusalem on the ordination of deacons. Besides, the succeeding context of Church history forbids such a supposition. It is an unquestionable fact that in the immediately post-apostolic time the co-operation of the community in the selection of their Bishops was accounted indispensable to the validity of the appointment. And to fancy that popular rights were the outgrowth of episcopal prerogatives is to reverse the whole teaching and tenor of history. But the word employed by St. Luke seems decisive. It means to elect to an office by lifting up of hands, and is accordingly rendered *chosen* in the second Epistle to the Corinthians, where St. Paul informs them that Titus was "chosen of the churches."

Again, the fact must not be overlooked that the ordination of elders took place on a second visit to the respective churches. They were in no hot haste to organize. They left the young societies for a time to partially shape themselves, and to find out the necessity of a more definite shaping. They allowed time for the manifestation of individual character and gifts.

The two Apostles effect a conjunction of the new work with the preceding, by returning to Antioch, *gathering the church together*, and rehearsing " all that God had done by them."

And now we come upon a page of primitive Church History of the highest interest and instructiveness. It shows most strikingly that the early Church was a law-abiding, though not a law-adoring community; that even in its seeming irregularity it was instinctively regular, and that, on the other hand, whatever uniformity it attained was the outbirth of spontaneity. The Garden of the Lord was not laid out in squares and circles; the City of God had not all its streets at right angles. 'T was "nature all." Everything was voluntary, vigorous, and vivacious. And why? Because everything was vital. An exuberant, irrepressible life burst out everywhere. True, the Apostles were the tribe-princes of the Church; but the rod of their rule was not a dry, dead, straight, rigid, polished stick: it bloomed with perennial beauty and vitality; it "budded . . . and bloomed blossoms, and yielded almonds." (Numb. xvii. 8.)

Whilst Paul and Barnabas were labouring at Antioch, on their return from their missionary tour, a terrible peril assaulted the Gentile churches. That movement was set on foot which, although repulsed for a while, was in after ages so fatally successful, and in our times is still in full and deadly force; namely, the attempt to confine the grace of Christ to certain external channels. "Certain men which came down from Judea taught the brethren, . . . Except ye be circumcised after the manner of Moses, ye cannot be saved. When therefore Paul and Barnabas had no small discussion and disputation with them, they" (the brethren at Antioch) "determined that Paul and Barnabas, and certain other of them, should go up to Jerusalem unto the Apostles and elders, about this question." (Acts xv. 1, 2.) In the first place, Paul and Barnabas, and the rest of the church at Antioch, heard patiently and candidly what these preachers of circumcision had to say. They attempted to settle the question by free and full discussion and debate before they made any appeal to authority. Second, Thorough ventilation and investigation of the point in dispute failing to secure unanimity, the church of Antioch sent a deputation to Jerusalem, consisting of the two Apostles and "certain other" less distinguished of their brotherhood, to consult with the eleven Apostles and the elders of the Mother-church "about this question." The two Apostles and their colleagues went to Jerusalem as delegates of the church of Antioch, having received their instructions, as well as their commission, from the whole body of the brethren. Third, The deputation were directed to submit the question in dispute, not to the Apostles alone, but to the Apostles and the elders, as co-assessors. Fourth, This act involved a recognition, on the part of the church in Antioch of the Apostles and elders in Jerusalem as the centre of Church unity and Church authority, as a Divinely provided and Divinely empowered Court of arbitration and appeal. Fifth, The reception of the Antiochian delegates at Jerusalem was given by the whole Church under the presidency of the Apostles and the elders: "They were received of the Church and the Apostles and the elders." Sixth, The delegates did *not* lay the matter about which they had come before *this general Church-gathering*, which was only *a meeting of recognition*. They confined themselves to a narration of the success of the Gospel amongst the Gentiles. But some members of the Church, who before their conversion had been Pharisees, rose and introduced the question, taking up a decisive position in favour of the partisans of circumcision. They were not put down either by authority or clamour; but allowed to state their opinion. Seventh, The question was *not* determined in this *general Church meeting*, before which indeed the delegates had not stated the question, but where it had been introduced by the eagerness of the Ex-Pharisees. Eighth, The questions were next discussed by the *Apostles and elders*, at a *subsequent* meeting, in which no other members of the Church took part, although they seem to have been present as hearers. Ninth, The matter was thoroughly and vigorously discussed, right and left, with "much disputing," and was determined at last, not by authority, but by argument. Tenth, The decision of the Apostles and elders was then reported to "the whole Church," who adopted it and became parties to the decision. "Then pleased it the Apostles and elders, *with the whole Church*, to send chosen men of their own company" along with the returning delegates to Antioch; and the decisive document begins thus: "The Apostles, and elders, and *brethren*," and these three estates of the Church conjoin in one compact *we*, and sum up at last in this style,—" It seemed good to the Holy Ghost, and to *us*, to lay upon you no greater burden than these necessary things." Eleventh, The *whole Church* at Jerusalem regarded itself as exercising in this matter the power of binding and loosing, of laying on a " necessary " burden, and taking off an unnecessary one; and the churches of the Gentiles viewed the matter in the same light.

That was the way they managed the most critical matters in the primitive Church. Everywhere we find freedom and force of thought and sentiment; and indulgence for the sideplay and the underplay of opinion and of prejudice. Apostolic inspiration did not overawe or supersede deliberation. The body of the Church was not treated as in a state of everlasting nonage. The Church was under the reign of law, but it was the law of liberty and love. Decisions were arrived at by the frank and cordial coalition of all the component parts of the Church. The Apostles did not act as an absolute

Directory or correctional police. The conclusive pronouncement of the Holy Ghost came through "the whole Church," differentiated as to office, but still "one body," animated by "one spirit." There was no crushing or cramping centralization; no absorption of the mind or the will of the Church in one absolute corporation; no annihilation of local self-impulsion. There was no congestion; on the contrary there was the freest circulation through every part of the system. The Church was alive all over. There was no torpor at the geographical extremities of the Church. The Gentile Antioch was one with Jerusalem, and Jerusalem was one with Antioch.

And in the Apostolic Synod argument was not based on authority; but, contrariwise, authority was enthroned on argument. Nay, rather, here argument and authority met together, Divine guidance and human good-sense did kiss each other. A spark from "the Fountain of light" lit up the lamp of honest insight: *in God's light they did see light.*

And what a consciousness that the Holy Ghost was with them and they with Him, what a sense of their own simplicity and godly sincerity spoke in the solemn style, "It seemed good unto the *Holy Ghost* and *to us!*" What a confidence in His patience with their personal prejudices inspired them with mutual forbearance, mutual confidence, mutual deference! They knew that the Spirit would pilot them into port even through the swelling surf and the conflicting currents of debate. Had not Apostles, Elders, and Brethren all knelt together and implored direction, assurance, unanimity? They were all alike seekers and scholars. They *called no man Master:* yet they were not Masterless; One was their *Master even Christ.* Here was no human domination either of crown or crowd. Here was no *voting by orders,* but an absolute deliberative equality;

here was nothing of democracy, and if possible, still less of absolutism or hierarchical pretension. The tone and accent of a studied or rather an instinctive moderation pervade the only two recorded speeches, those of Peter and James. A gentle and convincing light fills the place where they are sitting. Everything finds its exquisite equilibrium. That the debate had been animated, and attended by much *movement* on the part of the unofficial brethren, who, if they did not join in the discussion, gave vocal indication of their assent or dissent, is graphically indicated by the description of the effect of Peter's speech, " *Then all the multitude kept silence.*" The sum of Peter's speech is this: *God's Church is bound in spite of all personal predilections and preconceptions to accept God's own action as authoritative and conclusive. If the work of the Spirit in the world proves to be contrary to our Church-theories then our Church-theories are wrong, and must be corrected into accordance with the action of God. God has made no difference between the uncircumcised believers and the circumcised. He has purified their hearts by faith as well as ours. The correspondence between their heart-experience and ours is decisive of the whole question.* What a grand axiom is this—*the very charter and criterion of true catholicity!* Had this axiom been kept in view, bigotry could never have obtained foothold in the Church of Christ. *A universal re-affirmation of and recurrence to this principle is all that is needed to terminate the mutual unchurching of all true Christians.* I, for one, do most solemnly re-affirm it: *Heart-experience, shown in character, is the true basis of Church-recognition.*

The most unchurchly aberration from Apostolic Church-principles into which the Church can fall is to unchurch any to whom God has borne witness by stamping His seal upon their consciences and their characters. This, as St. Peter puts it, is essentially a perpetration of that terrible crime of tempting God—("Now therefore why tempt ye God? Ver. 10)—that is to say, dictating to Him as to what should be His course of procedure, and refusing to recognise His divinest action—that upon the human heart and character—unless it accords with our Church-theories. This is to place the Church in opposition to the Spirit; the Spirit witnessing to a fact, and the Church contradicting it; the Spirit conferring present and patent salvation on multitudes who have not passed through certain rites; and the Church avowing that unless you pass through those rites you cannot be saved! Peter, in effect, says, *We are the Church of God, are we not? Of God? Well; a work is wrought upon the hearts of these uncircumcised believers which God alone could work. If it were the Church's work to purify the heart, it might be competent to us, though not very charitable, to decree, There shall be no circumcision of the heart without circumcision of the flesh. But this is God's work, and not that of the Church. You, estimable brethren, who, when you became Christians, did not cease to be Pharisees, say, " But God has made circumcision necessary to salvation." " Why tempt ye God?" Do you not see that this is attempting to place the Omniscient in a dilemma, setting His Word against His Work? You have misread His Word: Go back, and read His Word by the light of His Work, and note well this text, " Thou shalt not tempt the Lord thy God."*

Re-read God's Word by the light of His Work:—That is just what St. James does in the speech which decided the whole matter. He shows that the discrepancy was not between the Work and the Word, but between the Work of God and a narrow, hasty, superficial, one-eyed mis-interpretation of the Word. And in this perfect unison between the Word and the Work of God, he sees the basis of union between the church of Antioch and that of Jerusalem, the churches of the Gentiles and the churches of the Jews. And this is the true and only firm foundation for a re-united Christendom. The kernel of St. James's argument lies in these words: "Saith the Lord that *doeth these* things." *Jehovah the Doer* is the Expositor of *Jehovah the Speaker*. On this broad, deep, strong principle was a decision based which was to affect the destinies of the Church to the end of time. It is idle then to quote isolated passages of Scripture in defence of Church-theories which are belied by the facts of history and of existing society.

Thus then was guaranteed to the Gentile churches an unrestricted and inviolable freedom of self-evolution and self-shaping. *Non-interference on questions of ceremonial* is decreed. St. James's "sentence is—that *we* trouble not them." What he above all things dreads is a meddling dictation which might impair or impede the Work of God amongst the Gentiles, and harass or hamper the workers. And yet this self-same decree effects the thorough unification of the Gentile and the Jewish churches.

The absolute unanimity with which this decision was arrived at was felt to be the work of the Holy Spirit. He had made "*men to be of one mind in an house.*" When they assembled there was wide divergence of opinion and keen contrariety of sentiment; before they parted they could say, "It seemed good to us *having become unanimous*" γινομένοις ὁμοθυμαδὸν. This was no Popish unanimity: it involved no suppression or dissembling of personal conviction; no abdication of individuality, or abandonment of Christian liberty and independence of thought. It was not a mere outward, surface, make-believe agreement. It was an honest, natural, *ex animo* concurrence of sentiment and judgment.

And the decision arrived at was regarded as authoritative,

definitive, decisive. Paul and Silas in the visitation of the churches of Asia Minor deliver them "*the decrees for to keep*, which were ordained of the Apostles and elders which were at Jerusalem." This did not at all imply the domination of the church of Jerusalem, over the church of Antioch and the other Gentile churches, for it was really the decision of the church of Antioch as of that of Jerusalem. For the Antiochian delegates were integral parts of the synod, and parties to the decision. So clearly was this the case, that Paul and Barnabas become now a moiety of the delegation from Jerusalem to Antioch; that delegation being the Apostles Paul and Barnabas, and the prophets Judas and Silas, "chief men among the brethren." (Ver. 22.) Paul and Barnabas were, in fact, members and representatives of both the churches, or rather, they represented the oneness of the twain who were in Christ, Himself " of twain one new man; so making peace." Thus love was the limiter of liberty, and the Holy Ghost Himself was the Harmonizer of opposite tendencies of thought.

It should also be borne in mind that this decree of the Council of Jerusalem, whilst it established the liberty of the Gentile churches, also regulated that liberty; and whilst it removed obstacles to progression for the future, it also established a harmonious connection between the new era and the past; in other words, maintained the historical continuity of the Church, and prevented its squandering the "holy legacy of a Divine post." To assert that this first great Christian Council was a normal Council might be saying too much; but assuredly it is a most luminously exemplary Council.

As we trace the further unfolding of the Church, we find it still to be richly natural, and yet accomplished by the most real and effective Headship of Christ through His ever-present Spirit. The Apostles still reverently adjust their formative action to that of the constructive Spirit. As we watch the germination of the living Word into the living Church, we see that " *God giveth it a body as it hath pleased Him, and to every seed its own body.*" We mark a refreshing individuality amidst essential sameness. The Spirit of God moves upon the primordia of the Church, and gives it configuration and Kosmic beauty. Thus that which became a universal Church-institution, the Eldership, is said by St. Paul to be, as to the selection of the individual members of the order, and therefore *a fortiori* of the origination of the order itself—the Spirit's act and deed. He tells the Ephesian elders that the *Holy Ghost has made* them "overseers over the Church of God." The Apostles by ordaining elders in every Church did, so to speak, decree *order* and *oversight*, and consequently *subordination*, as essentials in the Church.

III. The third principle implied in St. Paul's analogy between the human body and the Church is, that *the Church, like the human body, is built up of individual living particles; the members of the Church, like the particles of the body, being all homogeneous and related structures, and not unrelated atoms —as in some inorganic mass: and that, as each particle of the body contributes to the growth of the body, so every member of the Church is bound to be a "joint of supply,"* by which the growth of the whole Church, in knowledge, faith, love, holiness, in one word, spiritual manliness, is advanced: a joint as of the spinal column, "full of marrow," and replenished with nerve-force from the Living Head: " The Head, even Christ : from Whom the whole body fitly joined together, and compacted by that which every joint supplieth, according to the effectual working in the measure of every part, maketh increase of the body unto the edifying of itself in love." There is no little difficulty if not in ascertaining the exact meaning of the word ἀφῆς—rendered "joint" yet in giving it a precise and adequate translation. This results from the variety, breadth and subtlety of signification in which the word is used by Classical writers. Sometimes it means *joint;* sometimes a joining or meeting of two or more ends; sometimes *touch;* sometimes *grasp;* sometimes *feeling, sensation—perception, sense;* sometimes *function.* (See the lexicographers generally.) We shall not give the word its due force in this passage, shall not bring it up to the level of the context, unless we combine the five ideas—*joining, touch, grasp, sensation* or *perception, function*—in one; or rather take in the fivefold idea at once. It is clear that the word does not here mean precisely and exclusively "joint," in the ordinary sense, " *the articulation where a bone meets a bone.*" * It is not the word used in the New Testament with that meaning (ἁρμός Heb. iv. 12). Besides, to give it that meaning here would involve tautology, the word *joint* being included in the participle "joined" literally, *jointed together.*† It is a much more generic and inclusive term, and is used here to cover the "joints and *bands,*"—ligaments of the parallel passage (Colos. ii. 10). Hence "joining" (*Vulgate, junctura*), is a preferable rendering to "joint," and perhaps *coupling* better still. Bengel very strikingly translates—"every handle for mutual help,"—" *ansæ ad mutuum auxilium.*" *Handling* would be nearer the mark, according to his illustration of the classical use of the word. Alford (*ad loc*) says,—"The joints are the points of union where the supply passes to the different members, and by means of which the body derives the supply by which it grows." But the joints, in the popular meaning of the term, are not the only " points of union, by means of which the

* Johnson. † συναρμολογούμενον.

supply passes to the different members, and by means of which it grows : " else what would become of those parts of the body which are connected otherwise than by joints? If Alford means that the word here includes *all* " the points of union by means of which the supply passes, etc.," he is right. It would be hazardous to pronounce positively what the Pauline Physiology precisely was : * but the ideas of absolute individuality, on the one hand, and of sympathetic and effective connectedness, on the other, in the living particles which compose the body and the living members which compose the Church, are clearly and strongly expressed. This then is the practical point of the passage.

That the word means here much more than "joint" has been perceived, with more or less clearness, by all the ablest expositors. The Greek commentators, Chrysostom, Theodoret, with Meyer make it mean perception ($αἴσθησις$) or consciousness: "the perception of the vital energy imparted from the head." But Zanchius and Macknight have shown the deepest insight into the passage. The former says,—"The whole body makes increase so far only as it remains conjoined with Christ and with its individual members. $ἁφή$ signifies, First, the ligaments, nerves, and veins, by which the members are joined together amongst themselves, and at the same time connected with the head : Second, the actual mutual contact and cohesion of the various parts of the body. *Joinings of supply*, to be taken *actively*, because by them the vital spirit and

* To what extent the physiological principles laid down by St. Paul were in accordance with, or in advance of, his age, I have not been able to discover. But that Hippolytus (Circ. A.D. 200) held that the head is the focus of life appears incidentally from a remarkable passage in his *Refutation of All Heresies* (Bk. iv., chap. 51). "The brain . . . the whole frame participates in the spiritual energy."

nutriment are subministered as from the Head to each member, so by the members to each other reciprocally. *According to the effectual working of each member;* by which the gifts received are not kept buried, but each communicates to the others." (*Eatenus totum corpus,* etc.) Again " Grow up *into* Him " signifies, not local but spiritual motion. That is, he who grows up into Him, tends to Him as his consummation, and becomes ever more and more incorporated with Christ like to Him, one with Him. The accusative here has great force (Motuum, etc.)*

In the human body, the sensitive, vital energy, is transfused and interfused through every particle—molecule—vesicle of the entire tissue of the body. It is not merely *di*ffused, as if each part of the whole mass were independent of the rest and non-essential to the rest for its vitalization and growth, but the life-force passes from the head to every particle and through every particle to the rest: so that a devitalization or degeneration of any one vesicle of the entire tissue would entail an arrest or diminution of supply to the other vesicles; and a degradation of any portion of the tissue of a living body, involving a lessening of the energy and lowering of the function of that part, impedes, to that extent, the growth of the body, and to that extent depresses its tone. Every particle or vesicle of the human body is a " joint of supply " to the rest; in other words, forms an integral part of the system of supply from the head downwards, by which the vitality and power of growth of " the whole body " is sustained; so that each vesicle is a feeder as well as a sucker. If any vesicle were to be continually absorbing nutriment,

---

* So Grotius: " Christ in the Church discharges the functions both of the head and of the heart: whence both the blood are the spirits, by *many interconnected channels,* are conveyed even to the extremities, and supply increase to each." (Christus in Ecclesia, etc.)

and never giving it out or passing it on, that vesicle would become congested and diseased.

We are distinctly taught by the Spirit of God that mutual cohesion, mental and spiritual contact, sympathy and interdependence between the members which compose the Church, are as essential to the healthiness, vigour, and integrity of the Church as are mutual cohesion, sympathy, and interdependence amongst the particles that compose a human body to the healthiness, vigour, and integrity of that body. In short, all that has been affirmed of the particles of a healthy body may with equal truth be affirmed of the members of the Church when in its normal state; when it is as it ought to be, as it is to be, and as it is the urgent duty of every member of the Church to strive to make it. The Church is not a low invertebrate type of organization, but is as exquisitely articulated as it is intensely vitalized.

IV. The fourth principle implied in this analogy is that, as the growth of the body is in proportion to the "effectual working," the active and effective energy "in the measure of every part," even so the real growth of the Church is in proportion to the "effectual working,"—the active and effective energy "in the measure of every one of its members." In a healthy body there is an incessant activity in all its component particles,—an "effectual working in the measure of every part." There is in every vesicle a teeming faculty of growth, so that, if one may so speak, the right and the responsibility of growth is shared by every particle of the entire mass; each particle being a life-point. Thus the body, though not self-created, is self-built up by the continuous utilization of the life-force communicated from the head to each individual particle. The body is built up of rings—zones—which are united and nourished by what modern physiologists term "commissural growths,"—joining growths,

—(the very idea of the text); each vesicle budding towards its neighbour. Thus the whole body is made up of *budding* particles, closely related to each other, and formed into a unity of mass by the unity of a common and intercommunicated life; each particle being at once a depository and a distributary of the vital force.

And what, according to the teaching of the Spirit of God, are the analagous facts which constitute the Church of Christ, not only in the Divine idea, but also *in its normal state*, as real an organic unity as is the living body of a man?

Why, that there is in every living member of the Church a teeming faculty of growth: every living member is charged with grace—*charged* in a double sense—with stored-up spiritual energy, communicated from Christ, "the Head," for the benefit of his fellow-members as well as of himself. Hence if any member of the Church wilfully presume to absorb spiritual nutriment without contributing directly to the edification of others, that member inevitably becomes morbid and congested.

In the human body, the nutritive process, that by which the body "maketh increase to the building up of itself" in the mutual sympathy of its parts,—depends upon and is carried out, not by one organ only, but by the vital powers of its several particles. The body is built up by the living force, and out of the living matter which the individual particles contain. The binding force which makes it "one body," and the building force which makes it grow inheres —it is one force—in every particle of which the body is composed. Not only does a devitalization or degeneration of any member of the Church entail on the other members an arrest or diminution of supply, but sluggishness or self-containedness in any member inflicts an incalculable loss, and perpetrates an irreparable wrong on all the rest; inasmuch as it, to a very serious extent, impedes the growth and depresses the spiritual tone of the Church. Every individual member of the Church forms an integral part of the system of spiritual supply. Each member is required to be, both a depository and a distributary of light, faith, love, energy. We must all be "vessels, *instruments* of grace." The official ministry of Apostles, prophets, evangelists, pastors, and teachers, is not intended to supersede, nor even to supplement, but to set agoing, to direct and keep in full operation, the individual and universal ministry, which belongs inalienably to all and every member. Christ "gave some Apostles," etc. (Ver. 12), "for the perfecting of the saints for the work of the ministry,"—that separating comma has no business here; it diverts and distorts the sense.* At any rate one may boldly say that the natural and straightforward translation is—"for the perfecting of the saints to work of ministry or ministration,—πρὸς τὸν καταρτισμὸν τῶν ἁγίων εἰς ἔργον διακονίας. Nothing but the incapacity for making sense of the words, if rendered according to their simple and obvious meaning, an incapacity resulting from its contrariety to ecclesiastical usages and ideas,—caused the deflection of translators to a barely admissible and most unlikely alternative rendering. The words are clear enough, if translators and expositors would let them speak for themselves. It is the starting at the plain meaning of the words which has driven exegesis into such pitiable embarrassment.† The direct rendering of the passage is in detail: πρὸς—Towards,

---

* It is omitted in most editions of the Greek Testament. Scrivener omits it, and gives no various reading. Ellicott and Valpy omit it from the text, and insert it in the translation.

† For example, Ellicott might have been saved his dubious, hesitating, complicated, and somewhat perplexed note, had he not either shrunk instinctively from the simple significance of the passage, or failed to realize the idea of the text in actual working.

unto, for this end, viz.,—τόν καταρτισμόν—the perfecting, the fully-fitting of the saints—εἰς, unto ἔργον διακονίας—work of ministration (neither of the two "thes" is in the original), that is, effective and useful function (1 Tim. iii. 1) in the Church, in one department or another, according to the special grace-gift of the individual, in its Divinely designed and Divinely dispensed adaptation to the particular needs of the Church. To what ministerial work? *Unto*—εἰς—"the building up of the body of Christ," the advancement of the whole Church to a symmetrical spiritual completeness, its steady progress towards perfect holiness and love. Each of us has a benign duty to fulfil, and a blessed destiny to realize, in the building up of the Church, which nothing but one's own unfaithfulness or the wasteful malconstruction or maladministration of our Church-systems can defeat. The Church is self-built up by the active utilization of the lifeforce communicated from the Head to each individual member. It is " compacted by," literally *through*—διά—through in both senses—intermediately and instrumentally—every member.

According to, that is *in proportion to*, and as the result of κατά—" the effectual working in the measure of every part." In the ideal Church, the potential Church, and according to the plan on which we ought all to be working, " the whole body maketh increase of the body," by a system of mutual ministration,—the productive employment " of the manifold grace of God " distributed by Christ Himself to each one of His members. Reciprocal sustentation is a fundamental law in the sacred physiology of Christ's body the Church.*

* The reasons why this text has been so difficult of interpretation to commentators, as Matthew Pole says, "*locus difficilis*," are, First, its anticipation of modern physiological discovery; even the clear-headed Grotius being somewhat perplexed by its divergence from the physiology of his time: and Second, the fact that all their existing Church arrangements, with one exception, which did not come into existence till about

No living member of Christ's Church is without his speciality. Each is able, and each is under obligation; every one can, and every one is bound to contribute his share to the edification of the Church. Whilst all have an infinitude in common, each has a most precious gift of his own, which is yet not his own, but the property of the Church. " To *every one* of us is " literally *was* ἰδόθη "given " literally "*the* grace," ἡ χάρις. The common grace which the Head of the Church at His ascension received in trust for the self-

the middle of the last century, were so wofully out of harmony with the Apostolical ideal. Yet Hammond, as well as Zanchy and Macknight, saw clearly that the text announces the mutual adaptation of the members of the Church, the correlativeness of their graces and gifts, and the necessity of close connexion amongst them.

Beza, (from another point of view, but still with the same general idea,) " in the measure of every part, according to the capacity on the one hand and the need on the other, of every member" (*pro modo et exigentia*). Similarly, Mede and Hammond. Vetablus points out the fact that this mutual ministration is to be effective in the accomplishment of its purpose, is not to stop short of that purpose—not merely *towards*, but *unto* " *usque ad* "—the edifying of itself (not " for," as Ellicott weakly and inconsistently renders). Estius finely comments : " The building up,—both the enlargement and the perfect binding together. This teaches the end contemplated by this growth of individual members and its serviceable result, not only the member's own personal benefit, but the common advantage of the whole body ; for the sake of which every one has received from Christ whatever gift he may possess. *In love*, without which the body does not grow, and without which all the rest is nothing." (*Edificationem sive extructionen, etc.*). Whitby's comment is to the same effect : " By the assistance which *every* of these parts, thus *united* together, gives to the whole, according to the particular proportion of its gifts, increaseth or grows in love, and *so each member edifies one another.*"

Were not the fact so patent that institutions shape ideas, it would be strange indeed that all these able expositors, seeing so clearly as they did that the plain, the inevitable teaching of this passage and others is—that reciprocal edification is an essential part of Church-life, an indispensable element in Church organization, did not call attention to the glaring deficiency of the existing Church-organizations in this particular. Modern commentators, Ellicott and Alford, for example, though not upbuilding of His Church, and for the fulfilment of its mission to the world, is specialized in each individual believer. In the animal kingdom there are some species which include such a wide free range of individual peculiarity that each individual may be regarded as almost constituting a sub-species by itself: but in no kingdom is there such diversity of original gift as in the kingdom of grace.

All believers have equal Church-rights; the dignity of each being so lofty that none can possibly overtop another, all being " sons, heirs, kings, and priests unto God." There cannot be any difference of order, since each holds a rank than which there can be no higher; still there is a difference of office, a diversity of function. The one God works through all, yet diversely as to measure and manner. No real member of God's Church is without his speciality. Every one of us has a work to do, a function to discharge, for the building-up of the body, which no one else can do so well, because no one else has the exquisitely fitting gift for it.

According to the measure of the gift—the boon of Christ. That is to say, each individual member's gift for the edification of the Church is a definite spiritual, mental, bodily endow-

nearly so explicit as many of their predecessors, say quite enough to implicitly condemn the large majority of existing Church-systems for making *no provision* for this essential element of the Christian life— mutual ministration, reciprocal edification. Ellicott ever and again "*burns,*" to use an expressive child-phrase in the game of "hide and seek," but just when you think he now must put his finger on the point, his ecclesiastical pre-occupations send him off in some other direction. For example, on verse 7, he writes, " In the general distribution of gifts, ... no single individual is overlooked, ... each has his peculiar gift, each can and ought to contribute his share to—" What ? Surely to the matter in hand, namely, "the edifying of the body of Christ." But no, he resiles from *that* instinctively, and falls back on the comparatively remote context,—" preserving the unity of the Spirit." What but prepossession could drive such an accomplished and conscientious commentator to such an exegetical eccentricity ?

ment, determined as to its original extent and limits by Christ Himself. It is a Christ-given faculty, bestowed, not by the Church, but for the Church: it being the business of the Church to ascertain the special designation of each one of its members, as indicated by the special faculty. The neglect by the Church of the working power of its members is a wanton waste, entailing woful want. Whilst all the members form one Church, each member has his own strongly-marked, most interesting, important and serviceable individuality. And this individualization, so far from disintegrating the Church, constitutes its completeness, since the perfection of the Church is the perfect development and correlation of all its members. Every believer should reverence his own gift and recognise, respect, and rejoice in that of his brother.

It is by these universally distributed gifts, received by Christ from the Father and communicated by Him through the Spirit, that the One God and Father of all works "*through* all." Thus, while there is such diversity of gift, there must be no divergence of aim or effort.

When He ascended up on high. This grandly connects the Article on the Holy Catholic Church with that on the Ascension. It also shows that the Church was not really constituted until after the Ascension, although it had existed previously in a rudimental or embryonic state. *He gave gifts to* men and *for* men,—the gift and the office being the counterparts of each other.

From all this it is plain that in the view of the Holy Spirit the Church is a *living* organism, animated by the Spirit of Christ diffused through all its members; an organism of which in its healthy, normal condition, the mutual interdependence and the reciprocal sustentation are perfect and entire. Cuvier's descriptive definition of an organized being is precisely the Spirit's representation of the Church. " Each organized being forms a complete and specific system, all whose parts mutually correspond to each other and, *through their mutual and combined activity*, fulfil a definite aim." Or take the words of another great physiologist, Johannes Muller :—" *All* the parts are co-ordinated, so as to form one whole, and to combine in fulfilling the object of that organized whole. Some have believed that life, or the activity of organic bodies, is only the result of the harmony of their parts, the interlocking, as it were, of the wheels of the machine, and that death is caused by the rupture of this harmony. . . . But this harmony which exists among all the members of the whole body, is itself produced *by some power which operates through the whole body*. . . . And further, this *power exists before the harmoniously related members of the whole body*."* Dr. Radcliffe, again, says,—" Bones and vessels and nerves are *bound up in mysterious communion*, and *their harmonious reconciliation in a common purpose* may be presumed to indicate the probability of a common law of formation." † This sentence, too, might serve as a compendium of the Pauline physiology, on which rests his grand analogue of Church-organism, excepting that " the common law of formation " is laid down by the Apostle as an unquestionable fact, and the "harmonious reconciliation in a common purpose " is assumed to be the practical sequence.

V. The fifth principle involved in St. Paul's analogy is, that to the mutual ministration of spiritual life-force, coherence, contact, continuity of parts are requisite. The particles which compose the body cleave to those that are locally the nearest. Whilst—

<blockquote>
"Each part may call the farthest 'Brother,'
For head with foot hath private amity."‡
</blockquote>

* Quoted in *London Quarterly Review*, January, 1873, p. 280.
† *Proteus, or the Law of Nature.* ‡ George Herbert.

every vesicle fraternizes most practically with its neighbours. And thus it should be in the Church. But this can only be accomplished upon *system*. It must be at once voluntary and regulated. Of course in the present state realized communion must be modified by the cramping conditions of our mortal life. Thus, to some extent, Baxter's aphorism is correct, though it must be taken with strong modifications. " The Communion of Saints is, in this world, a matter of faith." Certainly, but like other matters of faith, it is also a matter for practice, of duty. What is the use of believing " in the Holy Catholic Church," whilst taking no steps towards identification with it? What, of believing in " the Communion of Saints," without endeavouring to realize it *so far* as the conditions of our earthly life will allow? Even in heaven, the finiteness of the creature must impose some limitations on realized communion. " The spirits of the just made perfect" do, doubtless, group themselves into " solemn troops and sweet societies," whilst they altogether form one harmonious household : for, as the Spirit teaches us in this Epistle, God is " the Father of Whom every *family*" —πᾶσα πατριὰ—" in heaven and earth is named." And, in this respect, too,—

"What if earth be but the shadow of heaven?"

and as in our " Father's house are many *mansions*," so the enthroned Apostles shall judge the *tribes* of Israel; and the good and faithful servant shall have dominion over *cities;* and " the *nations* of them which are saved shall walk in the light of the city of God?"

But the question fairly urged with regard to the etymology of the word *Ecclesia* may be put, with reference to the analogy between the human body and the Church, Is it not possible to press an analogy too far? And the answer is similar,—

Certainly: the analogy must not be pushed one hair's breadth further than the point of its accordance with Apostolic precept and procedure, and the institutions and usages of the Primitive Church. Let us then look closely and candidly at the injunctions of the Apostles with regard to reciprocal edification, and inquire what provision was made for it in the arrangements of the primitive Church.

And, first of all, Could anything be more explicit and more emphatic than the assertion of the Spirit, through St. Paul, of the universal diffusion of gifts for mutual edification, and the repeated insistence on the fact, that one grand department of the Spirit's work in the Church is the exquisitely balanced distribution of gifts amongst the various members of the Church for the express purpose of reciprocal upbuilding? The Spirit Himself distinctly affirms that "the manifestation of the Spirit is given *to every* man to profit withal" (1 Cor. xii. 7),—for *utilization*—πρὸς τὸ συμφέρον; as the context shows, not his own only, but that of his fellow-members.*—" Dividing to every man severally, as He will." (1 Cor. xii. 11.) It is also abundantly clear that the Christian gift of " prophecy," that is, of speaking on divine themes under a divine afflatus, in an elevated and elevating manner, was very far from being an exclusively official function.

The earliest description of primitive Church-life occurs in Acts ii. 42: " And they continued steadfastly in the Apostles' doctrine, and fellowship, and in breaking of bread, and in prayers." *Continued steadfastly:*—The word here employed by St. Luke is much stronger than this rendering προσκαρτεροῦντες. It is expressive of the most energetic persistence. They *gave themselves up* to it, as the word is

* So Valpy (*ad loc*) "*Ad Utilitatem.* Non propriam, sed *ecclesiæ*, in *communem populi fidelis* usum."

rendered in the sixth chapter, where the Apostles say,—
"We will *give ourselves* to prayer and the ministry of the word."

Now, what is meant by giving themselves to "the Apostles' doctrine" is very plain. They devoted themselves to the learning, to the experimental realization, and to the assiduous practice of the truths which it was the principal work of the Apostles to teach. But what is meant by "*fellowship*"? This is obviously a question of vital importance to the very conception of the Church. We must get to the root of this matter if possible. The word* here and elsewhere rendered "fellowship" means, in the first place, a having in common, a joint interest; then intercourse; next, an intimate and sympathetic sharing, as where St. Paul declares his intense aspiration to prove " the *fellowship* of " Christ's "sufferings;" then it comes to signify affinity, mutual attraction, coalescence, as where he asks, " What *fellowship* hath righteousness with unrighteousness? " next, a joint and privileged partaking, as where he terms the Lord's Supper " the *communion* of the blood " and " the *communion* of the body of Christ." Then, by a very natural crystallization of meaning, the word designates the parties to whom the privilege of joint participation exclusively belongs,—the initiated and registered society or brotherhood, the enrolled community, as when St. Paul reminds the Corinthians that they " were called unto the fellowship of—Jesus Christ," and hence exhorts them to have " no divisions among " them, but to " be perfectly joined together." It then comes to signify reciprocal recognition and co-partnership, as when St. Paul says that the other Apostles gave to him and Barnabas " the right hand of *fellowship*." Sometimes it means the actual

---

* κοινωνία.

communicating and conveying to others of sentiment, feeling, experience, and is so rendered in our English Bible, where the Apostle prays that "the communication" of Philemon's faith may become "effectual." Sometimes it signifies a Church-contribution, as where St. Paul tells the Romans,— "It has pleased them of Macedonia and Achaia to make a certain *contribution* for the poor saints at Jerusalem." Again, in writing to the Corinthians, St. Paul uses this word to designate their Church-charities, where our translators render the word "distribution."

Now it will be readily perceived that although this word has great breadth and elasticity of signification, yet all its meanings are closely related, and, so to speak, run into one another naturally. But our present question is, In which of these shades or phases of meaning are we to take the word in this description of the form which the Church-life of the first converts spontaneously assumed? That it must have been something substantive; something of which a description could have been readily given in answer to a candid inquirer, is plain from the connection. For this is but one of several details of the primitive Church-life. If Theophilus had written to St. Luke to this effect:—You speak of the new converts as devoting themselves to the Apostle's teaching,—what does that mean? He could have felt no difficulty in describing this usage and habit as it actually appeared at the time. Or if Theophilus had put the like question with regard to "breaking of bread," or "prayers," a descriptive answer would have been readily returned. Does any one doubt then that if Theophilus had written,— There is one part of your account of the Church-life of the converts of Pentecost which I find myself unable to realize,— "fellowship," one of the four things which you say they were given up to,—what usage or usages do you indicate by that word? What did it feel like to them? What did it look like to others? Does any one imagine that St. Luke would have had any greater difficulty in describing the *fellowship* than in describing the teaching, the breaking of bread, or the prayers? Clearly not: for St. Luke himself only used the word as a compendious expression for that which he had witnessed or which had been described in detail, and vividly, glowingly, amply narrated to him. This is rather obscured in the A. V., by an arbitrary and inconsistent punctuation and use of the word "*in :*" there ought to have been a comma and an "in" between doctrine and fellowship. The strict rendering is, "They devoted themselves to the teaching of the Apostles, and to fellowship, and to breaking of bread, and to prayers." Their Church-life had four principal departments, to which they all gave assiduous attention : First, the teaching of the Apostles ; Second, fellowship; Third, breaking of bread; Fourth, prayers. That some *special* usage is meant is plain. It cannot mean merely that they did not abandon their profession, did not renounce their baptism. The word here, then, cannot have one of its two most usual significations—community. But is there any objection to the other,—confidential intercourse? That there is no antecedent unlikelihood in the practice of close, familiar intercourse amongst them is obvious, and that such intercourse did form an essential element of primitive Church-life is abundantly evident from other passages in the New Testament, and from ecclesiastical and secular history throughout the first six centuries of the Christian era.

That the followship, communion, here spoken of, was not identical with that blessed solemnity to which we now emphatically apply the name—*the Communion*, is plain, inasmuch as that rite is mentioned next—under the descriptive title "breaking of bread;"* the two might be, and demonstrably were, generally combined. We know the Lovefeast and the Lord's Supper were so combined in primitive times. Often probably the four principal elements of Church-life—teaching; social intercourse; the Christian family-meal; the Lord's Supper; and conjoint prayers were united in one service. But still—*fellowship* must have been as distinct an element of Church-life—as were teaching, the Lord's Supper, and collective prayer. Fellowship, like the three other elements of Church-life, was a regularly recurring act, performed at set times. And this addiction to *fellowship*, hearty social intercourse, was in exquisite accordance with the self-surrender, the effusion, one might almost say the *abandon* of a community such as had never before appeared on earth; which as Baumgarten beautifully says "exulted in its own existence," and which, as St. Luke tells us, by its unearthly loveliness commanded at once "fear" and "favour," from those whose enslaving worldliness could not permit them to join it. Those who would not be its adherents were per-force its admirers.

The sense of mutual *belonging* is beautifully indicated in the word used by St. Luke in recording the action of Peter and John on their dismissal from the Jewish Council—"they went to *their own*." No sooner were they at large than they naturally gravitated to the confidential, privileged gathering of the disciples. That was the magnetic hearthstone to which their hearts were instinctively drawn. This closeness of union is further indicated by the strength of the expression employed by St. Luke in describing the salutary effect of the vindication of the holiness of the Church by the death of Ananias and Sapphira. "Of the rest"—contrasted with

* Bishop Wordsworth (*ad loc.*) maintains this on grammatical grounds. He sees that "external acts of fellowship" must be meant here.

believers—of those who were not sincere believers, durst no man join himself—literally *glue* or solder himself unto them, κολλᾶσθαι. (see Valpy *ad loc.*) The Church was a spiritually agglutinated mass.

But it may be said—this was peculiar to the Hebrew Church who had been accustomed to the free social services of the Synagogue. Let us see, then, whether there was anything like it in the Gentile churches.

In St. Paul's earliest Epistle, the First to the Thessalonians, he writes thus to these newly converted Greeks : " Comfort yourselves *together* and *edify one another, even as also ye do,*" are in the habit of doing. (Ch. v. 11.)

Again, in Col. iii. 16, the Apostle exhorts believers to the duty of " teaching and admonishing *one another* in psalms and hymns and spiritual songs." Here an important function of the Apostles, that of teaching and admonishing *reminding*—νουθετοῦντες—(see Ch. i. 28) is laid upon each individual believer; *teaching one another*, what was not before clearly known, *reminding one another* of what was in danger of not being sufficiently heeded—*one another—yourselves conjointly* ἑαυτοὺς, each conveying to himself and his brethren at the same time, instruction and admonition through the medium of psalms, etc. ; as did the Apostles and disciples when Peter and John returned from the Council, and as was customary in the Corinthian meetings—" Every one hath a psalm" (1 Cor. xiv. 26), and according to the good old usage of Methodist prayer-meetings, when any member of the meeting might give out a verse or two *admonishing* himself and his fellow-Christians by such a hymn as "A charge to keep I have, etc." The idea is plainly that of mutual and conjoint instruction and admonition by means of a varied psalmody adapted to the varied moods and phases of the spiritual life. " Speaking to one another (not *yourselves* exclusively,—Ellicott *ad loc.*,—more correctly still among *yourselves*) in psalms and hymns and spiritual songs." (Eph. v. 19.) This is strikingly illustrated by Pliny's celebrated letter to Trajan " *Carmina Christo quasi Deo dicere secum invicem.*" That these were social singings seems to be indicated by the context; the contrast between *being drunk with wine* and *being filled with the Spirit*, being implicitly continued in that between the Bacchanalian drinking songs, by which the intemperate excited each other to excess, and the psalms, hymns, and spiritual songs, by which the Christians were wont to intensify their social devotions and to challenge each other to heroic constancy and a holy rivalry of goodness, to stir the fire of sacred enthusiasm, and " consider one another to provoke unto love and to good works." It seems plain from 1 Cor. xiv., that in the earliest Christian times, under an afflatus of the Spirit, a sacred improvisation was common.

" Let us consider one another to provoke unto love and to good works: not forsaking the assembling of ourselves together, as the manner of some is; but exhorting one another." (Heb. x. 24, 25.) *Consider—earnestly regard* *— κατανοῶμεν (Acts xxvii. 29, "*wished* for the day," looked out longingly for it) " the assembling of ourselves *together:* " the word *together* here is not pleonastic but emphatic, being the translation of the επι in επισυναγωγὴν, which certainly suits better a close and confidential and an exclusively *Church*-gathering than a public assembly. (Comp. Matt. xxiv. 31, Mark xiii. 27, 2 Thess. ii. 1, Matt. xxiii. 27, Luke xiii. 34.) Well does Bengel comment on this passage. " For spiritual heat and ardour also disjoin things that are heterogeneous, and draw together those that are homogeneous. The exhortation which is required includes the *peculiar ardour* of

---

* " Regard with solicitude," (Williams *in loc.*)

every individual." (*Nam etiam spiritualis, etc.*) "Oneanother" is also very emphatic. The juxtaposition and organic connection of the clauses suggest that the *exhorting* one another, was one of the chief objects of "the assembling of ourselves together."

Nor is this idea of the mutual attraction of true believers, their vital affinity and interdependence, not only as a matter of faith, but also as a matter of fact, practice, usage, duty, and experience—not only as an ideal, but as an institution—confined to St. Paul. In St. John's view *fellowship one with another* is as real as our fellowship with the Father and the Son; fellowship one with another being the proper sequence of our fellowship with the Father and the Son.—He writes " Truly our fellowship is with the Father and with His Son Jesus Christ. . . . And if we walk in the light, as He is in the light, we have fellowship one with another." Assuredly fellowship with the Father and the Son is to the true believer a matter of experience and realization,—in prayer and thanksgiving on his own part, and in the communication of peace and joy and strength from God to the believer. Who could maintain fellowship with the Father and the Son without frequent, if not regular and stated acts of prayer and thanksgiving? How then can we be said to have fellowship one with another without Christian social intercourse,—frequent, if not regular and stated?

In like manner St. James enjoins mutual confession, and supplication for one another. "Confess your faults one to another and pray one for another."

It is true that nothing is said in any of the Epistles as to the precise mode of exercising all this mutual vigilance, and realizing this mutual membership, and discharging those reciprocal obligations, and condensing into an effective working force this strong and universally diffused sentiment of a

G

mutual belonging. The exact mode in which the Church is to accomplish its great work of self-upbuilding is not made matter of Apostolic prescription. What were the definite arrangements for the utilization of each member's special gifts; in what particular manner the primal and imperative Christian duties of reciprocal exhortation, confession, consolation, incitation to love and to good works, were to be fulfilled, is not laid down in any of the Apostolical letters; any more than the precise mode of conducting public worship, administering baptism, or solemnizing the Supper of the Lord. But it is just as unreasonable to doubt that there did obtain in the primitive churches usages of, and arrangements for mutual edification, heartening and confession, and the interchange of Christian sentiment, as to doubt that in some form or some variety of forms public worship was conducted, and that in some way or some diversity of ways baptism was administered, and the Lord's Supper was celebrated.

There can be little doubt that as to the mode of meeting these solemn Church-responsibilities and securing these invaluable Church advantages much was left to the genius of the people, and their previous religious and social usages and habits. Indeed this becomes apparent in comparing what we know from "the Acts" of the Church in Jerusalem with what we gather of the Corinthian church-customs from the Epistles to the believers of that great centre of Greek intelligence and energy. There are reasons at once obvious and conclusive why no rigid Apostolic regulations should form part of the rule of Christian faith and practice, and why no detailed descriptions should be given of the meetings for reciprocal edification and enlivenment, and why we are rather left to form a general idea of the several customs and institutions of the primitive Church from scattered and incidental intimations. There is such a terrible tendency in all ages to insist upon the form rather than the force, to rely upon the *opus operatum* rather than the spirit and life, that we may well thankfully recognize the wisdom and the kindness, the mercy and the justice of this chariness of detail as to Church organization and administration, and hoard up the golden silence of Scripture on this as on many other questions. But notwithstanding all this there are ample indications in the Epistles of most veritable and effective modes of manifesting the essential mutuality of the Christian life, and indulging and strengthening its strong family-instinct, in short of *building* itself *up in love*.

In the First Epistle to the Corinthians we have some very interesting and instructive glimpses of the internal structure of the Church. We first discover a system of classification of converts with reference to the various states and stages of the spiritual life; and how classification could be accomplished without classing, and how classing could be effected without classes, it is not easy to conceive. In the Second Chapter, the sixth verse, St. Paul tells the Corinthians, "We speak wisdom among them that are perfect,"—mature, "of full age." (Compare Heb. v. 14.) "We *speak*," says Bengel, "implies something private. (Compare Ver. 7, 13.) We *preach*,—a public act." ("*Loquimur habet, etc.*") Besides, the idea of privacy and confidentialness is suggested by the word "*among* them that are perfect." That to τελειοις should be here assigned its frequent meaning *mature, advanced, proficient*, seems required by the contrast in the subsequent context "babes in Christ." It is plain from the tenor of the second and third chapters that the Apostles supplemented their public preaching by private instruction, ascertaining the exact state of individual disciples, and addressing their teaching to that state. They formed inner circles of more advanced believers, among whom they spoke "wisdom . . . and the deep things of God."*

The utilization of the manifold and universally-diffused gifts of the Christian Society, and the earnest care of the Apostle to regulate, but in nowise to repress, the rich resources of the Church for mutual edification, are instinctively apparent from that very Epistle to the Corinthians in which he most severely rebukes license and disorder. First of all, he gratefully recognises the various and most precious endowments of the Church comprehended under the term "utterance" (1 Cor. i. 5), presenting an admonitory contrast with that reticence as to personal experience which in the present day has become a fashion and an epidemic.†

In Chap. xiv. 12, the whole body of believers is exhorted individually to "seek to excel to the edifying of the Church.". "Understanding" on spiritual matters is pronounced "unfruitful," if not directed to the edification of others. The Apostolic rescript is as positive as it is plain, "Ye may *all* prophesy one by one, that all may learn, and all may be comforted." The learning "all" and the speaking "all" are identical.‡

---

* Assuredly, the public and promiscuous preaching of the word—the present style of average and even of popular preaching, adapted to the present state of our congregations—is not sufficient for the formation of a full-grown, manly, robust, and high-toned Christian experience. The churches of the present day are kept to a large extent on a milk diet,—are treated as infantile, invalid, or convalescent. (See a Paper by the Lecturer in the *Wesleyan Methodist Magazine* for January, 1867. "*The Pew, etc.*")

† We ourselves have heard one of the most eminent and eloquent of Dissenting Ministers deduce from the expression "joy unspeakable," by a curious hermeneutical process, the wisdom and propriety of leaving altogether unspoken our spiritual joys.

‡ On this passage Bengel, with his usual insight, says, "*All;* the *univer*-

Again, the striking passage in the Epistle to the Colossians, parallel with our text, in which the Apostle holds up the ideal of a compactly and sensitively united and self-nourishing Church, is preceded by a glowing description of the actual state of the Colossian church. He writes, " I am with you in the Spirit, joying and beholding your *order*, and the steadfastness of your faith in Christ," which, as Bishop Ellicott says, has " reference to Church-fellowship." It is difficult to imagine how the Apostle could have chosen the words—τὴν τάξιν—regular array, as of an army on the field of battle, unless he had in his mind's eye some definite and well-observed arrangement for mutual support. The allusion is certainly to a well-organized body—probably to military service (Ellicott, *ad loc.*, who quotes a remarkable comment by Theophylact on the passage, showing that the *steadfastness* of a church as of a *phalanx* depends upon regular and compact disposition: as Charles Wesley puts it, its standing—

" In close and firm array,"

sality is to be noted; all may learn by conversing, asking, teaching, listening; they *all* being prophets. One learns by teaching; one learns by speaking and interrogating. Many remain foolish and languid as to spiritual things, because they *speak* next to nothing about such subjects. Sometimes the speech of another more effectually stirs us up, and sometimes our own." *Notanda universalitas, etc.*

Again, commenting on the twenty-sixth verse, " When you come together every one of you hath a psalm, hath a doctrine, etc.," he says, " The public meeting was then more fruitful than in the present day, when *one* person, whatever his mood of mind may be, is bound to fill up the time with a sermon." (*Fructuosior, etc.*)

The same consummate expositor, commenting on 1 Cor. v. 11, takes occasion to animadvert on the modern unsocial mode of taking the Lord's Supper, amongst nearly all the churches. He writes, " Let the Church of the present day see to it, in which the Eucharistic table companions are *not like children in one home,* but like a diversity of strangers in a huge hotel." (*Viderit, etc.*)

and being—

"In mighty phalanx joined.")

Whitby, too, sees clearly that "order" here means Church "discipline and union."

But we gain further light from a passage in the Epistle to Philemon, in which we catch some vivid glimpses of Church-life—as realized in Colosse,—Philemon i. 7.* In the opening paragraph of Paul's letter to his friend, one of the leaders of the Colossian church, we are incidentally admitted to a kind of privileged inspection of vigorous Church-life as manifested in the dewy youth of Christianity, and under the loving gaze of the Apostle. We become acquainted with the internal structure of the Church of Christ in its earliest formation amongst the Gentiles. We see what are the vital forces of the Church, what Church-life is in its essence, what it looks like in healthy operation. We see that the life of a church resides in its individual members, and is fundamentally the same life in all of them; that life being in its source and element, " Grace and peace from God our Father and the Lord Jesus Christ," and in its most distinctive manifestation "love and faith toward the Lord Jesus, and toward all saints." We further see that the life which individual Christians have in common naturally draws them together, and binds them and blends them into an associated life, the new God-breathed life in each individual heart being attracted by, and in turn attracting to itself, the same life in other hearts, until "like kindred drops," they mingle into one. Hence each is to the other " beloved," and each saint—*i. e.*, each one who manifests "love and faith toward our Lord Jesus Christ"— evinces "love and faith towards all saints." Hence arises

---

* The exposition of this passage is slightly abridged from a Paper on *Fellowship*, by the Lecturer, in the *City Road Magazine* for July, 1872.

a fellowship, not only the exquisite accord of sentiment, the delicious communion of affection, and the warm heart-grip expressed in the words "*thee, brother,*" but also a combination for work, and an enrolment for warfare, for mutual defence and conjoint aggression; so that they all become *fellow-labourers* and *fellow-soldiers*,—each one both a labourer and soldier, wielding at once the trowel and the sword, and all other serviceable tools and effective weapons; yet the one character and calling predominating in one Christian, the other in another Christian, so that Philemon may be specially a "fellow-labourer," and Archippus characteristically a "fellow-soldier" (Ver. 1, 2), whilst Paul is pre-eminently both.

We see, still further, that this love-united band of workers and warriors form themselves into an association for united worship and mutual instruction, advancement and enlivenment, in order to effect "the communication" to all of the faith of each, and especially the helping of the less advanced members by the unfolded experience of the more advanced, and the quickening of the less animated members by the zeal and joy of the more animated, —" That the *communication* of thy faith may become effectual by the acknowledging of every good thing which is in you in Christ Jesus. For we have great joy and consolation in thy love, because the bowels "—literally, the vitals, those parts of our nature which are most stirred by affection and emotion, —" of the saints are refreshed by thee, brother." (Ver. 6, 7.) We see, further, that this loving brotherhood of workers, warriors, worshippers, and fellow-students of the great science of salvation, must, by reason of its growing numbers, group itself into smaller associations, determined by the local habitation of its members; so that within the compass of the one indivisable Church of Christ, there may exist and flourish the church of God in Colosse, and within the pale of the church in Colosse there is a recognised church in Philemon's house. We see, still further, that this miniature church in a private house is none the less a *church*, containing within itself all that is *essential* to the Divine idea and definition of a church:—"The *church* in thy house." (Ver. 2.)

But the " grace "-*felt favour*, and the possessed "peace" of God in the believing heart did not exhaust their power there. Like an imprisoned energy they struggled for outward expression. And this outward expression was naturally threefold. First, upwards "toward the Lord Jesus" Christ, and then, if one may so speak, lateral, "toward all saints," and then downward, toward those who are not yet in the enjoyment of the felt favour and peace of God, urging to *labour* that they too might be brought into the same happiness, and constraining to heroic aggression on the kingdom of darkness, making believers *fellow-labourers* and *fellow-soldiers*. But what is most dwelt upon is the central movement—"love and faith toward all saints." There is a remarkable variety in the original which the usages of our own language do not allow a translator to represent, but which is invaluable to the expositor. It is, literally, love and faith toward (πρὸς) our Lord Jesus Christ, and *unto* or *at* (εἰς) all saints. The two prepositions have a local significance, the one implying the invisibility and bodily distance of our Lord Jesus Christ—so that love, in its expression is, as yet, *toward* Him, whilst it is *at* or *unto* all saints, because they are visible and near. There is a passage in the sixteenth Psalm which strikingly illustrates this, and is as strikingly illustrated by it: "O my soul, thou hast said unto the Lord, Thou art *my* Lord : my goodness extendeth not to Thee, but to the saints that are in the earth, and to the excellent, in whom is all my delight." The love of God shed abroad in the heart, which can now say unto the Lord, "Thou art *my* Lord," pants for some ample outlet : What shall I render Thee for the Divine sweetness and serenity wherewith Thou hast replenished my heart? My goodness, though it flows from Thee, *extendeth not* to Thee. Yet the up-springing fountain of love in the heart is ever-flowing and overflowing. It must extend; it must reach so as to enrich, and fertilize, and gladden; and it does extend to the saints that are in the earth; not yet to angels or perfected spirits who are on too high a level to receive direct consolation and refreshment from us, but to the saints that are in the earth.

But it is to be specially noted that not only love is to be toward all saints, but faith is to be toward all saints. How can *faith* be toward or unto saints? This is explained by St. Paul himself. Writing to the Romans, he says, "I long to see you, that I may be comforted together with you by the *mutual* faith both of you and me." The one word rendered *comforted together with*,* is another of those expressions for which the English language is not rich enough to form an exact equivalent. It means, to address one another in turn for the interchange of comfort, encouragement, hope, resolution : *That I may be comforted among you by confidential intercourse, by the interchanged faith of you and me.* The faith, then, of one believer towards or unto another believer, is, first of all, personal faith, communicated by one to the other for the purpose of reciprocal edification. This is still further illustrated in the twelfth chapter of the Epistle to the Romans, where, speaking of " the measure of faith," which " God hath dealt to " every Christian man, St. Paul adds, we are " members one of another:" not only all members of the same body, but each

* συμπαρακληθῆναι.

one a member of every other one, bound therefore to cultivate the quickest and strongest sympathy, and by *communication* to supplement each other's faith. That is to say, our personal faith, though given us for our own soul's salvation, in the first instance, is also given to us for the good of our fellow Christians, and whatever measures of light, conviction, confidence and comfort God deals out to us, He requires us to communicate to others. And St. Paul thanks God that Philemon's faith is not only toward the Lord Jesus, but *unto* all saints. How? By "*communication.*" "That the *communication* of *thy* faith may become *effectual;*" in other words, that thy faith being communicated, may become effectual,—operative and productive. A still-born faith is very like an abortive faith. The ensnaring fear of man, a fastidious shrinkingness of nature, misplaced or morbid bashfulness, over-indulged peculiarities of temperament, conventional codes of religious decorum, an unscriptural and unhealthy sentimentality, or erroneous teaching, may suppress the faith of even a sincere and earnest Christian; but such suppression is to the individual a grievous privation and a grave peril, and to his fellow Christians an indefensible wrong. It is, moreover, the wrapping up in a napkin—it may be a very soft, silken, and daintily-embroidered napkin, and very neatly and carefully folded, but still a funereal napkin—the personal experience of Divine light and love, the most precious and productive talent which the absent but quickly-returning Lord can entrust to any of His servants.

But to what end is this "communication" of individual faith effectual? To "the acknowledging of every good thing that is in you in Christ." The word here rendered acknowledging * is of much deeper and broader significance than

* ἐπιγνώσει.

any one English word available to a translator. It signifies, first of all, *careful and skilful inquiry*, in order to clear and accurate knowledge; then, the clear and accurate knowledge actually arrived at by careful and skilful inquiry, and last of all, the joyful and thankful recognition—"*acknowledgment*"— of the facts ascertained. The word has a root, a stem, and a flower. The root, *inquiry;* the stem, *knowledge;* the flower, *acknowledgment.* Now the flower cannot flourish without the stem, and the stem must grow out of the root. Thankful acknowledgment of every good thing that is in us can only grow out of an actual knowledge of such good, and how can knowledge be secured without inquiry?

Now, how would this work? how would it become a fact in the case of Philemon, and that portion of the church in Colosse which held its meetings in Philemon's house? This is not at all hard to realize. It does not require a very vivid historical imagination to call up the scene. First, Philemon would communicate his faith to the rest, by leading their prayers in an " effectual, fervent " spirit; and then, by *acknowledging* to them the *good that was in him in Christ*, by telling them what God had done for his soul—done not only at first in his conversion, but done since their last meeting. He would *communicate* to his brethren and sisters, at their stated gatherings, the advance he had been enabled to make from time to time. And what would be the effect of this? What would the *communication* of his faith *be effectual to*, which it must have stopped short of, if it had not been communicated? To " the acknowledging of every good thing that is in you in Christ." This first; then the *refreshing of the hearts of the saints.* Think we that to a company of converted Asiatic Greeks a man could tell in a glowing, fervid manner, of the glorious Gospel translated into his own experience, without evoking from some a burst of praise, from others an upward look of speechless gratitude? No; there would come from all "*acknowledgment*," in one form or other, of the good that was in Philemon, in Christ. Nor would it stop there. How many a heart would be "*refreshed*," "like a green leaf after rain!" How many would feel as Christiana felt after one of Greatheart's outpourings, when she exclaimed, "This is brave! . . . Though my heart was lightful and joyous before, it is ten times more lightsome and joyous now." And this is just as it ought to be. No man's spiritual enjoyments are intended for himself alone. If earthly property have its duties as well as its rights, surely the durable riches of Divine grace in the heart are designed for the good of others, as well as of the first receiver. Thus St. Paul valued the inward consolations with which God had so richly blessed him mainly on account of their power of indefinite multiplication. " Blessed be God," he exclaims, " who comforteth us in all our tribulation." For what end? "That we may be able to comfort them that are in any trouble, by the comfort wherewith we ourselves are comforted of God." The Christian is never intended to lie "like a worm in wall-fruit," embedded in solitary surfeitings. Philemon by the rehearsal of his own experience would call forth similar declarations from others. Hence multiplied encouragement to the little flock, and redounding glory to God: "The acknowledging of every good thing that is in us in Christ," —how important! how desirable! For want of it how lamentably is the Great Giver defrauded of the gratitude which is at once His due and His delight! How we defraud ourselves of joy and hope and strength! What a wrong to our fellow-Christians and to the kingdom of God in the world!

In the Apostolic times mutual edification was accounted one of the foremost and most essential duties of the Christian life, ranking with the obligation to pursue peace and holiness, "Follow after the things which make for peace, and things *wherewith one may edify another.*" (Rom. xiv. 19.) The duty of mutual reception insisted on in the Epistle to the Romans (Comp. Chap. xv. 7, xiv. 1), evidently implies confidential intercourse, according to the force of the Greek word προσλάμβανεσθε: rendered by Campbell (Matt. xvi. 22, Mark viii. 32) "take aside," and by a French translator in Matt. "*tiré à part,*" in Mark "*prit en particulier,*" drew apart, took aside.

To this also is related that mutual vigilance, frankness, and fidelity which our Lord implies as essential to His Church (Matt. xviii. 15) which "is after and beside that first συναγωγή of the Jews, the true united ἐπισυναγωγή, in which one takes care of the other, in which the *exhorting one another* (Heb. x. 24, 25) finds its living progressive exemplification." (Stier *ad loc*). Stillingfleet has shown that *Fellowship* was the first element of the religious services of the synagogue, and was thence transferred to the Christian Church. (Menicon, p. 263.)

We must not fancy, then, that in the Apostolic age there was no other alimentary apparatus for the body of Christ than the preaching of the Word by ordained officials, the merely ritual or liturgical celebration of the Lord's Supper, and the oversight of the associated primitive bishops. The very fact that the Christian Church was formed, not on the model of the temple, with its jealously guarded priestly orders, and its punctiliously regulated services, but on the free and social platform of the Synagogue, is in evidence of this. There liberty of prophesying, under necessary regulations, seems to have been absolute; the gracious young carpenter of Nazareth might *stand up for to read* and to expound, and the devout and likely-looking strangers at

Antioch in Pisidia, receive the prompt invitation "Brethren, if ye have any word of exhortation for the people, say on." Moreover, even the clustering courts around the temple itself were open for earnest religious inquiry and interlocution: there the boy from Nazareth might hold deep converse with the doctors of the law, and the all but proscribed Jesus of Nazareth might teach daily within the very precinct of the Holy Place.

In fact, we know that the gatherings at Corinth for social edification and religious heartening and enlivenment, and for the recognition and realization of the family relationship of Christians, formed not only a very large and prominent part of the Church-life of the Greek converts, but were marked by such spontaneity and universality in the exercise of individual gifts, that even St. Paul found it necessary to caution these ardent and vivacious disciples against a confusion which would not only hinder edification, but also bring Christianity into disrepute amongst the heathen. But the Apostle, in warning against confusion, and even in reproving scandalous irregularities, is sensitively careful not to discourage the social element in Christianity, which, according to his Gospel, was an essential part of the Church's life. He rebukes license, and enjoins that "all things be done decently and in order," but he uses his Apostolic authority to regulate only, and in no wise to repress or to restrict. He is " gentle among 'them' as a nurse cherisheth her children," and moderates but does not check the generous and healthful, though troublesome and even dangerous vivacity of his spiritual children.

The Lovefeasts, Agapæ, or spiritual symposia of the primitive Church formed a prominent part of its system of mutual edification; and the close connection between them and the Lord's Supper, gave a very different character to that solemnity from that which it gradually assumed, as hierarchical pretensions and ritual proclivities gained ground in the Church,—a character which still lingers even amongst Protestant communities. The Lord's Supper, in the Primitive Church, was much more accordant with the title, The Holy *Communion*. Neander justly observes, "Those Christian Agapæ formed one whole with the celebration of the Lord's Supper." (*Planting and Training*, etc., i. 249.) The pre-eminently social nature of Christianity was that which most struck an intelligent observer of Christianity in the second century of our era, as is apparent from Pliny's celebrated letter to Trojan. And even so late as the beginning of the third century, as is plain from the Apology of Tertullian, the social intercourse of the Christians was so intimate, and formed such a striking feature of Church-life as to bring them under suspicion of conspiracy against the State. (Apologeticus, Cap. xxxix.) Others accused them simply of forming an unworldly and therefore alien and obstructive community in the midst of mankind. (Cap. xli.) And the earlier Apologists are incessantly rebutting infamous charges brought against the Christians, on account of their close and confidential meetings. (See especially Athenagoras' Plea for the Christians, A.D. 177, Cap. iii.)

Dr. Paley in a celebrated passage enumerates amongst the principal elements and prominent features of the earliest Church-life, "conferences . . . exhortations . . . affectionate intercourse with one another," and with his unfailing open-mindedness, admits that the nearest approach to the "mode of life, in its form and habit" of the Primitive Christians to be found amongst existing Christian communities is that of "the *Unitas Fratrum*, or the modern Methodists.*

* "Evidences of Christianity," Part First, Chap. i. The late eminent expositor, Professor Tholuck, whilst spending some time in Oxford for

The objects of that sacred association named *the Church* cannot be accomplished without regular Christian intercourse. What was the design and what were the advantages of the gatherings for mutual edification in the Primitive Church? These may be briefly stated thus: the gratification and strengthening of the social instincts of the new nature; the supplying to the converts—in exchange for the frivolities and rivalries of the world, its " pomps and vanities," the frantic revelling of heathen sacrificial feasts, the circus, the theatre, the gladiatorial show—facilities for a safe and healthy social religious enjoyment and sympathetic spiritual excitement, and a vivid, rapid interchange of holy sentiment; for mingling their joyous and compassionate tears, and reflecting each other's smiles; the evoking the sympathy which exists between all the members of the body of Christ; to bring their kindred natures into spiritual contact; to turn the full stream of the soul's affections and affinities towards the people of God; to make keen and sensitive in every Christian heart the love of his brother "whom he hath *seen;*" the alternate communication and reception of light; the sheltering, nourishing, and manifestation of the spiritual life; mutual vigilance and mutual confession of faults, noting slight and stealthy relapses and the passive and half-conscious re-admission of banished failings—lest failings should become faults, faults sins, and sins of surprise should become sinful habits, and sinful habits issue in apostacy (Heb. x. 24—26; xii. 15—17)—to promote the overflow of confluent thought and feeling to the submerging of self, and the growing by each other's help to a common standard of experience,

the purpose of consulting its libraries, attended a Methodist Class Meeting, and declared to the resident minister that it was the nearest reproduction of the primitive Church-fellowship he had ever enjoyed.

character, and course of life—" the measure of the stature of the fulness of Christ."

Other kindred objects of these gatherings were to *draw out* the timid and retiring, to ascertain and utilize their gifts for the general edification, to afford to the comfortable classes that healthy contact with the robust piety of the poor, of the advantage and the necessity of which Dr. Arnold so well speaks; to show how the sentiment of loyalty to Christ dominates over all inferior sentiments, and—

"Like Aaron's serpent, swallows all the rest;"

so that the repulsions of education are overborne and reversed by the attraction of a common love to Christ; * and lastly what M. Rémusat terms " the common life of souls, or the associated search for redemption by means of confidential intercourse, and the solidarity of believers."†

Such mutual ministration is a most effective means of symmetrical growth up into the Head even Christ, and of advance towards the measure of the stature of the fulness of Christ. Mr. Bagehot's statement in his well-pondered chapter on " *Verifiable Progress Politically Considered*,"‡ is quite applicable to the progress of the Church in love, holiness, and spiritual manliness: " Man can only make progress in ' co-operative groups;' . . . the co-operation in all such cases depends on a *felt union* of heart and spirit."

It never was Christ's design to found a small aristocracy

---

* As Otway makes one of his high-born heroes say of a crowd of artizans who had given enthusiastic demonstration of devotion to the cause he had espoused,—

"I could have hugged the greasy rogues, they pleased me so."
Venice Preserved.

† *Revue des Deux Mondes.* Review of Lelièvre's " Life of Wesley."
‡ *The International Scientific Series*, Vol. ii., p. 213.

of sanctity and perfection, but on the contrary to make the attainments of the most advanced in light and love but exemplary and helpful to all the rest, "till we all come unto a perfect man, . . . unto the measure of the stature of the fulness of Christ." We are to " comprehend *with all saints* what is the breadth, and length, and depth, and height." (Eph. iii. 18.) " Let the peace of God rule in your hearts, to the which also ye are called *in one body.*" (Col. iii. 15.) This is the true, the actual union for which the churches are groping, gasping. The Church can only become a living self-conscious, self-perfecting organism, by means of some system of reciprocal edification. It is mainly by loving truthful speaking, as a habit and usage of Church membership that the equable growth of the Church is to be effected. " Speaking the truth in love," we " grow up into Him in all things, which is the Head, even Christ" (Eph. iv. 15), becoming evermore and more sensitively united with Him, and consequently deriving from Him a more intense, abundant, and closely correspondent life. " In all things"— in the whole of our spiritual being and in the whole of His perfections; the whole of our capacity being brought into effective relation with the whole of His fulness; the whole of our life being more and more animated by and conformed to His.

The word used by the Apostle (ἀληθεύοντες) includes much more than the merely speaking the truth; it implies living the truth, and maintaining the truth, but *speaking* it is a primary signification of the word. (See Gal. iv. 16.)* And this is far from being a merely negative injunction—that we must speak nothing but the truth. It is a positive direction, that we must speak it, and speak it *out*, and also practise it, live

---

* Ellicott translates *holding* the truth in the text, and *speaking* the truth in Gal. iv. 16.

it, and be in all things the firm and loyal adherents of the truth, whether as opposed to error in teaching, or "any indirection" in the mode of advancing the truth.

In love. This clause belongs to both the preceding and the succeeding words; the truth must be spoken and maintained in love, and in love we must grow up into *Christ.* Love is the beginning and the ending : speaking and living the truth in *love,* the Church is to edify itself in *love.*

If then spiritual ministration be an indefeasible right and an inevitable obligation of Church membership, what are the special functions of the officers of that grand society called the *Church,*—" Apostles, prophets, evangelists, pastors and teachers," etc? We have already seen that one main duty of the officers is to keep in full force and to skilfully regulate the mutual ministrations of all the members. But this is not the whole of their duty. The elders—presbyters—bishops or overseers,—all names of one class of officers—are under-shepherds of the Great and Good Shepherd : their function is to feed with Scriptural knowledge, and watch over and lead and console the Church. They are also to defend the Truth against all comers, and " by sound doctrine exhort and convince the gainsayers." St. Paul in his Epistles to the Philippians and to Timothy gives authoritative recognition to two distinct offices, that of the Elders and that of the Deacons; the former being the higher, and having oversight over the latter. Neither public teaching nor Church-rule formed any part of the Deacon's office. This difference is clear from the fact that aptness to teach and well-ruling, are insisted on as essential qualifications in a Bishop, but are not touched in the enumeration of the indispensable pre-requisites of a Deacon. The Bishop, as a ruler, must be no " brawler " or " striker; " the Deacon, as having charge of the Church-chest, was not to be " greedy of filthy lucre."

The elder is the steward, or house-governor, of our Lord's parable; he has charge of the spiritual commissariat, and the ethical economics of the household,—he has to keep order and by virtue of his duties and responsibilities, is "ruler over" it. It is his responsibility to watch for *souls as* one *that must give account.* Although those over whom he watches are parties to his appointment, he is not a removable officer, except on conviction of unfaithfulness or incompetence.

His responsibilities are the measure of his rights. How can he "give account" of them if he may not and do not *take* account of them? If one is lean or torn or missing he must answer for it. The flock must pass under his *hand* as "of *him that telleth them.*" Every spiritual shepherd must "tell his tale." To claim to be recognised as a member of Christ's flock, and yet to be free from all effective oversight would be ridiculous, if the interests involved were not so solemn and stupendous. The very fact that any intelligent serious person can make such a claim proves to what a sad extent the true, the Scriptural idea of the Church and the Ministry has faded from the consciousness of Christendom. To say to a Minister, We prefer your preaching, your service, your sanctuary, to that of any other Minister, but we have an invincible objection to your knowing anything about our spiritual state, is saying, in effect, We wish to be fed and folded, and we prefer your feeding and your fold to any other; but we have an insuperable objection to oversight, and we shall not submit to yours.

But oversight is not lordship, any more than it is hireling service. St. Peter makes it equi-distant from both, and contrasts it with both. He writes to his brother elders, " Feed the flock of God which is among you, taking the oversight—

not for filthy lucre—neither as being lords over God's heritage, but being ensamples to the flock." The eldership is rather leadership than lordship. The elders are themselves still members of the flock, and the whole flock, pastors included, are Christ's clergy and the Lord's laity at the same time. The distinction between clergy and laity, if the original meaning of the two words be adhered to, or if the distinction be made to mean anything beyond the co-ordinating and the co-ordinated, the regulating and the regulated part of the community—is utterly, intensely antiscriptural. Our Lord Himself teaches that distinctions of office do not in His Kingdom, as they do in worldly kingdoms, imply distinctions of rank. In the very nature of His Kingdom they cannot. So lofty and so sacred is the rank of the least of his little ones that it is impossible for the greatest in His Kingdom to attain a holier or a higher.

The Bishop is to be no " striker," either with his own hand or that of the State. He must "reprove, rebuke, exhort, with all long-suffering." On the other hand, however, the very warnings against a wrong rule imply a real and veritable right rule. The Holy Spirit would never caution a body of men against the exaggeration or misuse of powers and prerogatives which they did not possess. The election to the Eldership by the members of a church of one of their own number is the recognition of a Divine call to the Eldership; otherwise it has no validity or beneficial effectiveness whatever. He *receives* his "ministry"—" of the Lord Jesus;" his final accountability is to the Master and not to his fellow-servants, though those who put him in office are bound to put him out if his conduct is palpably and incorrigibly injurious to the interests entrusted to his charge. He is pre-eminently their servant, but not their servant *to command*. He is not the mere paid agent of the people committed to his charge. He is their ruling servant and their serving ruler. He is a labourer worthy of his meat and hire, but he is no hireling or kitchen-knave. He holds, directly from Christ, a free, an independent, a rightful, because a responsible oversight and administration. The Holy Ghost alone can enable a man to harmonize in spirit and practice these apparently irreconcileable functions and qualities. The Elder is the impersonation of order and harmony, the keystone of the arch of unity; and subordination was recognised as an essential Christian virtue. Nothing but spirituality in a church can preserve the equilibrium of power.

But the existence of a hierarchical caste in the Church of Christ is abhorrent to the spirit as it is contradictory to the letter of the New Testament. And to claim a Divine right for any rigidly specific form of government is, if possible, still more unwarranted in the Church, and certainly more mischievous, than in the State. The only *form* of government which can justly claim, at any time or in any place, to be in possession by Divine right, is that which most effectively nourishes the spiritual life, and wins most souls to Christ.

There must also be in the Church officers of finance as well as of order; in accordance with prophecy, " I will make thy officers peace, and thine *exactors* righteousness " (Isaiah lx. 17); but the primary qualification even of these is that they be "full of the Holy Ghost" (Acts vi. 3), and like the deacons of the Pastoral Epistles, their *morale* and their spirituality must be high-toned and unimpeachable.

VI. The sixth principle implied in St. Paul's analogy between the human body and the Church is, That, *as in the human body all the once extraneous matter which becomes part of the body, repairing its waste and constituting its growth, becomes so by assimilation, that is, by being brought under the influence and control of the life inherent in the body, so that nothing can become organized until it has become vitalized, nothing can become part of the body until it has begun to participate in the life of the body; so it should be in the Church.* This, at least, is the ideal of the Church as an institution, and the working plan according to which it is to be built up.

The Church was not intended by its Founder to be a mere aggregation of unassimilated atoms. One great object of the Church is to induce dead souls into its organism, so richly endowed with life, and to make them partakers of that life. No sooner did the ever-active Headship of "the Lord" manifest itself than it became vividly apparent that the Church is not only a definite community within a sacred enclosure, a ring-fence of appropriate restrictions and fixed conditions of membership, but still further, that it is a thing of life, which can only be encumbered and harassed, defaced, and deformed, not really built up, by the merely external attachment of lifeless material. Along with a boundless *inclusiveness* and an impassioned urgency of invitation and of summons, we find a most sensitive *exclusiveness*, an unyielding insistence on the announced terms of admission, namely, repentance, the confession of Christ as the Divine Redeemer, and baptism; " Repent, and be baptized *every one* of you in the name of Jesus Christ." (Acts ii. 38.) And what is the grand attractive privilege of Membership? It is the communication to each individual so admitted of the life which animates the community: " Ye shall receive the gift of the Holy Ghost." (Acts ii. 38.)

We have seen already * that the Church, as an institution, cannot always be kept entirely free from merely nominal

* Pp. 13, 14.

members, those to whom it may be said "Thou hast a name that thou livest, and art dead." (Rev. iii. 1.) But a name on a church-register imports at least an incipient life, or a life not yet totally extinct. Even in the case of the Angel of the church in Sardis, there are "beneath the ribs of death," "*things which remain*, that are ready to die." There must be at least the semblance of an incohate or lingering spiritual life in those who are admitted to or are permitted to retain membership in a church. The tolerated tares must be so like the wheat that mistake is possible. To admit any one into the Church except upon professed and seeming repentance, and express confession of faith in Christ, is not only to set at nought the very reason of the Church's existence, but is as futile and mischievous as it is unwarranted, being a mockery of God and man. For what is Church-membership worth either to the holder of it or to the community without Church-life? It is to the Church a bane, and to the individual a condemnation.

The numerical growth of the Church should be contemporaneous with, and proportionate to, its spiritual growth. Its members should be edified and multiplied at the same ratio. *The Lord* alone can really *add* to the Church; and He adds none but "such as are being saved," are in a state of initial and progressive salvation; whose salvation is not only provisionally accomplished and conditionally guaranteed in Christ, but is in process of personal realization. Christ is not the Head "of the dead, but of the living." External association without a common tendency to Christ is worse than useless to a Church. The most scientific juxtaposition of limbs, trunk, organs could not constitute a living *body*. And the Spirit of God alone can organize and animate the disjected members of spiritually dead humanity, making bone come "to his bone." He alone can conciliate the antipathies of race and education, and combine the antipodes of social position and surface-civilization into one exquisitely sympathetic organism, "tremblingly alive all o'er," with mutual love.

We must now glance at and endeavour to correlate the various passages in the New Testament, bearing on the legitimate constituency of the Christian Church.

We learn from the Head of the Church Himself, and from His Apostles, that not only His Church generally, but also every local church is authorized and required by Himself to enforce, on all who challenge membership within it, its appropriate restrictions, and is invested with the right of constitutional, not arbitrary, expulsion of all who transgress its peculiar limitations or frustrate by their habits the purpose of the association.

In addressing the various churches the Apostles plainly state the objects of their corporate existence : they are " called to be saints "—holy ones : they are assumed to be " sanctified in Christ Jesus;" to be, in fact, what they are called to be, "saints." They are " the faithful in Christ Jesus;" " the faithful brethren in Christ;" they are " elect—through sanctification of the Spirit unto obedience and sprinkling of the blood of Jesus Christ;" they are those " that have obtained like precious faith with " the Apostles. The direct object of their association is that they may " have fellowship " with those whose "*fellowship is truly* with the Father and with His Son Jesus Christ." The Church then is an association for moral, spiritual, and heavenly purposes: the aim of all its ministrations and arrangements is to " present every man perfect in Christ Jesus : " its consummation will be reached when Christ shall present to Himself the entire body of those who have kept, practically in view the ends of the association " a glorious Church, not having spot or wrinkle, or any such thing."

The point to be aimed at in, and by the Church is "that it may be holy and without blemish."

And this holiness clearly is not to be a merely constructive, inferential, hypothetical, make-believe holiness, as if by some legal fiction; a collective or corporate holiness attaching to a community the majority of whose individual members are palpably unholy. It is to be a real personal purity. To guard and nourish holy, heavenly dispositions is the immediate object of the society. Its principal officers have an inevitable responsibility to God, with reference to the individual members placed immediately under their care. It is not enough that they supply them with a sufficiency of wholesome spiritual food, they must also "watch for their souls as those that must give account."

St. Paul, addressing the Ephesian elders, describes the Church as the flock of God, who require oversight as well as sustentation, discipline as well as doctrine: "Feed the flock of God ... taking the oversight," and it is with reference to this duty that they are called bishops—"*overseers.*"

In the New Testament the Church is held responsible for its own purity of morals and soundness of doctrine; the Angel or presiding Representative of the Church, by virtue of his trust as presiding Representative; the collective church of a town or city; and, finally, the individual members of that church. Our Lord's injunction is* that the obstinately implacable brother is to be remonstrated with first by another brother alone, then by two or three brethren, and last of all admonished by the Church; of course the local church, which is for this intent and purpose "the Church," inasmuch as no one could imagine that an Œcumenical Council must be summoned to compose every mis-

---

* Matt. xviii. 15—18.

understanding between two private members, or that a remote central authority must be appealed to on every occasion when private remonstrance with an impracticable brother proves in vain. If, after Church-investigation and remonstrance, the offending brother prove still injurious or implacable, he is to be regarded, not only by the collective Church but by the individual member "as a heathen man or a publican:" "let him be unto *thee*, etc." This shows that an extortionate, reckless, profligate man may not be allowed membership in the Church, any more than "a heathen man."

"*If he neglect to hear the Church, let him be unto thee as an (the) heathen man and a (the) publican,*" that is, an object of yearning, pitying love, and earnest, hopeful desire, and the subject of fervent prayer, but not any longer admitted to that intimate association which mutual membership involves. "This implies the denial of Church privileges, exclusion from the Sacrament, etc.;"* and from the Lovefeast, of course. Moreover, the highest official is as amenable to this discipline as the lowliest member: as even Pope Sylvester II. himself (quoted by Baronius) said: "If the Pope of Rome were to sin against a brother, and after repeated admonition would not hear the Church; he should, according to the commandment of Christ be held as a heathen and publican." The evidences of habitual immorality must be conclusive before disciplinary action is taken. Penitent offenders must be restored. Though confidential fraternal relations are intermitted so long as the excluded offender remains obdurate, yet the most tender and hopeful relations must still be maintained. But the morals and the reputation of the Church must be resolutely and sensitively conserved.

Again, the entire Church is enjoined "not to eat"—

* Stier *ad loc.*

surely least of all at the Lord's Supper or the Lovefeast—with "any man that is called a brother," if he "be a fornicator, or covetous, or an idolator, or a railer, or a drunkard, or an extortioner." They are required to "put away from *themselves* that wicked person." The incorrigibly idle is "not to eat"—then surely not at the Lord's Supper or the Lovefeast, and not at the expense of the Church-funds. Individual members are directed to separate themselves from those who "walk disorderly."

All these oracles clearly make the Church responsible for the conservation of its own morals and its own true and good report, and do not allow the individual member to lose his responsibility in the collective Church, but make the purity of the Church every member's business, in such wise that it *is every* member's business.

Of course, discipline must be carried out in a regular and constitutional way, but it *must be carried out*. That the ratification in heaven of any Church-sentence on earth is conditional on its accordance with the Word of God is plain from our Lord's own dictum.

In all consistency and honesty of interpretation the extent to which the binding and loosing of the Church will be made effective in heaven is limited by the justice, mercy, and wisdom of its decisions; *unless* the expositor who would carry it further be prepared to maintain that the consentaneous prayers of any two Christians will be carried into effect by God, however foolish or wicked those prayers might be. If it be answered that the very promise implies the impossibility of any local church (for we have seen that the reference is to a local church) erring in judgment, then it must also be maintained that the promise involves an absolute infallibility in prayer, diffused through all the churches of Christendom. If so, then Professor Tyndall's proposed experiment would be quite fair. For what are the Master's words? "Verily I say unto you whatsoever ye shall bind on earth, shall be bound in heaven; and whatsoever ye shall loose on earth, shall be loosed in heaven. Again, I say unto you, that if two of you shall agree on earth as touching anything that they shall ask, it shall be done for them of My Father which is in heaven." (Matt. xviii. 18, 19.)

With our Lord's direction for preserving the peace, the purity and the unity of His Church, agrees that of His Apostle Paul: "I wrote unto you not to company"— (not to be *mixed up together with* συναναμίγνυσθαι,—not to have intimate association with indicating the closeness of connexion which the mutual membership of the Church implies. Comp. Wesley's "Mix our friendly souls in Thee.") "If any man that is called a brother be a fornicator, or covetous, or an idolator, or a railer, or a drunkard, or an extortioner; with such an one no not to eat; ... therefore *put away from among yourselves* that wicked person."

From this it is plain that the Church—every local church —is held responsible to God for the preservation of its own purity.

A kind of secondary, intermediate, temporary, provisional, or latter excommunication, or rather suspension from membership, seems to have been adjudged to those who were guilty of habitual indolence and its attendant vice, a wanton and mischievous intermeddling with other people's affairs. These were to be first *admonished;* then, if unreformed, *avoided, seceded* from, left behind (στέλλεσθαι—" to send oneself away from;" Parkhurst; 2 Thess. iii. 6); and, lastly, denied all the confidential and privileged intercourse of real Church-membership. The disciples were enjoined to have no company with "such." He was to be excluded "*in the meantime*" from the Lord's Supper, the Lovefeast, and other *fellowship*-meetings; the object being brotherly, the winning the delinquent to a better mind, "that he may be ashamed." And (καὶ) count him not as an enemy, but admonish him as a brother. He was still a brother, though a brother in disgrace; not to be counted like the implacable and unrepentant wrong-doer, "as a heathen man and a publican," or definitely *put away* as " a wicked person." Thus was Church-discipline graduated, and thus were idleness and gossiping reckoned grave, but still minor, breaches of Church-discipline.

Moreover, we have Christ's own commendation of intolerance of teachings which subvert the foundations of Christian faith and morals, and His stern and monitory condemnation of any sufferance of such teachings within the Church. And this is the more impressive from the fact that the leniency to depraved and depraving doctrine which the Head of the Church so terribly rebukes in the person of the Angel of the Church of Pergamos was connected with rightness of personal belief: "Thou holdest fast My name, and hast not denied My faith . . . But I have a few things against thee, because thou hast there them that hold the doctrine of Balaam . . . so hast thou also them that hold the doctrine of the Nicolaitanes. . . . Repent; or else I will come unto thee quickly, and will fight against them with the sword of My mouth." (Rev. ii. 13—16.) To *have*, to retain within the Church the holders of doctrines subversive of the very basis of the Christian belief, and fatal to the moral purity of the Church was a tolerance which Christ Himself would not tolerate, an official disloyalty which no personal loyalty could condone, a sin to be repented of and reformed without delay, "quickly," under penalty of the direct and summary hostility of the Redeemer Himself. The weak indulgence of this otherwise worthy Christian overseer towards his spiritual charge was as offensive to God as that of Eli to his profligate sons. Tolerance of gross evil within the Church is regarded as complicity, by the Head of the Church Himself.

On the other hand, the Angel of the church of Ephesus, though not faultless in all other respects, is applauded not only for sharing Christ's own doctrinal antipathies,—*hating* that which Christ also *hates*, but also that his was more than an intense repugnance to corrupt dogmas in the abstract, was a concrete and most practical repulsion of the holders of such doctrines, and the perpetrators of such practices. " Thou canst not bear *them* which are evil." On this Trench justly says, " The sphere in which the Angel of Ephesus had the chief opportunity of manifesting this holy intolerance of evil doers was, no doubt, that of *Church-discipline, separating off from fellowship* with the faithful those who named the name of Christ, yet would not depart from iniquity." (Com. on Epists. to Seven Churches in Asia, p. 72.) Habitual evil doers are not to be *borne* within the Church. Still further, mutual vigilance is required of all the members of the Church.

But are there not other sayings of our Lord, and other advices of His Apostles, which tend to relax the strictness of the above-quoted injunctions? Let us closely examine these converse directions, and allow them their full weight. Let us look first at the Parables of the Tares and of the Draw-Net, and St. Paul's similitude of the " Great House;" premising, however, that it is a violation of the simplest and most obvious canons of interpretation so to press one of our Lord's parables as to make it nullify or neutralize our Lord's positive precepts, or so to strain an Apostolic similitude as to bring it into violent collision with Apostolic directions. Neither parable nor metaphor must be pushed beyond their own proprieties, in order to silence other oracles of Holy Writ.

In the first place it must be borne in mind that in these parables our Lord does not say—*My Church* is likened unto —but "the kingdom of heaven is likened, etc." The Church and the Kingdom are not absolutely and unconditionally identical, though closely, related and concentric; the Church being the inner circle of the Kingdom. There is a Christendom outside the Church. And, *locally*, the church and the "congregation;" that is, the regular *attendants*, "hearers only," are not necessarily interchangeable terms. The "called" and the "chosen" are not always numerically the same. One error of Broad-Churchism and Broad-Chapelism is, the obliteration of this distinction. Yet the Kingdom includes the Church, although the Church does not include the whole Kingdom. The Church is "the household of faith,"—the homestead of mutually endeared discipleship. The Kingdom, as a historic phenomenon, takes a wider range. The leavening process works beyond the Church proper into the Kingdom, influencing public opinion and national law, and creating a Christian civilization.

So Baumgarten (Apostolic History, Vol. ii., p. 336, etc.), but unfortunately he mixes it up with less plain and pressing matters. He truly says, "We do find in this spiritual domain *two spheres of communion.*" No doubt the Kingdom and the Church will ultimately be identical. But at present Baumgarten's observation is full of significance and force: "As much as the ties of household and family are more intimate and fuller of affection than those of the native country or kingdom of a people, so the intimate and personal relations of the Lord towards the community of His saints must attain to a fuller realization and acknowledgment, exactly in the same proportion as *within this spiritual brotherhood the*

form of the Kingdom subsides into that of the family household.
This perfect configuration of the work of grace in the form
of a perfect community on earth has been at first disap-
pointed; therefore the Lord has now turned Him to individual souls, and on this, the deepest and most permanent
foundation of any in human life and nature, seeks to build
up eternal righteousness and holiness. These individuals
He for the time unites in the *communion* of the Church. . . .
As in the house the individual is always recognised in his
independence, and never can sink to the point of ultimate
insignificance, so in this ecclesiastical form of communion,
*the individual soul remains in Christ the ever present ground
and foundation for the life of the whole;* and on the other
hand the smallest community, even two or three, represents
the whole; because the whole—even in that extent with
which it shall fill the whole world—has simply the form of
the family and the household. And for this reason it is not
a matter of accident if the smallest assembly bears the same
holy name as belongs to the Church universal."—Vol. II.,
pp. 339, 340. "The two important expressions ἐκκλησία and
βασιλεία . . . are distinct notions, and are in fact supplementary of each other." (P. 354.)

The necessity for some such distinction as is here recognised between "the Kingdom," and "the Church" has
been felt by many earnest preachers. The Rev. Thomas
Dale, for example, discriminates between " the sheep of the
pasture " and " the sheep of the fold." (Exposition of the
XXIII. Psalm.) The early Church recognised that distinction. Even when God divides "the light from the darkness"
there is yet a twilight both of morn and eve. There is a
penumbra about the orb of the Church.*

---

* The History of the Church as distinct from the Kingdom has never

I

Notwithstanding this distinction, the bearing of the parables and the similitude upon the question of Church discipline and Church constituency is close and vital.

In the second place, *the world is the field*, not as all actually cultivated and enclosed, but as the sower's place of labour in contrast with the barn. Originally it was all *out*field, as all that part still is which is not yet *broken up* or enclosed.

The world is Christ's field in the sense of being both His property and the scene of His labours. Christ is the House-Master, or Landlord (οἰκοδεσπότης) of the entire world, enclosed or not yet enclosed, cultivated or not yet cultivated. It is not written "the kingdom of heaven is like unto a field," which field is the world, much less the Church is like to a field, which field is the world; but the kingdom of heaven—the Christian dispensation—is, in one especial aspect, like this whole agricultural apologue. To say, therefore with Augustine and the flock of commentators who have leaped after that great bell-wether of polemical exposition, that the world here is a synonyme for the Church, is a rich specimen of controversial exegesis which consists too often in correcting instead of commenting on Scripture. The *good seed* embodied in individual character forms "the children of the kingdom," the subjects of Christ by spiritual nativity, born into the kingdom; the *tares* are *the children of the wicked one*, the willing victims and embodiments of his falsehood and delusion, who yet present to human eyes such a resemblance to the children of the kingdom, in certain states and stages of the spiritual life, that any human hand attempting to clear the tares out of the way would be in danger of uprooting some of the wheat.

yet been written. Milner and Neander come the nearest to this conception; Milman's History is perhaps the most exclusively that of the Kingdom.

The inevitable alternative then is, either to let the tares grow side by side with the wheat, or to destroy some of the wheat in order to make a clear riddance of the tares. "Root out" of what? Out of that part of the field in which the good seed is sown. For the *sown* field is that wherein the devil *supersows*. It is not that the wheat is sown amongst tares, the children of the kingdom interspersed amongst the children of the wicked one. The parable does not refer to the wild and deleterious growths covering the land not yet sown upon; but tares are sown amongst the wheat, the children of the wicked one interspersed among the children of the kingdom.

"While *men slept*." The same inherent, and therefore inevitable, weakness of human nature, under cover of which Satan sowed the tares, incapacitates the servants for discriminating infallibly between tares and wheat. And it is the most watchful, keen-eyed, zealous and faithful of the servants, those who detected a spurious growth amongst the wheat, yet, whilst eager to uproot the tares, would not presume to do so without first consulting the Master,—the very servants whose discrimination and conscientiousness are manifest, who are pronounced incompetent to decide with certainty in every case, that such and such a person is a tare, and must be rooted out. No human vigilance can either keep Satan out of the field or surprise him at his work and compel him to declare himself. He does not spoil his work by overdoing. He treads so softly that he does not even leave his footmarks. He is quite content that men should deny his very existence.

The danger is not so much that the poison-grass should be mistaken for the wheat, but that wheat in its immature state should be mistaken for the poison-grass. And better let ten thousand blades of poison-grass cumber the ground, than let one grain of wheat perish. The difficulty arises from the fact that neither truth nor error always *heads out* before the close of life. There may be a blade of wheat of which one can say with confidence, That is wheat certainly; but there is no darnel of which one can say with absolute certainty, That is darnel. It is a gross and glaring violence to the parable to apply it to openly immoral people, or downright deniers of the Godhead of Christ and the Trinity in Unity, since the very point of the Parable is, the perplexing resemblance of the darnel to the wheat, whilst yet there is unlikeness enough to convince all sensitive observers that there is in the Society an admixture of darnel with the wheat.

It is plain that the parable sets forth a specific difference amongst " those who profess and call themselves Christians;" between the true evangelical cereal and the mere professing Church-weed : and the point of the Parable is—the impracticability of distinguishing infallibly between a specious but spurious professorship, and a genuine but immature Christianity. It is in vain to tell the Gospel grain-grower, You cannot always distinguish a blade of wheat from a blade of darnel, therefore you have no right to weed out *twitch:* you cannot invariably discriminate between a spurious Christianity and an immature Christianity, therefore you have no right to exclude from the Church a notoriously and habitually immoral man, or a denier of Christ's Godhead and of the basal and baptismal faith. It is within the range of fundamental orthodoxy that the spurious Christianity springs up. *Practical* Antinomianism is not ethical darnel; it does not bear the remotest resemblance to Christianity. Socinianism is not doctrinal darnel; it is not the counterpart of fundamental Christian truth, but the contradiction of the fundamental Christian truth. In *practical* Antinomianism the devil does not stealthily sow, and go "his way." He stops on the ground in broad daylight. And so in all those audacious systems which impudently claim the name of Christ, and yet reject His avowals as to His own conscious personality; the demon of deliberate doubt and desperate denial does not slyly sow his seed and slink away, but strides across the servants' path to face it out with them.

Moreover, the Parable shows that there are servants in charge. When rejecters of all Christian discipline, or "disciples" who set themselves above their Master, even as to His knowledge of His own personality and that of the Father and the Spirit, claim to be recognised as members of the Christian Church on the strength of this Parable, they turn the Parable into a fable; in which the *twitch* says to the servants whom the Lord has left in charge, "Keep your hands off me: remember your orders are to let *tares* and wheat grow together." To which the servants should reply, "Yes, but the fact that we cannot get rid of the tares, makes it all the more urgent that we should clear out the twitch: for with tares and twitch together the wheat would be sadly overmatched."

Moreover, this Parable does not refer to the terms of admission into the Church, but to the question of uprooting from the cultured glebe of Gospel labour persons who are already rooted in it. It can only refer to evangelized people; but those who reject Christ as a Divine Redeemer refuse to be evangelized. To make it a plea for the abolition of terms of admission into the Church, is to make the "servants," if not deliberately the sowers of tares in the Church-field, yet effectively subservient to the enemy;—a gross injustice to those who show such a godly jealousy as do the servants in the Parable.

Do let the enemy have his own work to himself, and do not make Christ's servants his accomplices. The Parable contains nothing in favour of an indiscriminate admission to the Church.

The primary lesson of the Parable is the tenderness which the Master feels towards the most dubious beginnings of the spiritual life. He will not trust to human discretion the distinguishing between a specious profession and half-developed Christian growths. And the whole of His own action during His personal Ministry, as also the whole bearing and teaching of His Apostles, is accordant with and illustrative of this principle. His gentleness with Nicodemus, with Zaccheus, with the Apostles themselves, is in perfect harmony with this, as also the maternal character of Apostolic discipline. How readily an eager zeal might grub up irregular or imperfectly developed growths of spiritual life. The second lesson of the Parable is that there are servants left in charge of the field. But the great tendency of zealous, prompt, decisive and perfervid men, whose strength of character marks them out for the overseership, is to deal with defaulters in a rough and ready manner. Their "gather up" (Ver. 28), the Master perceives, would in effect be "root up" (Ver. 29), and in many cases, as the history of Romanism shows, to *burn* up. For to such men these parties are things that do offend (Ver. 41), and occasions of stumbling both to their intellect and their sensibilities, nay often of actual uncharitableness, and are also sources of danger to the sincere and inexperienced, offending some of Christ's little ones. Moreover, the tares cast a cloud of suspicion on those who are "weak in faith" (Ver. 43). And, besides, they who make a heartless profession of religion, "mere outside Christians," as Wesley calls them, "do iniquity," by that unreal profession, as well as by the worldliness which they have never thoroughly abandoned.

The difficulty which some able expositors find here melts

before a closer inspection. Ministers may be quite sure that there is a great deal of hollow profession in the church, and yet be incompetent to say to this or that person whose outward life is not grossly disreputable, Your profession is altogether hollow, we cannot have you amongst us any longer.

The consistency of the Parable itself no less than its adjustment to the rest of the New Testament teaching, forbids its being pressed to the abrogation, or even the relaxation of Church-discipline. For, not only must the Master have had a reason for selecting darnel rather than any other weed which infests the wheat-field, but the *uprooting* which the Master prohibits is a widely different thing from that hopeful, reformatory, and in intention temporary exclusion which repentance will speedily reverse. It must not be supposed that Christ made the pronouncement recorded in Matt. xviii. 17, in forgetfulness of His teaching from the ship; or that St. Paul's decreeing the putting away of the immoral Corinthian, or his injunction to reject a heretic after the first and second admonition, was in contravention of his Master's orders. In that terrible and exceptional rooting out of the field entirely, the doom of Ananias and Sapphira, it is not to be doubted that the act of God *in so far as it removed them from the Church* anticipated the action of the Community. The death of Ananias and Sapphira was an awful vindication of the holiness of the Church.

What complicates the matter is, that in each human heart there is incessant danger of some "root of bitterness" springing up amongst the good seed, and whilst the tares may by conversion become wheat, the wheat may by heart-backsliding become tares.

The state of the Corinthian church, and St. Paul's treatment of it, afford a fine practical illustration of this Parable.

They were "babes in Christ," "yet carnal" walking as men; yet what patience! excepting with the openly immoral, who was not finally rooted up, but put away until his repentance. Thus lukewarm Laodicea, is still *loved*, warned, rebuked, chastened, and for a season, spared.

The most audacious violators of the Master's commands, as conveyed in this parable, are the Roman Catholics and the Calvinists—Genevans, Scotch and New Englanders,—who instead of making excommunication on the ground of even fundamental error, provisional, hopeful and *pending penitence*, have rooted up and in some cases even burnt the offenders, thus cutting short their space for repentance.

The Parable of the Draw-Net refers distinctly to the vast and larger inclusiveness of the Church; but the fish must be within the meshes of the net, in order to be within the Church at all. And what are those meshes, if the leading truths of Christianity — the Divinity of Christ and His death for our sin according to the Scriptures—and a strong effective Church-discipline—are not? A man who slips through those meshes has got out of the net again into the sea, and one who evades those meshes has never been in the net.

The net is, in the first place, the preaching of the Gospel. It encloses within its meshes all that come within its sweep. The evangelization of a country is the casting the Gospel net into the midst of its population. Its net-work includes not only its communicants, but also its hearers and scholars, and consists of all its appliances and agencies for drawing men out of the troubled element of worldliness. The sea is the world as really as the field is the world; and the sea is the world in the same sense as the field is the world. But that part of the field where darnel and wheat grow together is not limited by the boundaries of the Church-proper, but comprises all that is brought under some kind and degree of evangelical culture. The draught of fishes consists of all who are brought within the range of Gospel ministrations.

The Augustinian interpretation, which Archbishop Trench pronounces to be that of the Church, and which certainly has been copied by the mass of interpreters, as being most accordant with the actual condition of the professing Church, would turn the net itself into a " great and wide sea, wherein are things creeping innumerable, both small and great beasts." (Psalms, b. iv., 25.)*

But what is the significance of the " vessels ? " and who are they that drew the net to shore, and sat down and gathered the good into vessels, etc. ? Those eminent Apostles who were themselves fishermen would naturally and necessarily conclude that those who cast the net and drew it to shore were those who sat down and gathered the good into vessels, etc.

* It is much to be regretted that Archbishop Trench's interpretation of these two parables is not nearly so firm or skilful as that of the rest. It is indeed little more than a second-hand comment—Trench upon Augustine—instead of a direct, unbiased exposition. Thus the learned theologian degenerates into a controversial commentator ; not first expounding the two parables on their own merits, and then judicially arbitrating between the polemical one-sidedness and extravagance of Augustine, and the polemical one-sidedness and extravagance of the Donatists, but at once ranging himself as a partisan of Augustine. Hence he puts down all who cannot accept the dictum of Augustine, that in the Parable of the Tares, Christ by "the world," means the Church, by curtly pronouncing, " It must be evident to every one not warped by a previous dogmatic interest that the parable is, as our Lord announces at its first utterance, concerning the kingdom of heaven or the Church." But it would have been much more to the purpose, though not quite so easy, if the erudite expositor had proved that " the kingdom of heaven " and the Church are in every aspect identical. Is the Church then the " one pearl of great price ?" or the field-hidden treasure ? Would he venture in a new edition of his admirable *Synonyms of the New Testament*, to give " the World " as a synonyme of the Church ? He has not the hardihood to say *point blank*

Any one who has watched the process would instinctively adopt the same supposition. What Trench says of the affinity of tares and wheat may be as justly said of the fact that the fishermen themselves are wont to sort their fish—" it makes much for the beauty of the parable and is full of instruction." Indeed, the consistency, the holding together, of the parable necessitates this interpretation. It is in possession, and there is no other legitimate process of eviction but the proving it to be irreconcilable, either with the rest of the parable or with the direct teaching of Christ and His Apostles. But is it so? Is it impossible to harmonize the statement—" So shall it be at the end of the world "—with the propriety of the parable? This is done at once if we take ούτως " so " in its frequent signification of *appropriate sequence*, and not of direct correspondence or comparison, as the narrative "then" "so then" "and so." (Comp. Acts xx. 11; xxvii. 17; xxviii. 16; Rev. iii. 16.) This is a meaning quite in agreement with classical as well as New Testament usage.

What then is the work of the angels? Clearly something different from that of the tired fishermen who "sat down and gathered the good into vessels, etc." The angelic attitude and function is in contrast with that of the fishermen. The former "sat down;" the latter "shall come forth."

..." the Church is the world," but coolly emends our Lord's statement into " 'the field' was 'the world,' namely, before it became the field." Yet, on one point, he happily diverges from his master, and in so doing refutes Augustine's aberrant exposition and his own, by admitting that " it makes much for the beauty of the parable and is full of instruction, that wheat and tares are not seeds of different kinds, but that the last is a degenerate or bastard wheat." (P. 91.) But "open" immorality is not degenerate or bastard Christianity, and the largest "numbers" cannot make it so. Yet the Archbishop agrees with Augustine in sheltering under the title of "tares"—" open offenders who from their numbers may not without greater evils ensuing be expelled!" (P. 85.) Wordsworth follows St. Augustine slavishly.

Their work does not begin till the fishermen's proper work is ended. The net is drawn to land; the fishermen have sat down—in contrast with their former eager and exhausting toil—for quiet, deliberate examination of the result of their labours; they transfer the marketable fish from the net to vessels, the necessary complement of the net, and cast the rest away. So far all is familiar and natural to Peter, Andrew, James and John, who were henceforth to be "fishers of men." But those who catch the fish, and put the wholesome into vessels, and cast away the unwholesome, do not burn "the bad," or subject the fish in the vessels to a second and severer scrutiny. That is left to the angels, the sanatory inspectors * of the City of God.

The first anxiety of a true hearted fisher of men like Peter, Paul, Whitefield and the Wesleys, is to have *a good haul.* He does not restrict the range of his invitation for fear lest some improper characters should get entangled in his evangelistic appliances. He is not content with dreamy angling, by rippling shallows or by waveless pools. His passion is for deep-sea dredging, with stout tackle, and in craft well-found. But when his net is full he draws it to shore, and examines his prize. Then those whom he has cause to think truly sincere, he puts into the vessels of Church-privilege and oversight;† whilst those who do not "bring forth fruits meet for repentance," he rejects. But the contents of the vessels must undergo a subsequent and far more searching scrutiny, and the worthless and useless,

* The ἀγορανόμοι and ὀψονόμοι of ancient cities; the latter were especially charged with the inspection of fish (Becker): the Ædiles of the Romans. The fishermen of Capernaum, Gadara, and Gergasa knew these officers well.

† Whitefield's mistake, however, as he himself afterwards admitted, was that he was so intent upon catching men, that he neglected too much the duty of putting them into vessels when caught.

whether in the vessels or on the beach, whether in the Church or out of it, will be burnt.

The Similitude of the Great House: 2 Tim. ii. 16—21. The teaching of this passage is clearly in favour of maintaining the doctrinal and moral purity of the Church. The tenor of the Apostle's argument is:

Although, by false teachers, the faith of some is overthrown, yet "the foundation of God" was not shaken by the falling faith which had for a time been placed upon it. What then is that Divine foundation whereon the Christian faith is built? According to St. Paul's teaching throughout, it is "Jesus Christ," and the truth concerning and in Him— "the truth as it is in Jesus." "Other foundation can no man lay than that is laid, which is Jesus Christ." (1 Cor. iii. 11.) That foundation is "the foundation of God" in an absolute and unapproachable sense. Whatever rival foundation, even though it should assume the dear and sacred name of His Church, may be placed beside this, and however numerous the "unstable souls" who are beguiled away from it, it still "nevertheless . . . standeth firm." And it bears this twofold inscription, on the one side, "The Lord knoweth them that are His;" and on the other, "Let every one that nameth the name of Christ depart from iniquity."

This is obviously intended to mitigate the shock inflicted by the discovery that false teachers and unstable hearers may appear within the Church, "the great house" built on the sure-standing "*foundation of God*," and further to give practical directions as to the action of Church-members, and Pastors especially, towards the overthrowers of the faith of unstable souls.

The principles implied are, 1st., That Church-membership affords no absolute guarantee for loyalty to Christ and His truth. The allusion to the insurrection of Korah, etc., is clear; the first inscription being a direct quotation from the Septuagint version of Numbers xvi. 5. The two inscriptions and the admonition, "If a man purge himself from these," form a kind of double echo to the warning of Moses: "Depart, I pray you, from the tents of these wicked men, and touch nothing of their's, lest ye be consumed in all their sins." (Numbers xvi. 26.)

The second principle implied is, that although the profession of Christ's religion affords no absolute security of holiness in the professor, yet it clearly implies the renunciation of iniquity. A profession of the Christian's "most holy faith" is, in itself, a most solemn engagement to lead a holy life. And then the first principle is recurred to, and further illustrated: In the Church, as in a royal palace, there cannot but be, by reason of the present condition of human nature, "vessels to dishonour," as well as "vessels unto honour." False teachers and heresiarchs serve the former purpose: they carry off from the Church the impurities which might otherwise defile it. A parallel passage is 1 Cor. xi. 19: "There must be also heresies among you, that they which are approved may be made manifest among you." Heretical leaders are not without sanitary serviceability. They carry off from the Church incongruous and unhealthy material: as saith St. John, "They went out from us, but they were not of us; for if they had been of us, they would have continued with us: but they went out that they might be made manifest that they were not all of us."

The practical deduction is plain and positive: "If a man therefore purge himself from these"—"vessels to dishonour"—"he shall be a vessel unto honour, sanctified, and meet for the Master's use." Now how can a man purge himself from vessels to dishonour, except by avoiding close contact with them? But the very idea of the Church involves, as we have seen, fellowship, communion, intimate union amongst all its members. To say that it is right to take the Lord's Supper—an act involving the most confidential spiritual contact—with persons whose friendship we dare not cultivate, for fear of moral or spiritual contamination, is to violate the very principles on which and to frustrate the very purpose for which the Church was founded. True, even in a palace there must be the footbath and the charwoman's bucket; but even in a palace some sort of decency and discrimination should be preserved. Surely some outhouse of the Church, some decorously divided scullery, is good enough for vessels to dishonour. And yet this passage has been alleged as justifying not only the retention of disreputable Church-members, but even the tolerance of profligate or misbelieving preachers, prelates and popes.

When David exclaimed "Moab is my washpot," did he imply that the ancient decree was repealed, "A Moabite shall not enter into the congregation of the Lord?" (Deut. xxiii. 3.) Yet many writers from Augustine downwards have made this similitude, and the parables of the Tares and Draw-Net the Magna Charta of undisguised worldliness and wickedness within the pale of the Church, and have interpreted them as setting the Church free from strict responsibility for the preservation of righteousness and purity in the life of its members. They thus reverse the teaching of the passage, which is not only "Let every one that nameth the name of Christ depart from iniquity;" but that "a man" should "purge himself from these" *vessels* to dishonour.

To point as even Rutherford,* for example, does to Corinth, Sardis, and Thyatira in proof of the dogma that no degree of connivance at evil in the Church involves complicity in

* See Dr. Walker's "Theology and Theologians of Scotland," p. 99.

that evil and participation in its guilt, is strangely to misread the Word of God. It is quite true, instructively and significantly true, that the Apostle did manifest a motherlike forbearance towards the partisanship and irregularities of the Corinthians; but he insists upon their *putting away* a scandalously immoral man; and our Lord Himself holds the Angels of the churches of Sardis and Thyatira strictly responsible for their tolerance of corrupt teaching and corrupt living.

The Augustinian principle, adopted by so many subsequent writers, that "communion with notorious offenders cannot pollute the united body of Christ,"* must not be received as an unconditional affirmation, seeing that Christ entrusted to His Church, locally and individually, the maintenance of right-dealing and peaceable relations amongst its members, and holds the authorities of the various churches responsible for purity of doctrine and morals within their several charges. Moreover, as Augustine himself asserts, "the good" alone hold the high prerogatives of the Church; and therefore surely the responsibilities attached to those prerogatives. What is meant by *polluting the body?* Clearly according to the course of Augustine's argument, the involving the good in the guilt of complicity, resulting from connivance. Christ, by laying upon His Church the responsibility of conserving its own purity and peaceableness, assumed that His Church would never be without constitutional means for the discharge of this responsibility, through its angels or representatives, the overseers of its own election, which it had the power of displacing and replacing in the event of their palpable dereliction of this duty. Christ never conceded to a community destitute of the apparatus of effective discipline the title of Church.

But to what extent does membership in a church involve

* De Baptismo, Bk. v., Chap. v.,—i. 1.—" Nulla Malorum, etc."

responsibility for the purity of that church or complicity in any errors or corruptions that may have crept into it?

In order to a correct and conclusive answer to this question, it is necessary to put a few preliminary inquiries: 1. Is any degree at all of moral purity and integrity, or any amount of positive truth, necessary to a church or the Church? May a church or the Church tolerate within its bosom any extreme of immorality or false teaching or forbidden worship whatsoever? 2. If some degree of moral purity and integrity and some basis of revealed truth is absolutely necessary to a church or the Church; if there be any limit whatever to the Church's tolerance of gross immorality, fundamental error or forbidden worship, who is responsible for the maintenance of the necessary purity, and the exclusion of intolerable vice, error or impiety? Surely the Church is responsible to God for the insistence on some minimum of piety in all its members, some modicum of revealed truth in public teaching, some safeguards against the intrusion of forbidden worship. If this be undeniable, then, where does the responsibility rest? Is it confined to elders, bishops or angels of churches, whatever modern names they may bear? Or is it diffused through the whole body of the Church? Does it inhere in each individual member, from the least to the greatest? If it be replied that the elders, bishops, angels or otherwise designated overseers of the Church are the only responsible parties,— then, what is to be done in the event of their gross neglect of duty, or of their being themselves the scandalously immoral, the perpetrators of forbidden worship, or the teachers of doctrines directly at variance with the Word of God, "speaking perverse things," as St. Paul prophesied (Acts xx. 30). Clearly, every individual believer is bound not to join in forbidden worship, is bound to watch over his brethren, to admonish and to warn openly every brother, whatever may be the offender's office, and to protest against corruptions in living, teaching, worship. Every one is under obligation to refuse to obey man rather than God, or to do, affirm, or be party to anything clearly contrary to God's holy Word, even under peril of excommunication. If for his loyalty to God and truth and purity he be put out of the pale, those who put him out are the separatists, the schismatics, and not he.

What condition of a church, then, can justify or necessitate secession from the church of one's spiritual parentage? In the first place, nothing can justify it which does not necessitate it. What Burke says of political revolution is equally true of ecclesiastical secession: it will be the very last resort of the thinking and the good.

It must also be remembered that a faulty church is still a church in the authoritative nomenclature of Christ Himself. So long as there are " a few *names*" (persons entered on the Church register) "even in Sardis, which have not defiled their garments," and discipline is not wholly defunct—"the church in Sardis" still survives. In the spiritual Babylon God has His people, as plainly appears even from His solemn and final warning, " Come out of her, My people." No precise rule can be laid down applicable to all cases. Every one must discreetly and duteously follow the leadings of the Spirit and of Providence. Above all no man must judge his brother or set at nought his brother, as to motive. Isaiah (Chap. vi. 13) compares the Church in its winter state to a deciduous tree, whose trunk is firm when it has shaken off its withered leafage: " as a teil tree and as an oak, *whose substance is in them, when they cast their leaves: so the holy seed* shall be the substance thereof."

To allow no inner bolt to Christ's fold, but only an outer latch which any stranger may open, is to invite into the fold the thief and the robber. To make out, as Augustine attempts to do, that the moral character of Christian pastors is no more the concern of Christian people than the moral character of the Scribes and Pharisees was the concern of the disciples, is at variance with Christ's own statement that every true Shepherd *goes before* his flock, and that Christ's sheep know not the voice of strangers, and *a stranger they will not follow*. All Christ's shepherds must themselves be members of the flock—they are made " overseers" "amongst" —*in*—the flock.

The claim put forward by certain respectable seatholders in Christian sanctuaries to be admitted to the Lord's Table and into the Church *sub silentio*, and to be excused from all inquiry as to their religious beliefs, convictions, experience, and habits, and from all confession of Christ by the mouth unto salvation, is directly at variance with the whole plan and purpose of the Christian institute. To maintain that the Church has no collective representative or reciprocal responsibility, as touching the faith, earnestness, and spiritual growth of its members, but that it is quite at liberty to throw or leave the entire responsibility of the faith of its members in the foundation facts on which the Church rests, as well as of their Christian habits and daily life, upon any individual who, from whatever unascertained cause, would like to be regarded as a member of the Christian Church and partake of the Supper of the Lord; that the obligation of the Church terminates with the providing the ordinances of Christian worship, the periodical celebration of the Lord's Supper, and the invitation of all " seriously disposed " persons to join; and that all necessary " fencing of the tables " is accomplished by reminding the intending communicants what is the proper state of mind for the reception of that Sacrament—this betrays a notion of the nature and functions of the Church of Christ and of the significance, sacredness and obligations of membership therein, widely differing from that of Christ and His Apostles.

But, alas! the Augustinian notion adopted by Roman Catholicism, Erastianism, extreme Broad-Churchism, and other theories made to fit the actual condition of affairs, throws upon the forbearance of God and individual accountability that responsibility for the open wickedness of Church-members which Christ laid upon the churches themselves. Thus no resolute disciplinary effort to make the Church as an institution approximate to the Church as an ideal is insisted on. Christ's representation in the Parable of the Tares is reversed. It is the wheat that is sown among the tares, not the tares among the wheat. According to this theory, so far is the Christian Church as a historic institution from being an advance on Judaism in its best days (much less the realization of the ideal of the ancient Theocracy), that it does not allow to the Christian Church as effective moral guarantees as those of the Mosaic Dispensation.

The true Church is represented as a small minority in the factitious Church. In Christ's fold the goats may be allowed to outnumber the sheep, and hustle them at will; nay, an episcopal wolf must not be turned out, for fear he should carry a sheep away in his mouth. The Church-field may be overrun by all kinds of palpable poison-grass, with thorns, briars, and thistles to boot, till the vineyard of the Lord is like the sluggard's garden. Christ's threshing-floor must not be situate upon a breezy summit, that the chaff may be blown away, but in some sheltered depression, that it may have every chance of overlying the wheat.

The prophetic pictures of the multitudinousness, the territorial vastness, the external grandeur of the Church are proudly pointed to ; the pictures of its contemporaneous and co-extensive purity and righteousness are lost sight of. Of two such pictures, why forget the grander, the lovelier, and the holier one?

To swell the numbers of the Church by an indiscriminate inclusiveness is to make an Esau-like exchange, to barter the Church's sanctity for specious statistics and "a fair show in the flesh," and to sacrifice the might and majesty of spiritual loveliness to "the weak and beggarly elements" of worldly influence and position. Earthly extension without a correspondent heavenly elevation, spoils the symmetry of the City of God, which "lieth foursquare. . . . The length and the breadth, and the height of it are equal." (Rev. xxi. 16.) The beginning of the great apostasy was the disloyal compromise with the Canaanites; the ignoble policy of Issachar. The Church became "a strong ass couching down between two burdens: and " she " saw that rest was good, and the land that it was pleasant; and bowed " her " shoulder to bear, and became a *servant unto tribute*." (Gen. xlix. 14, 15.) The church that accepts endowments as the price of a laxer spiritual discipline, becomes "a servant unto tribute:" her secular elevation is spiritual servitude. And the unendowed church which, yielding to the seduction of splendid statistics, or a Satan-suggested numbering of the people, should abandon the requirement of a confession of personal faith and a statement of personal experience in order to membership, because such requirement keeps out of Nonconformist churches many virtuous, intelligent and cultivated individuals, and thus lessens the numerical imposingness and the political influence of Nonconformity, would become "a servant unto tribute." If any unendowed church which has been brought by the Spirit and providence of God to recognise the essentiality of "fellowship" as an element of Church-life should cease to insist upon the *duty* of fellowship, in deference to the distastes of respectable communicants, it would become "a servant unto tribute." *

It also behoves the various Nonconformist churches to remember that freedom from State establishment and endowment constitutes no infallible safeguard against the de-spiritualizing tendency of worldly prosperity and popularity. The dominant influence of an unspiritual millionaire might be at least as pernicious to a church in England as that of a half-evangelized king of some island of the sea to the native converts.

The error of the main body of the Church in the Dark and Middle Ages was that "with fleshly wisdom" it came to terms with the worldliness against which it was sworn to wage a war without truce or terms, and in addition to all its other fond and childish Judaising it "put the Canaanites to tribute."

The most effective as well as the most legitimate influence of the Church is that of holiness. Even when in its infancy it was exposed to deadly persecution and was the subject of a social ban, many were attracted towards it by intellectual affinities and sentimental sympathies who had not yet yielded to deep spiritual convictions. That tremendous vindication of the sacredness of Church-membership, the death of

* Such motives for this strange innovation in Puritan churches are not hastily imputed. They are avowed and eloquently insisted on by some of its able advocates (notably in an Essay by a leading Congregationalist minister in the remarkable collection of essays entitled *Ecclesia*.) We heartily congratulate our Congregationalist brethren on having escaped this terrible temptation. The *Christian Witness* did good service in the discussion, and the Rev. Eustace Conder's speech from the chair of the Congregational Union was a noble manifesto on the subject. Let us hope that the laxity of spiritual discipline which has so often and so justly been denounced as one of the peculiar evils of a State-church will not be allowed to invade the sanctuaries of Voluntaryism.

Ananias and Sapphira, was intended to purge and protect the Church from the debilitating and demoralizing effects of such incongruous accessions. And what was its practical result? It was, of course, in the first instance, repellent. "Of the *rest durst* no man join himself to them" (Acts v. 13); the rest of the class of unspiritual aspirants after Church-membership. "Christianly disposed" persons who were not yet resolved, by Divine grace, to live holy lives *durst* not join the holy Church. But did the Church consequently lose public influence? Just the opposite: "the people magnified them." (*Ib.*) The honest, healthy, popular instincts gave willing homage to a really spiritual society, flourishing amidst and testifying against the corruptions of the unregenerate world. But was the numerical increase of the Church thereby really checked? Just the contrary: "*Believers* were *the more* added to the Lord, *multitudes* both of men and women." (Ver. 14.) The excision of a few unspiritual members, and the warning off of a few unspiritual applicants for membership, was richly compensated by a vast ingathering of true, living converts. Believing men were not repelled by the doom of Ananias, nor believing women by that of Sapphira. For that which guards and guarantees the sanctity and spirituality of the Church enhances its public influence and multiplies its converts.

The claim of admission to the Lord's Table *on demand*, without spiritual investigation or oversight, is inconsistent with even the lowest view of the Communion of the body and blood of Christ. Take for example the elegant dogma of "Ecce Homo:"—"The Christian Communion is a club dinner: but the club is the New Jerusalem; God and Christ are members of it." (P. 173.) Surely the *New Jerusalem Club* has the right of every other club to decide on the eligibility of applicants for admission to its privileges. It should have no honorary members: "having men's persons in admiration because of advantage." (Jude 16.)

The Church as a vital and organic unity, which, though like an animated body, it cannot be totally unaffected by outward influences, should yet demonstrate its living individuality, and protect itself from decay and decomposition by not permitting the world around to encroach upon and assimilate it; but, on the contrary, should conquer and appropriate the world by *converting* the world into the Spiritual Church.

Yet, on the other hand, it is plain from the Apostolical Epistles, that the discipline of the Apostolic Church was marked by extreme forbearance towards all but incorrigible offenders and active corrupters and seducers. Not only was the immature and feeble Christian to be *received*, but one of the primal obligations of the Christian fellowship was the restoration by the "spiritual" of any brother "*overtaken* in a *fault*." This is an essential part of that mutual sympathy and mutual help which makes the Communion of Saints a reality and not a myth. The most invaluable help which we can render to each other is spiritual help in the great fight which we all have to fight, the fight of the Spirit against the flesh. And the most kindly and effective spiritual service which we can either render or receive is help to recover ourselves when we have been worsted in the battle with evil: our very *brotherhood* binds us to this, as also our companionship in arms. "Brethren, if a man be overtaken in a fault ye that are spiritual restore such an one in the spirit of meekness, considering thyself, lest thou also be tempted. Bear ye one another's burdens, and so fulfil the law of Christ."

"*Brethren,*" as much argument as appeal is enclosed in that word. It not only awakes the family-feeling of true

Christianity, but also suggests the fact that amongst children of the same Father, sharers at the same board, kneelers at the same household altar, equals around the same hearth, a fault in any one of them cannot unloose the relationship, and ought not to deaden the affection. There is a terrible predisposition in unspiritual strict livers to neglect and abandon an erring brother, as if the only Christian duty to the fallen were to censure and to shun. Against this egregiously un-Christ-like tendency St. Paul found it necessary to warn his converts. But the very expressions employed clearly show that the " fault" to be thus tenderly dealt with is something very different from presumptuous, deliberate, habitual sin. The fault which the Church of Christ is to condone is not the sin which a man pursues and OVERTAKES, sets himself to find occasion for committing, making " provision for the flesh to fulfil the lusts thereof," but one that overtakes a man assaulting him from behind.

" Babes in Christ," whose lingering carnality forms a serious harassment both to themselves and others; " him that is weak in the faith;" " the bruised reed and the smoking flax;" the awakened sinner *desiring* "to flee from the wrath to come;" the penitent backslider; the sincere soul as yet " unskilful in the word of righteousness," or for a time " bewitched" like the Galatians by the specious dogmatism of false teachers, or like some of the Corinthians beguiled for a season by the refinements of a seductive rationalism; the subjects of religious declension, in whom some spiritual " things remain " although they be " ready to die;" even the " lukewarm," until utterly rejected by God and abandoned by His Spirit—all these must be retained within Christ's Church, so long as they do not resist the decent and orderly arrangements of its gentle house-rule; but not the habitually immoral, the incorrigibly quarrelsome, the pertinacious propagator of destructive error. That connivance at these evils involves complicity is taught by St. John (2 Epis. xi.), and by St. Paul (1 Tim. v. 22).*

In what then does the *holiness* of "the Holy Catholic Church" consist? The holiness of the Church as of the individual Christian, is real and actual, and not merely imputative, though not yet in every respect absolute and unprogressive. As every true, living believer is a saint, according to the Scriptural conception of saintship, although his sanctity may be as yet incohate and germinant only; so the holiness of the Church is a real, and not a merely ideal, forensic or constructive holiness, although it be not yet " without spot, or wrinkle, or any such thing." The holiness of the Church, like that of the individual believer, is not an abstract but a concrete holiness. The Church has no collective holiness distinct from the holiness of its members. As the public health is no mere abstraction having some mythical existence apart from the individuals who compose the public, but is nothing more than the totality of the health of those persons regarded as a community, so the holiness of the Church is no mere abstraction, with some mythical existence apart from the individuals who compose it, but is nothing more than the totality of the holiness of those persons regarded as a brotherhood or fellowship.† The Church is the Holy Church inasmuch as it is the aggregate of " the churches of the saints." (1 Cor. xiv. 33.)

---

* The question of the relation of baptized children to the Church my space will not allow me to touch at present, as it involves the whole doctrine of Baptism, and other much mystified theological questions.

† And yet, as the public health may be pronounced good, whilst some are sick, or even dying, and very few in perfect health, so the Church is still "the Holy Church," though some of its members are unsound, and very few perfect.

The holiness of the individual believer, and consequently that of the Church, is, first of all, a holiness of relationship and of obligation. The term *holy*, as also the term saint, is in the *first* place descriptive of relationship and obligation, and then of those moral and spiritual qualities which befit that relationship and obligation. And this holy relationship to God in Christ is most real in every believer, and the holy obligation grows out of the relationship; and nothing but the utter neglect of the obligation entails the forfeiture of the relationship. This sanctity of relationship and obligation appears very strikingly on the first occurrence of the word " saints " in Scripture (Deut. xxxiii. 2, 3), where it is applied in common to angels and God's covenant people. (Comp. Psa. lxviii. 17.) The Old Testament definition of saints is "those that have made a covenant with Me by sacrifice." (Psa. l. 5.) This covenant with God by sacrifice establishes the holy relationship and involves the holy obligation. Hence Moses reminds the Jewish nation—" Thou art an holy people unto the Lord ; " which he was far from intending as perfectly descriptive of their moral character, at the time, but as a memento of the lofty responsibilities resulting from a lofty relationship. Now although a persistent disregard of the responsibilities ultimately destroys the relationship, yet through the tender mercy of God, the perfect sanctity of the relationship does not await the perfect sanctity of the individual or the community ; is not held in abeyance till that sanctity be complete, does not fluctuate with the advances and recessions of purity in the Christian or the Church ; is, in fact, not the terminus but the starting point in the pursuit of holiness by the individual or the Church. The leniency of God, through the propitiation and advocacy of Christ, condones, to an extent which man cannot measure, the shortcomings of His as yet imperfect people, individually and as a community. Not in vain does our Advocate present the plea of Hezekiah: "The good Lord pardon every one that prepareth his heart to seek God, the Lord God of his fathers, though he be not cleansed according to the purification of the sanctuary." (2 Chron. xxx. 18, 19.)*

Yet there is a point of backsliding whereat apostasy is accomplished, beyond which this relationship does not extend, although none but God can pronounce when it is reached by this or that particular church. This point was almost touched by the ten tribes at a time when the two tribes were yet many removes from it; as saith the Spirit by Hosea (Chap. xi. 12): "Ephraim compasseth Me about with lies,

* In this respect the Church ought to imitate the clemency of God: "Bear ye one another's burdens, and so fulfil the law of Christ." The heaviest burden a believer has to bear is the burden of his regrets his stumbles and his slips—his "faults." And the first and highest duty of Christian brotherhood is to help one another to bear this burden. "Confess your *faults* one to another, and pray one for another, that ye may be healed."

Trench calls attention to the fact that the word rendered "bear" in Gal. vi. 2, βαστάζειν, is the same as that so translated in Rev. ii. 2,— "Bear ye one another's burdens." "Thou canst not bear them that are evil." On this textual coincidence he well remarks, "The infirmities, even the sins, of *weak* brethren are burdens which *may* be borne, may, which we are commanded to bear; these, however ('them that are evil'), are not weak brethren but 'false;' and there must be no such toleration of them." (Ps. cxxix. 21, 22.; Com. on Epis. to Seven Churches.)

But the ancient Church, like its Lord, *hated putting away*. "Judgment," excommunication, was "strange work." To cast a man out of the ark of the Church into the raging monster-peopled abyss of heathen society, was more repugnant to them than was the throwing overboard of Jonah to the seamen of Tarshish. Even when the ecclesiastical tempest was so "mighty . . . that the ship was like to be broken," "they rowed hard to bring it to land," and it was only when they saw that the alternative was the utter foundering of the Church, that they at last, with vehement deprecation, cast the incorrigible disturber and corrupter "forth into the sea," the devouring surf of the world "*without.*" In the view of the primitive Christians excommunication, like relapse or apostasy, was a terrible thing, a *delivering* to *Satan*.

and the house of Israel with deceit: but Judah yet ruleth with God, and is faithful with the saints." A state of incorrigible pride and lukewarmness may be reached at which Laodicea would be rejected with disgust; but the Omniscient alone is competent to declare when that state is fallen to and fixed. Moreover, the defection of any Christian community, is not the defection of the Church. So long as two or three faithful people meet together in Christ's name the Holy Catholic Church survives. Nay, a church is not extinct so long as one resolute confessor of Christ remains, one Abdiel-spirit "among the faithless." Even had Elijah's moody census of God's people been correct, when he cried, "I alone am left," the Church had still survived.*

Again, the very purpose for which the Church exists is the cultivation and conservation of holiness. Its administration and arrangements should all be directed to this end, and as we have seen the acceptance or retention of Church-membership implies a solemn engagement before God and man to make the pursuit of holiness the great object of life. The Church, then, is the Holy Church, as possessing and enforcing a holy discipline, a Christ-like intolerance of "the works of the flesh" which "are manifest" (Galatians v. 19—21).

The Holy Church then is not an aggregate of unholy individuals made nominally holy by their aggregation, but a community of "saints"—holy persons in the Scriptural

* A gallant illustration of this truth occurred at the meeting of the Young Men's Christian Association in Paris, in 1857. The representative from a village in the South of France being called for, an *ouvrier* in a blouse stepped forward. Being asked how many members there were in the Association of which he was the delegate, he replied, "One; myself. There were three, but one is dead, the other removed, and I shall never rest till I have persuaded others to join me. I represent the Association past and future."

sense of the term, persons who have voluntarily joined an association, the object of which is holiness, and are pledged to abide by, and maintain the holy discipline of that association.

But we shall see more clearly in what the holiness of the Church consists by inquiring, what constitutes its unity.

Having ascertained that the Church of Christ, according to its Divine ideal, is a vital and organic unity, and that according to the working plan of that "wise master builder" St. Paul, it must be as such self built-up, it is now necessary to ask, In what does that unity consist? By what is it constituted? How is it manifested? How maintained? How violated? What is true catholicity? and What is schism?

The Holy Spirit, in our text represents the unity of the Church as sevenfold. There is (1) one body; (2) one Spirit; (3) one hopeful calling; (4) one Lord; (5) one faith; (6) one baptism; (7) one God and Father of all.*

When St. Paul alleges as the first inducement to the endeavour "to keep the unity of the Spirit in the bond of peace:" "There is one body;" what idea is intended to be conveyed by the word "body?" The only fair and safe mode

* We do not find here *one episcopate*, which we certainly should have found had God allowed His Word to be tampered with, and as we surely ought to find if the "High Church" theory be true. But, as many High Churchmen are now candid enough and sufficiently regardful of their scholarly reputation, to admit, there was at the date of this Epistle no such thing as the episcopate, in the High Church sense of the term, namely, prelacy. Their theory makes the Apostolic statement "There is one body," an unaccountable anachronism. If it be replied, Though there were no prelates, yet there were Church-officers bearing the *name* of bishops ; then how does it occur that the episcopate, which Roman and Anglo Catholics make to be *the* element of unity, is not mentioned at all even as *an* element of unity ? The very Apostolate was not regarded by the Spirit as an element of unity co-ordinate with those which are enumerated.

of arriving at an answer to this question is the allowing the Apostle to explain his own term, that is, by consulting the passages in this and other Epistles, in which he employs the same word to designate the entire Church. The first of these is the last verse of the first chapter of this Epistle, "the Church which is His body." Now the constituents of this body, as the entire preceding and succeeding context shows, are those who have "trusted in Christ," have been "sealed with that Holy Spirit" (Chap. i. 13), "quickened" made alive—"together with Christ" (Chap. ii. 5), and "are saved through faith" (Chap. ii. 8). Christ's one body then is the totality of true believers, not the organization which they may be led to adopt, nor those members of the body, as distinct from the rest, who are invested with a special oversight and ruling function. This aggregate of believers is "the body of Christ," "the whole body" of our text (Ver. 12, 16). In what respects we have already seen. They form Christ's "one body," as all having the one "Head, even Christ," being each livingly united to Christ. Their oneness is no more metaphorical or mystical than that of the members of a human body, which has one *sensorium*, one nervous system. There is a continuous current of life streaming from Christ to each one of them, in proportion to his faith; the weakest, the most ignorant, the most obscure, as well as the strongest, the most advanced and the most distinguished. They are all one, inasmuch as the life which is communicated to each and all of them is the self-same life; not only flowing from the same fountain, but the same vital force, being no other than the Spirit of God Himself. They form one body again, all necessary to each other, so much so that no one single believer can attain full growth, or retain vigorous spiritual health, without help from others, and the collective Church can in no wise fully accomplish its mission on earth but by the conjoint action of each member.

As with the human body so with Christ's body, the Church: the life that is in the body assigns to every new particle that enters into its composition its own place and function. The exquisite mutual adaptation of the different parts of the body, and the consummate harmony of the whole, constituting it one body, result from the oneness of the formative and all-pervading life-force. Bodily health might be defined as the perfect correspondence of organ with function; and the normal state of the Church is the perfect fulfilment by each member of his own part in the grand work of general edification.

That the present state of the Church is glaringly not its normal—its healthy condition—does not prove that the body is disintegrated. The health of the daughter of God's people may yet be recovered.

Thus the Holy Catholic Church, which is an article of Christian belief is "the Communion," the fellowship "of saints." This is the original, the historical, the true meaning of the Creed: "The Holy Catholic Church, which is the Communion of Saints."* It is the Catholic Church, as embracing all, of whatever nationality and whatever denomination, who *hold* "the Head," though differing very widely in their modes of worship and forms of government. The word "Catholic" as an epithet peculiarly appropriate to the Church, indicated originally the ubiquity and equality of Church-privilege and Church-power, independent of locality or numbers. This is clearly its meaning on its first occurrence in Christian literature, which is very early indeed.†—

---

* See Hagenbach, Vol. i., p. 185.
† Soon after the death of St. John.

The Epistle of Ignatius to the Smyrneans, (8) "Wherever Jesus Christ is, there is the Catholic Church:" ὅπου, etc., in evident allusion to Matt. xviii. 20, "Where two or three are gathered together, etc."

And this is the real Church "the *very* Church," as even St Augustine terms it. All other, merely external members, are heterogeneous accretions, or Satanic insertions. If so, then the real visibility of the Church must be the character and course of life of the believers, and the historical continuity of the Church the unbroken succession of true believers; not of bishops but of saints.*

The continuity and the uniformity for which the Apostles were most solicitous were the continuity and uniformity of Christian character and life. Thus St. Paul congratulates the Thessalonian converts on their having fallen into line in the grand procession, the sacred march of the followers of Christ: the Christian societies of the Holy Land forming the head of the column which is to stretch through all ages and all climes: "Ye, brethren, became followers of the churches of God which in Judea are in Christ Jesus."

A Jesuit theologian † has given a true definition of the visible Church, or rather a just indication of that in which its visibility consists: "The Church," he says, "is the Christian religion itself in its objective form, its living exposition." This being the fact, the real unity of the Church is the unity of the Christian religion in its objective form, its living exposition. And what can this be but the homogeneousness, the correspondence in character and course of life of all the sincere disciples of Christ throughout the

---

* This even Montalembert, with all his resolute ultramontanism, is obliged to admit. See his *Life and Letters.*

† *Theological Prelections.* By J. Perrone, of the Society of Jesus. (Tom. i., p. 192.)

world? The essential oneness of the Church, then, cannot consist in uniformity of government or ritual. These must be secondary, and that after an immeasurable interval, to "the unity of the Spirit." Neither Christ nor His Apostles ever gave the slightest intimation that any particular form of Church-government or ceremonial is essential to the objectivity or "living exposition of His religion." In order to see in what Christ placed the visible oneness of His Church we must ascertain what He regarded as the visibility of His Church; in other words, the embodiment, the clear and convincing presentation of His religion to the eyes of men.

According to the Master's own pronouncement, the visibility of the Church, its splendid conspicuousness, the mountain elevation which makes its obscuration impossible, is the light of a truly Christian character and course of life, so shining "before men" as to constrain them to the reverential acknowledgment of God, in presence of the filial resemblance to Him apparent in the disciples of Christ (Matt. v. 16). Something far more patent and far more potent, more convincingly and convertingly obvious than the tangled and corroded concatenation of bishops, made Christ's Church visible to the world: "love one to another;"—"faith that worketh by love;"—"keeping the commands of God;"—active and well-directed benevolence, and sensitive, vigilant purity, visiting "the fatherless and the widows in their affliction," and keeping themselves "unspotted from the world;"—all this was at the beginning the true visibility of the Church. These are the Divinely indicated and Divinely impressed marks or notes of the true Church. So long as these are apparent in the various Christian Denominations, the visible oneness of the body may, by our sectional distinctions, be for a time obscured, imperiled, but not destroyed, or irreparably impaired.

L

But let us proceed with our examination of St. Paul's use of the word "body," as denoting the Church.* The second passage is Chap. ii. 16: "That He might reconcile both (Jews and Gentiles) unto God in *one* body." "In one body" here is parallel with "into [εἰς] one new man" in verse 15, which, as the preceding context proves, signifies the incorporation of Jews and Gentiles into one regenerated community, the old religious distinctions being abolished, and thus "the middle wall of partition broken down," and the mutual "enmity" slain by the Cross; and by the fact that through Christ "we both have access by one Spirit unto the Father." Here, again, the oneness of the body is grounded on the oneness of the atoning Lord, the oneness of the common Father, and is secured by the oneness of the near-bringing Spirit. But as the result of all this reconciliation and one-making, there does arise a new *sympolity* (Ver. 19), a fellow-citizenship of the saints, a new family—"the household of God," which both by absorption and expansion, supersedes the ancient "Commonwealth of Israel" (Ver. 12), being henceforth "the Israel of God;" succeeding to all the spiritual affluence and dignity of the olden Israel, guaranteed by "the covenants of promise," and to infinitely more.

Hence the Church of Christ becomes a grand social fact, a signal social phenomenon, a theme for history. It is not a bodiless abstraction. It is a society of souls, but of souls embodied; it is the aggregate Christian discipleship, but the

---

* "A body," says Dean Goulbourn, "is something visible and external, something which may be handled and seen, something which has locality, which takes up a definite room and space."—*The Holy Catholic Church*. Clearly, and is not a Christian life as visible as the succession of bishops? Would not all the true believers in the world take up as large and as "definite room and space" as all the bishops in the world?

discipleship in aggregation. It must, and in fact did, body forth its hidden life in institutions. It has overseers invested with constitutional authority, its officers of finance: God fulfils His promise to make the Church's "officers peace," and her "exactors righteousness." It has its privileged meetings for instruction, confidential intercourse, conjoint worship, consultation, legislation. It has its two simple, yet most significant ceremonies. It has its appliances for gathering in new members—since it is ultimately to include the whole human race—and for raising all its members as closely and as rapidly as possible to that heavenly standard of character which is the great purpose of the association. It has its outward and visible side; else what business has it in this outward and visible world? As its geographical distribution extends its area, the various local churches must strive to maintain a vital, sympathetic, serviceable connexion with all the other churches. Provision must be made against the vacancy of its offices "by reason of death," or defection, or hopeless incompetence, or honourable old age. But as we have seen, that organization was not rigidly fixed. Earthly law did not lord it over heavenly life. The only government by Divine right was the perpetual dual reign of wedded Charity and Common Sense. To interfere with "diversities of operation," "differences of administration," is to call to order God's "free Spirit," to "limit the Holy One of Israel." That there should be a succession of "faithful men" to whom the oversight of the churches should be committed was decreed; but the mode of their induction was left wide open. The only factors in the validity of ordination were the integrity of the commitment and the faithfulness of the men to whom it was committed.

The Church, then, is not only the mystical body of Christ, but is also the manifest body of Christ. The thousands who, on the day of Pentecost, and "daily" through the subsequent weeks of the first great spiritual harvest, were "added to the Church," were added not only to the invisible, but also to the visible, Church: first to the invisible, then to the visible. "The Lord added to the Church daily such as were being saved;"—in other words, added to the visible Church such as by repentance, faith and confession of Christ were already members of the invisible—to the manifest body of Christ; such as were already members of the mystical body of Christ. The oneness of the body, then, is something distinct from the oneness of the Spirit, though vitally connected with it. The oneness of the body must not be sacrificed to the oneness of the Spirit, much less the oneness of the Spirit to the oneness of the body. *Much* less: because so long as "the unity of the Spirit" is *kept*, the unity of the body cannot be destroyed. Hence the Spirit does not say,—Resolving to keep the unity of the body in the bond of authority: but, "Endeavouring to keep the unity of the Spirit in the bond of peace." Seek ye first the unity of the Spirit, and all these things—such a degree of coincidence or correspondence in modes of administration and forms of worship as may be better than diversity—"shall be added unto you." Uniformity is only valuable so far as it grows out of, manifests and conserves unanimity, and so far as it facilitates the objects for which the Church was instituted. Uniformity, like diversity, is an element of beauty when, and only when it is a manifestation of life. Uniformity may exist without unanimity, unanimity without uniformity. If the alternative be inevitable, uniformity must be sacrificed to unanimity.

It is very noteworthy that the Apostle connects the one body and the one Spirit more closely than any other of the elements of unity. He does say, There is one body, one Spirit, as he says, "one Lord, one faith, one baptism."

The Apostle would scarcely have put the "one body" before the "one Spirit" except with design to intimate that the oneness of the body results from the oneness of the Spirit. And this he explicitly states in the First Epistle to the Corinthians: "For as the body is one and hath many members, and all the members of that one body, being many are one body,"—their very multiplicity and diversity being essential to their oneness or unition as a body,—"so also is Christ,"—Christ and His Church being regarded as one corporate personality;—"for by one Spirit are we all baptized into one body, whether we be Jews or Gentiles, whether we be bond or free; and have all been made to drink into one Spirit." Here again we are plainly taught that external association can no more constitute a Church than the most scientific juxtaposition of limbs, trunk, organs could constitute a body. The social antipodes of slavery and freedom, all stages of barbarism and civilization, all degrees of secular ignorance and culture, all diversities and divergencies of temperament and taste have been brought together and bound together in the Church, not only by common convictions, but also by a common inward experience, each corresponding to each as face answereth to face in a glass. Where antecedently and naturally there was the strongest mutual repulsion, there is now the mightiest mutual attraction. What power but the "One Spirit" could accomplish this?

It is this Spirit-breathed sympathy, this conscious affinity which constitutes the true unity of the Church as really as it is the sense-diffusing soul which constitutes the oneness of a human body. Believers are not one by reason of their membership in the same external community; on the contrary, it is the spiritual oneness which constrains them to unite in outward fellowship. "We know that we have passed from death unto life, because we love the brethren:" not because we have read our names in a baptismal register, not because we have access to the Table of the Lord; but because "we are," as a present fact of consciousness, baptized by one Spirit, and have been made to drink into one Spirit.

Christ Himself declared that the unity of the Godhead in the three Persons of the Trinity is at once the Archetype, the Basis, and the Consummation of the Unity of the Church; that living Church-membership is essentially "fellowship one with another," the ground of which is individual fellowship with the Father and the Son, through the Spirit: that this unity of the Church is, and cannot but be in its Source and Essence invisible and spiritual; since it flows out of the soul-union of each real member of the Church with the invisible God; and Church-unity in its essence, along with the common individual life of believers, " is hid with Christ in God." The essential unity of the Church then is " the unity of the Spirit;" unity of faith, of hope, of love, of *life*, in both senses of the term. But as the life of the individual believer is to be manifested to the world, so it was designed that the unity of the Church should be manifested to the world. It was no part of Christ's plan that His body should be disjointed — *disjecta membra ;* that His Church should be split up into rival, mutually repellent, or even isolated and altogether mutually independent fragments.

The fact must never be lost sight of, that the Church is a noun of multitude, in which the idea of unity predominates over that of plurality. To say the Church *are* divided or the Church *are* agreed would be very false theological syntax.

It was Christ's own prayer that the hidden unity of His Church should not only be realized and recognised by the Church itself, but should also be manifest to the world in a striking, faith-compelling form.

It is equally plain from the New Testament and the Christian literature of the first two centuries and a half of our era, that the oneness of the body when it was most vital, sensitive and sympathetic, and most realized by mutual edification, was most strikingly apparent to the world. It was not a bare matter of faith, but a palpable matter of fact, even to hostile heathen eyes. If a man avowed himself a Christian, he was at once understood to assert his membership in a definite association, multitudinous indeed and widely spread (catholic), yet most sacredly, sensitively, vitally united. Everybody knew that the Church-tie was not a merely nominal but a true tie; closer, stronger than either the national tie or the family tie. When a convert was baptized he was well assured that he was not merely entering a local club, but was being initiated into a grand world-wide, international, catholic fellowship. The unity of the body grew out of the unity of the Spirit, and could not long survive that spiritual unity; but the one was not confounded with the other, and must never be confounded. The corporate oneness is one element of the sevenfold unity, and only one. It must neither swallow up the rest nor be swallowed up by them.

How, then, was this oneness of the body manifested and maintained in the Apostolic Church?

(1.) It was a oneness of confession—confession of Christ; which involved a confession of faith, namely, faith in Christ as the Son of God. No one could obtain admission to the Church who could not asseverate, "I believe that Jesus Christ is the Son of God." There was "one faith."

(2.) Then, there was one rite of admission into the Church and no other, "one baptism," the essential elements of which were the same everywhere, namely, confession of faith in the Son of God; the formula prescribed by Christ Himself, " in the name of the Father, etc.," and the invocation of Christ by both the baptizer and baptized. And the spiritual baptism, that of the Holy Ghost, symbolized by the outward baptism, was one :—

"One the pure baptismal flame."

(3.) There was also the unity of Apostolic teaching. "As God is true," and "this was not yea and nay." Timothy, in bringing to remembrance St. Paul's teaching at Corinth, showed how he "taught everywhere, in every church."

An Apostolic anathema was in force against the Apostles themselves and the whole hierarchy of heaven, if they preached even an alternative Gospel. (See Gal. i. 8, 9, which Luther rightly calls "a text like a thunderbolt.")

(4.) The unity of the Church consisted still further in the perfect correspondence of the cardinal traits of the Christian character throughout all ranks and races and ex-religions, Jew, Greek, barbarian, Scythian, bond, free—male, female; the oneness of the type—*Christian*—"*so* is every one that is born of the Spirit"—the family features of Christianity, the pervading Christ-likeness of the Christian brotherhood. Even an enemy on reading the Gospels, and then inspecting the lives of the disciples might exclaim, " As *thou*—so *they;* each one resembled the children of a king."

(5.) And allied to this was the oneness of living, the family mannerisms of Christianity, the "*norma vivendi,*" the Catholic canon of the new creature, of which Paul speaks when he says: "In Christ Jesus neither circumcision availeth anything, nor uncircumcision, but a new creature. And as many as walk according to this rule, peace be on them, and mercy, and upon the Israel of God." (Gal. vi. 16.)

(6.) Moreover along with a living freedom and a beautiful diversity in the modes of conducting their meetings for worship, teaching and mutual edification, there was amongst the primitive Christians a certain decorous correspondence of usage, fencing off unseemliness and preventing liberty from degenerating into license. To this St. Paul alludes, or rather appeals (1 Cor. xi. 16), "If any man seem to be contentious, we have *no such custom, neither the churches of God.*" The good precedents of older churches were urged upon the younger. (1 Cor. xiv. 36.)

(7.) Again, the unity of the Church was further guaranteed by the one standard of appeal—the Gospels and Epistles; and for the settlement of serious questions of Christian obligation, before the New Testament was written, a direct appeal to the Apostles in conjunction with the Mother Church in Jerusalem was open to all the churches.

(8.) Add to this the intercommunion amongst all the churches, including access to the privileged gatherings— the Lord's Supper and the Lovefeast—everywhere by means of Fellowship certificates.

(9.) Still further, the visitorial authority of the itinerant Apostolate, now superseded by their recorded decisions and their permanent epistles, formed a strong bond of union during the first age of the Church; as the community of ministers, through the itinerancy, is the binding cord of Connexionalism; as the superintendence of the brothers Wesley at the first, and afterwards of John Wesley alone, formed the bond of "the United Societies," and as the itinerating bishops now do in the Methodist Episcopal Church in America. The earliest Christian churches were, in fact, United Societies.*

* Before the death of the last surviving Apostle it was felt that a centre

The endeavour to make the oneness of the Church a cognizable fact was very strong in the Apostolic age. It was this which made Paul feel "bound in the Spirit" to pause in the midst of his missionary labours, and undertake a long and perilous journey to keep the anniversary of the Christian Pentecost in Jerusalem. This was one great object of the first great œcumenical, Catholic or connexional collection in Church history, that for the poor saints in Jerusalem. This it was that determined Paul to take with him to Jerusalem seven converts from various Gentile churches,* that Jew and Gentile might feel in "the right hand of fellowship" the strong pulse of spiritual consanguinity.

of local unity was requisite, and this was found in the institution of the episcopal office, or the appointment of a local Superintendent of the presbytery as well as of the people (distinct but not separate from the presbytery), the angelship of the Apocalypse; an arrangement recognised, though not enjoined, by Christ Himself in His messages to the Seven Churches of Asia. It is now admitted by candid High Church advocates that the bishop's relation to the presbytery was at first simply that of permanent president. They were his colleagues, not his subordinates; not merely consultees, but co-assessors. And is not this the shape which affairs take in every Protestant church where things are working well, whether Methodist circuit, Independent congregation, or Church of England parish? A judicious and effective Methodist Superintendent, a Congregationalist Minister with such talent and force of character as invest him with legitimate influence, like John Angell James or Mr. Binney, and an earnest, sensible, active parish clergyman, what are they all but the angels of their respective churches?

The bishop being chosen by the suffrages of the entire church, his presidency was for life, unless forfeited by apostasy, immorality, or false doctrine. It was not only competent to the presbytery and people to depose an immoral or heretical bishop, or one who had proved himself a hireling by deserting his post in the hour of danger, but it was incumbent on them to do so.

* "Sopater of Berea; and of the Thessalonians, Aristarchus and Secundus; and Gaius of Derbe, and Timotheus; and of Asia, Tychicus and Trophimus." (Acts xx. 4.)

The Apostle in his description of the Church as "one body" unquestionably had before his mind not only its spiritual, but also its external relations as a mundane institution of which the world " without " could take knowledge.

Like the Divine Founder of the Church Himself, he contemplated exultingly the historical continuity of the Church, its permanence and indestructibility as a definite association: "The Church . . . throughout all ages, world without end." And in the Apostolic times the Church actually was one body: it had all the elements and characteristics essential to unity. So palpably was this the fact than when this Epistle was first read in the Ephesian church, the affirmation, " There is one body," would be felt not only as axiomatic, but as the simple statement of an undeniable fact of contemporary history. It may well be questioned whether an Ephesian convert could have conceived of the Church otherwise than as one body. There was to the primitive Christian as plainly " one body," as " one faith " and " one baptism."

And to the early Christian writers, the idea of an externally disunited Church was an object of agonizing deprecation and holiest dismay. Could any one of them have seen the Church in its present abnormal, unnatural and ungracious state, he would, like Daniel, have been "astonied" at the vision. Yet, for the first two centuries, the churches saw that the essential unity was the unity of the Spirit; that external unity without this would be hollow and hypocritical, and that it could only be preserved by mutual endeavour and in the bond of peace. The first difficulties which threatened the unity of the Church were local, arising out of diversities of taste and divergencies of thought amongst Christians resident in the same town or city. These manifested themselves in murmurings, partialities, partisanships and faction-feuds, or were all but contemporaneous with the foundation of the Church itself, as in Jerusalem and Corinth. But they were healed by conciliation, remonstrances and exhortations, to obedience to their rulers, and by mutual forbearance, mutual submission, mutual deference, and mutual indulgence—even more than by mutual concessions—and by talking and praying each other into the same mind.

The motherhood of the Church was manifested, not only in swift help and soothing tenderness to the fallen, in watchful sympathy for the weak and ailing, in strengthening the weak hands and confirming the feeble knees, in succouring the "ready to halt, in a fond and almost proud," though vigilant, indulgence of the boisterous vivacity and adventurous energy of its healthy children ; but also in her respect for the individuality of her children and her reverence for the freedom of the sanctifying Spirit. So long as the promise was fulfilled, " I will pour . . . My Spirit on Thy seed," she marked with loving interest all varieties of expression and of action. She saw in this a close fulfilment of the prophecy, " One shall say, I am the Lord's ; and another shall call himself by the name of Jacob, and another shall subscribe with his hand unto the Lord, and surname himself by the name of Israel." She did not insist that there was but one right way of carrying out religious convictions and making an open religious profession.

The importance, in a sense, the autonomy of every individual member of the Christian Church being so profoundly respected, it required a very strong sentiment of unity and mutual belonging to render the cohesion of the brotherhood perfect and permanent. But the feeling of the oneness and wholeness of the Church among the primitive Christians was powerful enough, in the main, to keep under control the sense of personal freedom and responsibility. The units which constituted the totality of the Church, whilst each conscious that he was an integer, yet none the less realized the sacredness and grandeur of the aggregate of which he formed a part. Patriotism, the sense of nationality, never reached in Roman, Jew or Englishman to a higher pitch than was attained by the Church-feeling of the ancient Christians. The intense individualism was to a wonderful extent adjusted to Church-claims. Love generally asserted its primacy over Faith and Hope. But still an undue egotism did manifest itself, and that most disturbingly, in the early Christian communities. It was thus that schisms and heresies began within the fellowship of Christ.

Moreover, the oneness of the body was not impaired by the acknowledged rights and responsibilities of the local churches. It is clear from our Lord's directions for the settlement of grievances between two members of the Church that the authority of the Church for the settlement of such grievances is ubiquitous and equable. It may be, and has proved to be, a great advantage to have a central court of final appeal and arbitrament, deferred to by an indefinite number of voluntarily associated churches. This is one amongst innumerable advantages of association. But still Christ is in the midst of every little local church-court, met for the composing of differences arising within that local church: and where He is, there is the Catholic Church.

After the death of the Apostles, on all questions of doctrine and the universal, simple, and invariable rule of Christian life, the Apostolic writings in the Gospels and Epistles supplied the place of the Apostles, and the application of the rule of faith and morals was left, at the close of the Canon of Scripture, to the local authorities in the various churches. There is no trace in paulo-post-apostolic times of the jurisdiction of any one church over other churches; that is to say, of any central authority having any right of a more direct or formal interference than that of influence or persuasion, or that of voluntarily elected arbitration. The angel of the church of Ephesus, Smyrna, etc., respectively was responsible for the doctrinal and ethical soundness of the church of which he was the constitutionally elected and appointed representative and overseer.

Yet the Church was none the less *one* body because of the autonomy of the various local societies of which its totality was composed. It was, and styled itself, the Catholic Church, in the absence of any geographical centre of unity or any primatial authority whatsoever. Its unity was still Apostolic because the writings of the Apostles (the Gospels and Epistles and the Apocalypse) were the common standards of appeal on all matters of Christian doctrine and life. Where the standard was silent there was the utmost freedom and diversity. Hence Congregational, Parochial, Circuit, Diocesan, District, and national distinctions within the Church neither divide nor dilute the unity of the Church, so long as the oneness of the fundamentals of the faith and the standard of universal appeal—the Scriptures—and the oneness of experience, character and moral habitudes are maintained. The various churches are only so many municipalities within the limits of the City of God, each holding, or voluntarily sharing with others, its autonomy, within the limits of the unity above described. And so of each denominational distinction. Each church with such forms of administration, worship and fellowship as it deems best, is none the less an integral part of *the commonwealth of Israel*, because it uses its freedom as to forms of administration and worship. Hence a true believer may attach himself to whatsoever existing organization he deems best fitted for nourishing the spiritual life and bringing that life to bear effectively upon others. Thus the oneness of the baptism is not a oneness in the details of administration, but consists in the fact that wherever or however administered, if in the name of the Trinity, it is admission into the one Church of all climes, all ages and all denominations. Every Christian community holding fast and holding forth the fundamental truths of Christianity, whereby sinners are called to repentance, and penitents pointed to Christ, and believers built up on their most holy faith, so that "the common salvation" is experienced, and "like precious faith obtained," is an integral part of the Church,—of that Zion wherein God promised to "place salvation." A man is none the less a true Catholic Christian because he is a Methodist, or Baptist, or Episcopalian, or Presbyterian of whatever type. When he definitely enters this or that local or denominational church he definitely enters *the* Church : his membership is in the grand whole of which these sections are but parts. Thus, to the Church, at this day, there is in reality "one body."

Is then membership in one church membership in each and all? What do you mean by membership in any particular church? By assuming the name of Friend, Baptist, etc., or accepting that of Methodist, you surely do not mean either on the one hand to discard the name of Christian, or on the other to make your distinctive designation equivalent to the title Christian ! By entrance and enrollment in this or that denomination of Christians who hold the Head, you do not forsake the Christian, the Holy Catholic Church : on the contrary, you connect yourself with the Christian, the truly Catholic Church, at that particular point. Methodism, Congregationalism, or some other denomination becomes your point of contact with the universal Church. A Methodist is not a Baptist, nor a Baptist a Methodist, but what of that ? They are both Christians : Christian is the *genus,* Baptist, Methodist, etc., is the species.

So long then as the various Christian communities retain faith in the foundation-facts of Christianity, a common standard of appeal for doctrine and for morals and a common life in Christ, the essential unity is not broken, although it may be obscured and disturbed, by the temporary interruption of the external unity. As in the days of the Apostles each local church was as really a church as if it had been singly constituted by Christ, so now each local and each denominational church is as really a church as if it had derived its organization as well as its life directly from the common Head.

Regular admission into a denominational church is admission into the one Church of Christ, or transference, as the case may be, from one section of the Church to another. An accredited member of any Christian community which holds the Head should be admitted to communion by every other Head-holding community, and the community which rejects such proclaims itself schismatical by that very act.

What then is the significant force of rightful, constitutional exclusion from any denominational church? Is it exclusion from the one Church of Christ in all its branches?

If the exclusion be on the ground of a denial of any foundation fact of Christianity, or an egregious and habitual violation of the common rule of Christian morals, plainly it *is* an exclusion from the one Church. If, on the other hand, the exclusion be on the ground of the repudiation of some speciality of that denominational church, it is simply a dismissal to any other section of the one Church with which the dissident may be more nearly in harmony. Excommunication *proper* belongs to the Universal Church, but as each local church in the Apostolic age had not only the right, but also the responsibility, of excommunicating corrupt, disreputable, or fundamentally misbelieving members (*e.g.*,

Corinth and the Seven Churches of Asia), so now each denominational church has the right and the responsibility of excommunicating corrupt, disreputable, and fundamentally misbelieving members.

In like manner, in the primitive Church ordination was universal ordination; a presbyter anywhere was a presbyter everywhere.

Seeing that the Church, as at present existing, has not only geographical, but also denominational distinctions, it is quite competent to every believer to make choice of that section of the universal Church, which he, on examination, regards as most nearly approximating to the ideal of Scripture, and as affording the amplest facilities for nourishing the spiritual life and exercising one's own gifts for the advantage of others. Of course, the church of one's spiritual parentage and training has the first claim on one's adherence, and a man must be quite clear that he is by the change approaching nearer to the ideal Church of Scripture, and thus helping forward the historical realization of that Church, and is, moreover, by the change decidedly improving his opportunities of personal edification and usefulness, before he can blamelessly leave his birth-church for another.

It is the duty of every believer to maintain union and communion, as much as lieth in him, with all who have not abandoned the foundations of the faith or the rule of Christian life. So far as it is not sinful, by clear pronouncement of Scripture, to have fellowship with a church or individual professor, it is sinful to refuse such fellowship. The Church-theory, which leaves no room for a lenient and generous construction of motives; for a frank, fervent and all-embracing recognition of the family features of the household of faith; for a reverential acknowledgment of God's finger-mark upon the character; and for its own correction on the sight of God's signature on the dispositions and habits of those who do not belong to our particular community;—that Church-theory, call it Catholic, Anglo-Catholic, or what you please, is glaringly uncatholic and anti-catholic. Yet this venerable word " Catholic " has been so irreverently treated by those who use it most, that it is made the password of a pretentious party, the cuckoo-cry of an ecclesiastical clique. Every Church-theory which will not let its adherents love a brother of any other denomination when seen, or will not let him be seen for fear he should be loved, is as uncatholic as it is unevangelical.

It is, then, a truism, but none the less necessary to be re-affirmed, that the real, the essential oneness, visibility and continuity of the Church is not that of a mere corporation, such as may legally hold property, and dependent for its existence on formal official succession, and such as jurisprudence, politics and unspiritual history may take cognizance of; although it is the sublimest of all social phenomena, and the most significant fact of human history, one express design of which is the education and enlargement of the highest orders of created intelligence, " to the intent that now unto the principalities and powers in heavenly places might be made known by the Church, the manifold wisdom of God." It rests on a basis, not only of revealed, but of realized supernatural facts. What boots it that the chain of bishops has become, at least over a great part of episcopal Christendom, inextricably entangled and unmendably snapped? Council, Convocation, Consistory, Congregational Congress, Conference, might be (though Heaven forfend!) as they have been for hundreds of years nonexistent, and the Church would sadly miss them or their equivalents; but there would still be the Church to sadly miss them. The unity of the Church lies deeper than any organization, ordinance, or officiation whatsoever. The vital principle, the great life-force and will-force within all its institutions and agencies, is the Spirit of God. Its unity, which it is the duty of every one of its members to "endeavour"—to labour diligently—" to keep" is "the unity of the Spirit," the unity which the Spirit creates, constituting that "one body" which would otherwise, even under the most compact and consummate organization, be a heterogeneous heap. It is this which makes it "the Church throughout all ages."

This Catholic Church may be partitioned, not only by material, but also by mental barriers. The Vaudois might solemnize their simple worship amidst Alpine solitudes, all unknown by and unknowing of their brother Gospellers in Britain;—the baron in his hall, the schoolman in his cloister, the ploughman in his hut,—and many a holy monk, spending his peaceful days in "works of faith and charity." Howe, Baxter, and the Goodwins may find themselves on one side in a great civil and ecclesiastical contest; Taylor, Fuller, Hall, and Sanderson on the other: yet the oneness in Christ of them all is not destroyed by geographical interspaces, chronological chasms, intellectual divergencies, or the fiercest paroxysms of political and ecclesiastical conflict.

The extremest separatism, whose mission and witness might seem to be to demonstrate the infinite divisibility of the Church, has yet its tiny catholicity; and Plymouth Catholic is not a more real contradiction in terms than Roman Catholic or Anglo-Catholic. Nay, the most sectarian sects, whether numerically small or large, the most fanatical assertors of the damnableness of doubting the newest fiction of the Papal brain, and the latest subdivision of the Plymouth-Brethren have this at least in common, they all claim to be legitimate representatives of the primitive Apostolic

Church.*   They all claim to be built upon the old " foundation," that " of the Apostles and Prophets, Jesus Christ Himself being the chief Corner-stone."

Without some strong sentiment of the historical continuity of the Christian Church, secession must be endless, and separation will beget separation to the end of the world. The wanton or wayward spirit of standing off pulverizes the Church. No church will rise high or spread wide in the future which does not strike its roots deep into the past.†

---

* Dean Goulburn, in his new book, " *The Holy Catholic Church*," which I was providentially hindered from reading until after the delivery of this Lecture, and after its earlier sheets were in the press (it might have tempted one into a too polemical tone), says (p. 18) that he is " utterly at a loss to see how you can belong to the very Society which Christ founded by the ministry of St. Peter "—" unless your community can trace historically back to the ministry of St. Peter." Well, we can relieve the Dean's mind on this point : there is not a Nonconformist Church in the country but " can trace historically back to the ministry of St. Peter," and that without researches into the mouldy records (wherever such exist) of episcopal consecration. But the Dean adds this caveat : " Remember there must never be any new beginning made, if it is to be Christ's Society." What does the Dean mean by "a new beginning ? " Does he mean, " there must never be any " recurrence to first principles after they have been long lost sight of? Any recovery of usurped rights ? Any reconquering of privileges violently or fraudulently taken away ? Alas, this is but a new edition of the old romance—Roman story—of Apostolical Succession. When and whence was there a newer beginning than when the bishops first assumed to be the sole consignees of the grace of God ? No existing Nonconformist Church ever dreamt of making a new beginning of the Society of Pentecost ; unless it be the Irvingites, who proclaim a " New Apostleship." But, as Dean Goulburn's book is the latest and most plausible manifesto of High Churchism, we must notice it in our supplementary chapter on the History of the Doctrine of the Church.

† It was this sentiment, not any partiality for a State-church, which made Wesley cling so fondly to the Establishment. It is clear from his writings that he had no leaning to a State-church.

No earnest, conscientious seceder from the church of the majority ever dreamt of seceding from the Church of Christ, the Apostolic Church. On the contrary, however mistaken, and however culpably hasty and wrongheaded, they withdrew from the existing arrangement and administration, and the contemporary administrators, because they deemed them to have drifted or diverged from Apostolic precedent and precept. And there is no church whatever that has a history at all, or any life left it, but is passionately historical in its watchwords, and enthusiastically traditional in its reminiscences. A denomination scarce a century old already venerates its juvenile antiquity, and cherishes with reverence its infantile traditions. And this is right. Not converted Hebrews or Covenanters only run the race set before them with the more ardent fortitude, because from their own ranks many have gone to swell the ancient "Cloud of Witnesses."

Some of the straitest sects of our religion, notably the Cameronians and the Society of Friends, have never abandoned the conception of the Catholic Church, as the universal Communion of Saints. The most meteoric fragment of the Christian system, split off explosively from some larger orb, is still a cosmical, a catholic body, so long as it revolves around the common centre CHRIST.

Yet the visible unity of the Church may be temporarily disjointed whilst the vital unity survives. The tenacity and redundance of life in some churches seem to equal that of those organisms which, when cut to pieces, not only retain vitality, but a vitality endowed with such constructive force as to supply each fragment with the organization necessary for the purposes of life. And, still more wonderful, reciprocal anathemas have sometimes almost as little availed to exhaust the life of the anathematizing as to extinguish that of the anathematized.

And is not the conception of the Church as an integral whole, with a compliant and expansive framework, as much grander, nobler, heavenlier as it is more Scriptural than the Roman and Anglo-Roman notion of a Church whose vitality is so precarious, so skin-deep, and its unity so outward, superficial and mechanical, that a flaw in episcopal succession ruins all, and makes the body of Christ tumble to pieces,

> "And like the baseless fabric of a vision,
> Leave not a wreck behind."

O, but they cannot mean that! Then why do they persist in saying so, and in building their Church-fabric on a fiction?

Thus the headspring of the Church's life is the headspring of its unity, and that is not the turbid Tiber, but the river of the water of life, flowing "from the throne of God and of the Lamb." The river is the same, its continuity is unbroken, although the silt of earthliness which it has brought down with it in its course of centuries has by deposition formed a dreary desolate delta, dividing it into many arms. All spring from the source, and all reach the sea. A stream may indeed be more serviceable by reason of the multiplicity of its channels, and thus denominational divergencies, during a certain stretch of the Church's course,—"until we all come, etc.,"—may be so overruled by "the manifold wisdom of God" as to further rather than obstruct its fertilizing effect. Not denominational distinctions, but denominational contentions and internecine rivalries, by turning into the living current the fœtid sewage of carnality, polute and poison the "exulting and abounding" stream. The historical connection of the various churches, denominational as well as national, is distinctly traceable. By threading their course upwards, their point of divergence is readily reached. And what unfathomably low-Church principles those must be which make the continuity of "the river of the water of life" to depend upon a certain description of stakes driven in upon its banks, or a certain mode of driving them in, however worm-eaten and worthless those stakes may be, rather than on the life-current itself! in plain words on the succession of bishops—good, bad, and indifferent—rather than the continuity of Christian witness, character and course of life, in all Denominations which have retained the fundamentals of the faith, the Scriptures as the common standard of appeal, the Apostolic rule of holy living and dying, the spiritual life which flows only from the Head of the Church, and the means of instruction, edification, and oversight. It is in glaring opposition to the patent facts of the case, to say that the life-stream of Christianity, even though like the river of Eden it may be parted into four heads or more, has evaporated or been lost in the sand.

Where then is the main stream? Where the strongest current of life flows. The holy Roman Catholic St. Cyran said of his own church: "Now that which looks like water is nothing but mud: the bed of the beautiful river is the same, but not the stream that flows through it." Is the dry or slimy channel, or is the copious current the "river that maketh glad the city of God?" "Where civilization is there is Greece!" exclaimed the Hellenic patriot: "*Where salvation is, as a realized fact, there is the Church,*" for God has said, "I will place salvation in Zion."

The notion of a succession of bishops conveying by digital contact from age to age the whole volume of Divine grace—remission of sins, regeneration—the Holy Spirit—to be distributed through baptism and the Lord's Supper, by those only who have received such digital contact, and by the imposition of episcopal hands at confirmation—is as contrary to the letter as to the spirit of the New Testament.

But although all the responsibilities, right and privileges of the Catholic Church inhere in every local church, and no one local church can without audacious usurpation assume predominance over others, much less over all, yet congregational disconnectedness is very far from the Divine ideal and the New Testament working-plan of the Church. A voluntary federation of churches is not only legitimate and lovely and of proven practicability on a scale of indefinite magnitude, in either hemisphere, and already in almost every nation under heaven, but is the most accordant with the Spirit's own delineation of the Church's normal and ultimate condition. Such a voluntary federation on the basis of the fundamental verities of Christianity, and a common and communicated experience of those verities; with a well-defined and well-balanced constitution; with a system of mutual help and effective sympathy; the people having a forceful voice in the choice of candidates for the ministry—including an absolute veto on incompetence and inconsistency—and in the choice of their local pastorate; and with periodic councils: no new rule or regulation being binding upon any until accepted by the majority of the churches—is an arrangement as behoveful as it is beautiful; so far and so soon as churches m anifest a power of combination and coalescence. For this association to be valid must be vital, and to be vital must be voluntary.*

How then is "unity of the Spirit," without which all external union is hollow and precarious at best, to be main-

---

* The Apostolic system of Œcumenical, Catholic, or Connexional collections for the most needy churches, and the universal usage of reciprocal hospitality, and of effective pecuniary help to all who were travelling on evangelistic errands, conduced much to the realization of the oneness of the Church, and its visibility to the heathen. That it was manifest is plain from the witness of the literary assailants of the Church.

tained? It cannot be conserved amongst a vast association of human beings without strenuous endeavour. Irritability is a property of life. Hence exquisite spiritual sensitiveness and intense earnestness may tend to divergence or disruption. "The contention" may be "so sharp," even between Paul and Barnabas, Wesley and Whitefield, that for a time they part "asunder the one from the other." Family feuds may sometimes interrupt family fondnesses and not be fatal to family feeling. Although the Spirit is the Giver and the Guarantor of the Church's unity, yet here, as in every other moral sphere, man's free will must coalesce with His; our endeavour must carry out His prompting. The unity of the Spirit can only be kept "in the bond of peace;" and what the stronds are of this lovely cincture, the Apostle tells us, "all lowliness and meekness" intertwined with "long-suffering, forbearing one another in love." The resuscitation of that instinct of union which is natural to the new man, the desire, the tendency, the effort, the "endeavour" to unite, the movement towards each other, is one of the strongest signs of a revival of religion.

In order to the conservation of spiritual unity, we must be patient of intellectual dissent from one another. We must not count a brother a barbarian because he cannot "frame to pronounce right" our provincial shibboleth. The Spirit is the Spirit of love and light: in His love-light we shall see what is essential and what is not. The root of Church unity is not as Bishop Pearson puts it,[*] "the being all of one mind:" this is not always or absolutely the case. Heart-unity is the only firm basis of intellectual unity: our "hearts" must be "knit together in love *unto* the riches of the full assurance of understanding." The order is, not first understand one another, and then love one another, but first

[*] On the Creed, Art. IX., Sect. v.

love, and then understand. The unity of the Spirit cannot be conserved in the bond of an enforced or affected uniformity.

We are taught further that all Church-membership which is not rooted in spiritual experience is utterly fictitious and delusive. One cannot be a real member of the Church, unless one is a member of Christ, one cannot be a member of Christ, unless one have life in Christ, communicated by His Spirit. And, conversely no intellectual error or mystification which does not stop the flow of spiritual life into the soul can exclude one from the Church of Christ. This is clearly indicated in our text: "Even as ye were also called in one hope of your calling." It is very striking and significant that the foremost illustration and attestation of the unity of the Spirit is the oneness of the Christian hope excited and authenticated by the Christian calling. We become truly incorporated into the body of Christ by a duteous and hopeful response to the call of Christ. Living members of the Church are "holy brethren, partakers of the heavenly calling;" *heavenly*, since it comes from heaven and invites to heaven, and brings the earnest of heaven into the soul that obeys the summons. It is, moreover, as St. Paul shows in the first verse of this chapter, into a high order of nobility, with lofty associations and expectations, and therefore with stringent and exalted proprieties of conduct, bearing and habit: "I beseech you that ye walk worthy of the vocation wherewith you are called." Church-members must be all hopefully pressing towards one lofty standard of experience, character, and habits.

One Lord. The oneness of Christ involves the oneness of the Church: there can no more be two Churches than two Christs. "Is Christ divided?" is the appeal which rebukes the incongruity and impiety of divisions in the Church.

Christ's sole and absolute Lordship in His Church forbids all faction, all repellent sectionalism within His domain. Fidelity to each other is an essential element in our loyalty to Him.

One faith. The faith of Christ's Church is one both in its object and its nature; in fact, it derives its nature from its object, for it is " the faith of Christ." The oneness of the faith follows necessarily from the oneness of the Head and Lord. He is not only the Object of faith to each and all, but also its Author and Finisher, its Chief and Consummator. Whilst this does not imply an absolute uniformity of expression, it clearly does import the obligation on all sides round to *endeavour* after as near an agreement as can be honestly and lovingly effected, even in the verbal Confession of faith. But no faith can be the ground and guarantee of Church unity but faith in the Head of the Church, Who unless He be God cannot be what He is here affirmed to be—the Source and Sustainer of life to the myriads of His members in earth and heaven. Nothing can give oneness to the faith, but the oneness of its Object, which does not however imply an absolute oneness in the scientific systematization of revealed truth, termed *Theology.* The unity of the faith is that of unfissured foundation rather than that of the symmetrical superstructure. The very foundation of the Church was an objective faith to be met by the corresponding subjective faith. The Church was built at the beginning, and has rested from the beginning, on certain facts revealed by God concerning Himself and the invisible world, and on the spiritual and eternal significance of certain historic facts—the Incarnation, Crucifixion, Resurrection and Ascension of Jesus Christ, and the gift of the Holy Ghost on the Day of Pentecost, as an abiding, ever-active, and realized Power. Away from these facts the Church has nothing to stand upon, no *raison d'être*, nothing to justify or account for its existence as a distinct association. The Church was not built on the slipping sands, or the tossing surf of speculation. Its foundation-faith was as firm as its foundation-facts. No one could enter the Apostolic Church until he had confessed his belief in the Son of God. No one could continue in the Church after rejection of Christ's Godhead and atonement, "even denying the LORD that *bought*" him. But on this broad, firm foundation there was a wide range of doctrinal recognition. The "weak in the faith" was to be received. Given a man with an unfeigned faith in Christ as his Divine Saviour and Sovereign Lord, and in the one Father, the Giver of the Son, and in the Holy Ghost, Who sheds abroad in the individual believer's heart the Father's love and communicates the life that is in the Son,—although that man yet held defective or erroneous views on minor, though in themselves momentous questions,—his imperfect and erroneous views were not supposed to countervail his faith in and love to Christ and the Father, and his experience of the Spirit's work upon his own heart. The error on secondary points of doctrine did not vitiate, neutralize or counterpoise the cardinal truth; the secondary unbelief did not make the primary "faith of none effect."

No community can call itself a Christian church—without violating the original and distinctive meaning of the word—that does not rest on some fact of religion capable of being expressed in words, in answer to the natural question, What is the fact of religion which constitutes the basis of your association?

What then is that doctrinal basis without which no community can form part of the Christian Church, and no individual can justly claim recognition as member of the Church? The answer to this is, Whatever amount of revealed truth is sufficient, when heartily believed, for the initiation of a rudimentary Christian experience, the enkindling and sustentation of the spiritual life and for tracing the outlines of a truly Christian character, is sufficient to entitle any individual to recognition as a member of the Christian Church. The precise amount of doctrinal belief which is necessary to salvation is necessary to Church membership. But who is to settle that? It is settled already. First of all: Surely a belief in the Divine truths embodied in the formula of admission into the Church ordained by Christ Himself must be necessary to membership in His Church. But still further, St. Paul has distinctly stated the doctrines, belief in which is necessary to salvation. To the Corinthians he writes: " Moreover, brethren, I declare unto you the Gospel which I preached unto you, which also ye have received, and wherein ye stand; *by which also ye are saved*, if ye keep in memory what I preached unto you, unless ye have believed in vain. For I delivered unto you first of all that which I also received, how that *Christ died for our sins* according to the Scriptures; and that He was buried, and that He rose again the third day according to the Scriptures."* An effective belief that *Christ died for our sins* and was raised from the dead according to the Scriptures is here asserted to be essential to the salvation of *evangelized* people.

Those who deny the Divine facts embodied by Christ in the baptismal formula which He constituted the Confession of faith indispensable to admission into His Church cannot, without gross disregard to their own convictions and those of others, claim membership in the Church of Christ. Surely every intelligent, candid Unitarian must see at a glance that a community based upon the Godhead and atonement of Christ, the love of God the Father, and the experienced

* 1 Cor. xv. 1—4.

activity of the Holy Ghost, the very reason of whose association is to conserve, contend for and witness to these truths, are not at liberty so far to indulge their own sensibilities, at the expense of their convictions and obligations, as to admit into Christ's Church those who brand as gross superstition the facts with regard to His own Nature and Personality and the meaning of His life and death on the ground of which He Himself instituted the Society.

To concede the claim of Unitarians to be regarded as members of the Church of Christ were to violate the basal principles of Apostolic catholicity, which embraces "all that in every place call upon the name of Jesus Christ our Lord, both theirs and ours." In the first place, the Unitarians do not "*call upon* the name of Jesus Christ." In the second place, "Jesus Christ our Lord" is not the Jesus Christ of the Unitarians and Rationalists. Our Lord Jesus Christ is "over all God blessed for evermore," "theirs" is a mere man, or less than that, a *Christ-idea*. Our Jesus Christ is the historical Jesus who announced Himself as the eternal, omnipresent, infinitely trustworthy, infinitely competent Son of God; their Jesus Christ is a modern myth, whose Bethlehem is the brain of imaginative speculation, an unhistoric hero-sage, who changes his identity to suit every new phase of fashionable thought. The Christ of Unitarianism and Rationalism is not the same Christ as the living Head of the living Church; even as a conception of the speculative intellect he is not the same for two consecutive decades: Jesus Christ, the Author and Finisher of our faith, is "the same yesterday, to-day, and for ever." The two rival Christs, of whom one must be an antichrist, cannot be the objects of the like affections. Christ regarded as a merely human professor of ethics, whose pronouncements are open to the egotistic eclecticism of any one who may choose to patronise His professorship, and as the most successful cultivator of piety and philanthropy who has yet appeared, cannot be worshipped in the same *sense* as the historic Christ Who announced Himself as a Divine Personality. Channing, whilst denying the Godhead of Christ cultivated towards the Jesus of his theory a reverence and devotion bordering on worship, such indeed as ought never to be offered to a creature; but this enthusiastic hero-worship was altogether another sentiment, an alien passion, an antagonistic principle to the unbounded adoration, trust, devotion which believers render to the Divine Redeemer.

The first mark of the Spirit of truth and love given by St. John is doctrinal, namely, the confession "that Jesus Christ is come in the flesh." And the harmonious teaching of Scripture is, that living love grows out of genuine faith in, and experience of, revealed verities. Nothing can be more explicit than the testimony of St. John, St. Paul, and of Christ Himself, that faith in Christ as the Son of God is essential to a truly Christian life: " Who is he that overcometh the world, but he that believeth that Jesus is the Son of God?" (1 John v. 5.)

But *where is your charity?* What charity is it to admit men who avowedly do not need and will not have a Divine Redeemer and Atonement into the Church, which so soon as it ceases to witness to and worship the Divine Redeemer and to preach His redemption, has no reason for its existence as a distinct association?

To demand the inclusion of Unitarians in the Church of Christ is to demand that the Church shall accept two rival, alternative and optional Christs; the one being God, the other merely man; and either the one or the other an audacious and impious pretender. Not only is the Church a totally different structure as resting on the Divine Christ, on the one hand, or a merely human Christ, on the other, but the Church founded by Jesus Christ, the Church according to its Divine ideal, as a living organism, vitally united to Christ through the communication of the Holy Spirit, were on Unitarian *principles*, utterly impossible and inconceivable. To attempt the amalgamation of two such utterly incompatible views of Christianity and the Church, under the name of opposite tendencies of Christian thought, is to violate the sanctity of language, in order to effect a hollow coalition equally discreditable to the sincerity and earnestness of both parties. To ask the Church to make the Godhead of its Founder and its own character as a Divine institution matters of indifference, is to require it to decree its own triviality.

And all that Unitarians could gain by inclusion in the Church, which could never be anything more than nominal, would be the turning a philosophy into a heresy. But surely their own self-respect would keep them outside the Church of the Divine Redeemer, so long as they reject both His Divinity and His Redemption.*

* Yet a reverential shrinking from an unwarranted extension of the boundaries of the Church beyond the limits which its Founder Himself described, is in no wise inconsistent with the cultivation of a charitable persuasion that the self-excluding unbelief of such men as Firman and Channing had far less in it of that self-will and pride which form the damning element in unbelief, than of over-indulged intellectual idiosyncrasy, the disproportionate and therefore abnormal development of certain faculties at the expense of others, or of an educational bias which it was almost impossible to rectify. May we not, without disloyalty to the faith once delivered to the saints, cherish a self-diffident hope, nay, a humble expectation of meeting some in heaven with whom on earth we could have no honest Christian fellowship ; even as Wesley hoped to meet Marcus Antoninus there ? But surely the Apostolic reserve befits us here. "What have I to do to judge them that are without ?" Yet it behoves us to remember that the virtues of a Firman and a Channing will judge the practical Antinomianism of the orthodox as sternly as

But the original baptismal formula and the compendium of revealed truth above quoted (1 Cor. xv. 1—4) form the legitimate basis of a truly catholic inclusiveness, embracing precisely that which is absolutely necessary to even a rudimentary Christian experience, inasmuch as, if the creed of the heart, it livingly connects the soul with Christ, admitting it into true fellowship with the Father and the Son through the Spirit. Surely no Protestant, nor even any Roman Catholic, would affirm that the amount of doctrine rightly imposed as terms of communion comprises the whole body of doctrinal teaching provided for the nutriment or delectation of the flock.

The rule of inclusiveness in the Christian Church, then, is to insist on faith in the fundamental facts of Christianity and to allow liberty of discussion on all other doctrines. This involves no disloyalty to revealed Truth, inasmuch as true Christian discipleship does not imply a perfect perception, but the sincere and ardent study of revealed truth. For a time the less advanced in the school of Christ may be "otherwise minded" than the more advanced. The

those of Epictetus judged the vices of the zealous contemporary Jew. Still, to make good the parallel, even as it would have been absurd and impious to admit to the Church privileges of the Old Covenant any virtuous heathen who refused to submit to circumcision, so it would be preposterous and irreverent to admit within the pale of Christian discipleship any philosophizing or practical philanthropist who should refuse to be baptized "in the name of the Father, and of the Son, and of the Holy Ghost." For he who will presume to manipulate Christ's teaching, even about His own personality, that he may shape it to his individual preconceptions or proclivities, whether under the shallow pretence of historical criticism,—making nineteenth century notions the test of what was actually said and done in the first century,—or of his own individual "intuitions"—is not a disciple of Christ, but a dogmatizer of his own mental preferences ; and if not a disciple of Christ, not a member of Christ's Church.

temporary disparity of attainment does not involve a divergence of aim or a discordance of sentiment or a discrepancy in character or course of life. "Let us, therefore, as many as be perfect, be thus minded : and if in anything ye be otherwise minded, God shall reveal even this unto you. Nevertheless, whereto we have *already* attained, let us walk by the same rule ; let us mind the same thing." It is no small matter to be "established in the present truth."

But to leave the Church of Christ without any distinctive doctrinal basis whatever, with a view to a universal inclusiveness, would be to disband the Church, in order to extend it; to consummate the Church's destiny by resolving it into an indefinite number of philosophical schools, with nothing common to them all, but the delusive name and the fast fading prestige of the Church.

Without the oneness of its object the Christian faith would be a jumble of idiosyncrasies, "a feeling, fond and fugitive," a thing of moods and tastes. Still, this faith is not in its essence the unity of a tradition, but the unity of a life; though unity of tradition as to the One Spirit, One Lord, and One God and Father of all, can never be lost so long as unity of life survives; and conversely, the unity of life can by no means survive the unity of this tradition. Hence a Church without a creed, a confession of faith, written or unwritten, without *unity of the faith*, is a contradiction in terms; it may be a school of thought, a mutual improvement society, or a debating club, but a church—never. But a mere verbal faith—letter without the Spirit—can in nowise create or conserve Church unity.

And as there is one faith in the one Lord, so there is one profession of faith, *one baptism*. Since there is but one Christ, there can be but *one baptism*. There may be diverse modes of administering the one baptism, but the baptism is one, both in the significance of the rite, and in the experience of the thing which always accompanies the rite when it is accompanied by the faith and confession of the recipient, or follows the rite when it is followed by the faith and confession of the recipient. No one can have any idea of the significance and efficacy of baptism who does not see that there can be but one baptism, and that the oneness of the baptism is an essential element in the oneness of the Church. For the baptism of a believer is baptism into Christ. Baptism owes its institution to the one Lord, Who ordained it as the form of initiation into discipleship, and no one has a right to impose any other form, or to dispense with this. In like manner the oneness of the Spirit involves the oneness of the baptism, without Whose baptism of fire the baptism of water is a mere form, and without Whose new birth the birth of water is abortive.

One God and Father of all, Who is above—over—all, and through all, and in you all. The unity of the Church is here pronounced to be absolute, having its root and life in the unity of the Godhead. The adoption which is consummated by the advent of the Spirit of Sonship into the individual believer's heart, and is thus the privilege of every real member of the Church, is not inconsistent with that universal Fatherhood, from which, while sinners have disinherited themselves, they are not effectively cut off except by final impenitence; any more than His sovereignty in the Church presupposes an abdication of His sovereignty over the rest of the human race—He is *over all.* But the living Church is, not only by relationship, but in reality "in God the Father," inasmuch as the *life* of its individual members is *hid with Christ in God.* Besides, it is of the Church that the Spirit is here speaking. *Our Father* is the fitting address of Christ's *disciples, when* they *pray.* In the Church that blessed consummation is initiated wherein God shall be *all in all.* " The things that are freely given to us of God" are "the deep things of God"—the *abysses* of God, "the depths of Deity:" by the ever-expanding experience of its individual members, the Church is being "filled with all the fulness of God."

And with this accords, and from this flows, the unity of experience in all true members of the Church; and this is only another way of saying, *all members of the true Church.* They all have the moral features of one Father; they have all a conscious affinity, so soon as they begin to converse together on experience, however divergent or mutually repellent their natural tendencies and tastes may be. Their spiritual intuitions are the same: their spiritual instincts are the same. There is a Christian *common sense* which reveals and rests upon unity of nature.

This obtains through all ages and all sects and all schools of Christian thought. It is the same in Paul and the last converted Sunday scholar that triumphed over death. The same in à Kempis and Wycliffe, Luther and Pascal, Dr. Arnold and Dr. Marsh, Joseph Entwisle and Augustus Hare, in Archbishop Sumner and Elizabeth Fry, in Fijian convert and sad-hearted, sorely-bewildered, yet spiritually minded Ultramontanist,—all have underlying their prodigious differences the same life and the same love. One touch of grace makes the whole Church kin. An Œcumenical Lovefeast is the true eirenicon. The true believers through all the range of time and thought can sing each other's songs, and echo each other's sighs, and understand each other's speech. Spurgeon quotes Keble in his prayers. Their aims are identical even when their methods are opposed. As to "the root of the matter," God has already, from the beginning, given His people "all one way." And since this is substantially the fact, can it be fanatical to expect that it will be ere long conspicuously the fact. There is already ample evidence that the Church is one to those who have heart-eyes to see it, or are not blindfolded by theory. The Spirit of God has decided the point, both in the Bible and in the facts of Christian society, that the Church is not so feeble a thing that it cannot exist except by a certain official lineage.

Who is over all:—So that no man upon earth may be called our Father as holding an ultimate, conscience-binding authority. The relation and the access of each member to the Father is too direct, sacred and endearing for that.

He *is through* all:—He acts on all and in all His children; but His action should in no case terminate on the individual, but should work through each individual on his brethren who are already in the Church, and on those who have not yet joined themselves to the Lord.

And in you all:—The Divine energy which through each reaches others is not spent by communication; on the contrary, the more freely it flows through, the more richly it abides in the individual recipient.

Since there is but *one God* there can be but one Church, and that Church not bound to Him or bound together by the clamps of an outward mechanism, but by the sympathy of filial and fraternal love.

The Divine indwelling of the Church is not merely official or collective : " God is in you *all.*" The temporary episcopal, clerical, or numerical predominance of error does not destroy the continuity of the witness to the truth, so long as there remain a faithful few. God has not left His Church and His truth at the mercy of bishops and clergy, as some good men still persist in affirming;* in short, He has not *left* His

---

* *E.g.,* Dean Goulburn ; *Holy Catholic Church,* page 42. The Old Catholic movement is a protest against this dogma.

Church. We often say, "The best of all is God is with us;" but the very best of all is, God is *in* us. The all-illuminating intuition, "the unction from the Holy One," is the endowment of the Church in its individual members (1 John ii. 20—27). And the duty of *trying the spirits*, that is, all tendencies of theological thought, and all dogma propounded by ecclesiastical authority, is incumbent on all the "beloved." (1 John iv. 1.)

The strength of the Church is not in external supports, which may so readily become impediments and restraints, not even in internal acquirements and distinctions, such as the erudition or high social *status* of its ministry, but in the spiritual vitality and the consequent mutual affinity and heart-cohesion of its members. Yes, the glory of the Church, the secret of its might, the equipment for its mission, is the indwelling God—the possession of a Divine element, a life, a force, a combination of spiritual forces, "the powers of the world to come." And its commission is to bring these powers to bear upon surrounding society, to make them felt by all within its sphere. It is by the perpetual emission of spiritual influence, and by the witness to revealed and realized truth in word and life, that the Church must conquer the world. This strength Zion must "put on;" must wear and wield. It is the reality of godliness in its members, their influential holiness and spirituality, which draws souls to Christ and His Church. It is this in her public assemblies for worship and instruction which affects "outsiders." St. Paul describes the process and the scene: "If there come in one that believeth not, or one unlearned, he is convinced of all,—he is judged of all; and thus are the secrets of his heart made manifest; and so, falling down on his face, he will worship God, and will report that God is in you of a truth." It is this which demonstrates the Church to be "a supernatural society."* The heretofore unbelieving one, finding "the secrets of his heart made manifest," will fall "down on his face," "not daring so much as to lift up his eyes;" "and will report, that God is." He will confront and give the lie to Atheism, in whatever form it meets him —vulgar Atheism, stolid Atheism, political Atheism, scientific Atheism. He will confront and give the lie to the arrogant dogma that God is "the Unknowable." He "will report that God is among you of a truth." The *quondam* unbeliever has had in the Church-meeting experience of God. He reports the very present God as among you, as a verifiable, a verified fact. Thus the Church is not only the perpetual witness to, but also the perpetual demonstration of the supernatural.

We must now inquire, What is the relation of the Church to the world? It is at the same time that of contrast, antagonism, aggression, and that of rescuing, regenerating, reconstructive beneficence. First, *contrast:* the character of the Church, as the Ecclesia, the *called out*, was put in the fore-front at the very beginning. The substance and the application of St. Peter's Pentecostal sermon is thus stated: "With many and words did he testify and exhort, saying, Save yourselves from this untoward generation." And the untoward generation from which they must save themselves by flight, as Lot from Sodom, was none other than that which had up to that very morning composed the visible Church; and to return to it was apostasy, as the Epistle to the Hebrews elaborately proves.

St. Paul appends to his magnificent plan and elevation of God's great temple, the Church, this urgent practical deduction: "This I say, therefore, and testify in the Lord, that ye

* Hooker.

walk not henceforth as other Gentiles walk." (Ver. 17.) Out of unity of life must grow a striking uniformity of living. Christians are, throughout the New Testament, regarded as enrolled members of a distinct community, who are required to live according to the laws and usages of that community, and not to fall disgracefully below its standard of morals and decorum. They are bound to a manner of life very noticeably diffcrent from that of persons who are not members of that fraternity. They have their own especial and acknowledged rule of living—that rule being "the Gospel of Christ." The difference between a member of the Christian Church and one who is not a member is to be strongly marked and readily recognised. True Churchmen have a cherished code of manners and fondly reverenced traditions, to which it is their dignity and ambition to conform their entire spirit and habits. Church members are a spiritual peerage or Knights Companions, who, having high honours and peculiar privileges, are expected to observe a rule in keeping with their elevated position: the Gospel being the patent of their nobility must also be the standard to which all their habits must be accurately adjusted. Church-membership is admission into a glorious society and investiture with a celestial dignity, and demands a befitting character and course of life. Hence the "tares" must in any case bear such resemblance to the wheat that it would require a sensitive and solicitous eye to detect any difference, and not give to them "that pass-by" the impression that the Church is the paradise of weeds, and not the field of wheat.

But it is said, The "other Gentiles" were heathen people, and not the inhabitants of a Christian country. It is universally admitted that, in the early ages of Christianity, to become a member of the Church was a very solemn and momentous matter. All candidates for admission were required to " come out from among" the worldly and be separate. Then friendship with the world was enmity with God: but, it is argued, now there exists a Christendom; this requirement is out of date: as if "the world" which Christians must renounce, came to end, in Western Europe generally, at the conversion of Constantine ; and for the English, on the evangelization of the last kingdom of the Heptarchy, and has ever since been an interesting piece of ecclesiastical antiquarianism. But the features of the world which Christians were called upon to renounce are too plainly drawn in Scripture to allow of any honest doubt that it still survives. If the inclusion of a country in the map of geographical Christendom were any guarantee for the exclusion of " the lust of the flesh, and the lust of the eyes, and the pride of life ;" or if baptism, unaccompanied by repentance and faith of heart, involved the subjection of the carnal mind, then the introduction of baptism amongst the customs of a country might render obsolete within its latitude and longitude the summons to " come out from among " the worldly and be separate. But, alas! it is a gross historical error, and betrays a strange blindness to existing facts, to imagine that the christianization of Christendom has ever been so nearly complete as to make the ancient distinction between the Church and the world a question to be determined by reference to a school geography.

That " vanity of mind " in which " other Gentiles walk " (Ver. 17), that infatuated preference of the perishing to the eternal, of the creature to the Creator, which is the very *virus* of Gentileism, is so far from being antiquated like Druidism or the worship of Thorr, that at this very day it constitutes the most staring feature of English Society. Hence the Apostolic demand for a noticeable contrast between the " walk," the habitual manner of life, of members of the

Church, and "them that are without" is as timely and as urgent in the England of the Nineteenth century as in the Ephesus of the First. St. John's antithesis between "the world," and those who "have fellowship one with another," and "with the Father and His Son," holds good to-day. But the antithesis which has, to a great extent, been substituted for this, namely, that between the visible and the invisible Church, has been most unwarrantably exaggerated. The Apostles and primitive Christians knew nothing of this glaring contradiction between the Divine ideal and the reality of the Church; this acquiescence in that repulsive discrepancy as if it were a foredoomed thing; this concession of a time-established right of worldliness to form the largest element in Christ's heavenly society; this claiming for Satain a right of way into the wheat-field of the Church, with licence to sow in broad daylight not only tares but all other noxious weeds. This doctrine is itself Satan-sown. It is this which has made the so-called "visible Church," that institution which was nominally the representative of Christ and the living embodiment of His religion to become, in countries where it has not been checked by the witness and rebuke of spiritual associations, either seceding or ejected from, or secluded within the external pale,—the grossest misrepresentation of the religion of Christ; till the conscience and common sense of society "hiss at the daughter of Jerusalem, saying, Is this the city that men call the perfection of beauty, the joy of the whole earth?" What sort of *visibility* is given to the Church by the unchristian living of the great majority of its members? It was this, along with the twin-heresy of sacerdotal succession, which changed Jerusalem into Babylon.

It is this, too, which more than aught else prevents the external unification of the Church. According to the prayer of Christ, the unity of the Church and the spirituality of the Church must progress equably, and the consummation of the one is the consummation of the other: " I in them, and Thou in Me, that they may be made perfect in one." To despair of the holiness of the Church is to despair of the outward unification of the Church;* and to despair of the holiness and unification of the Church is to despair of the regeneration and reconciliation of the human race. The maintenance of a discipline maternal yet effective is the direct way to the ultimate unition and universal inclusiveness of the Church, and the accomplishment of its benign and holy mission in the world. Because the Church cannot yet be " without spot or wrinkle, or any such thing," must the ghastly scales of moral and spiritual leprosy cleave to it from generation to generation? *The* Church is "clothed with the sun:" because the sun has spots, must the Church be allowed to become a comet, with a little nucleus of spirituality and sanctity to draw after it a portentous tail of worldliness and wickedness? The visible glory, the glorious visibility of the Church in the view of its Founder, and in the view of the world, is its Christ-likeness, and its world-winning oneness of holy love.

The relation of the Church to the world, then, is that of sworn antagonism to its spirit, of avowed, unrelenting aggression on its vices, its vanities, and its hereditary ungodliness. She is the ruthless invader of its pestilential pleasaunces, the unsparing spoiler of its most worshipped pomps. She wages against its customs, its maxims, and its gods a war without truce or terms. She has on her hands a great work of disturbance, demolition and subversion. Although her birth-song and her battle-cry is, " Peace on

* Canon M'Neile avows his despair of the latter, on the ground of his despair of the former.—*The Church and the Churches*, p. 138.

earth, goodwill toward men," yet the first result of her attacks is "rather division." God's great gathering-process by her agency begins with, separation. Her "calling" is "to bring to nought things that are:" "the weapons of" her "warfare are mighty through God to the pulling down of strongholds." She walks abroad as with a wand of universal disenchantment, "casting down imaginations." When she goes forth in the strength of her Almighty Head, "her steps are earthquakes" turning "the world upside down," shaking "terribly the earth." It is in "this mountain" of Zion that God "will destroy the face of the covering cast over all people, and the veil that is spread over all nations," that many-coloured, miasmatic mist of delusion, the delusion of creature-worship, which has crept over the fair and pure creation of God. All this must vanish like the gorgeous mockery of the desert. What desolations must she make in the earth! The unhealthy frivolities of fashion, the polluting pageantries of superstition, and the barbaric pomp of war—all must be dissipated like a shimmering marsh-mist. But her work of spoliation is only preliminary to her work of benignant reconstruction. To her it is said, "Thou shalt be called The repairer of the breach, the restorer of paths to dwell in." How can it be otherwise since the Church is, as we have seen * the continuator of Christ's own work on earth?

The work of teaching and preaching and casting out devils, and thus reclaiming the lost souls of men was the principal part of Christ's personal ministry on earth, but it was not the whole of that ministry. He was the great Healer, the great Helper, the great Sympathizer, the Promoter of social gladness and grateful God-regarding hilarity. He was "*the* Son of Man" as well as the Son of God, and "the Son of Man came eating and drinking" alike at the

* P. 15.

humble, homely marriage-feast in the Galilean village, and "with publicans and sinners," in large commercial centres. He "went about doing good, and healing all manner of sickness and disease." And His Church's work is like His own: First *spiritual*, that of witnessing for God, warning and inviting sinners, preaching repentance, preaching the Kingdom which "is righteousness, peace, and joy in the Holy Ghost;" turning men "from darkness unto light, and from the power of Satan unto God, that they may receive remission of sins and inheritance among them that are sanctified through faith that is in" Christ. But the work of the Church is secondly, *social* and *physical*. Its mission is to mitigate misery, to soothe and solace poverty, to fight against ignorance, disease, pauperism, squalor, and the fiend of filth. The Church is to be eminently a sympathizer. This keen, vivid, prompt, practical sympathy with human sorrow is one of the essential marks of the true Church. Social evils are amongst the "works of the devil," which Christ came to destroy; "the first-born of death" which sin brought into the world, which "devour" the "strength" of poor humanity. Whatever tends to mitigate the hardships of labour, to "comfort us concerning our toil, because of the ground which the Lord hath cursed," that commands the interest of the Church of Christ, and is an integral part of its commission. It is called to confront and conquer crime, vice, sin, and want. The poor are the special wards of the Church. The first office instituted in the Church after the Apostolate was that of the Poor-steward. Hence every genuine revival of Christianity has been marked by a brave and laborious philanthropy.

And it is the aim of Christ's administration through the agency of His Church, not simply to mitigate human misery in detail, but also to advance towards perfection the external condition of the race. The Church is the executrix of His enterprise, the legatee of His aims and the claimant of His resources. That enterprise is, not only to form in " the land that is very far off " a glorious community rescued from the wreck of worldly society, but also to elevate, purify and beautify the earthly life of man, until the prayer is answered, " Thy will be done in earth as it is in heaven." It is the commission of the Church to raise to the highest possible pitch domestic peace and order; social kindliness and honour; political perfection—that is, the voluntary submission of nations to benign and equitable laws and their loyalty to well-adjusted institutions; education, that is, the unfolding all the potentialities of the human intellect; scientific discovery and induction, that is, the familiarizing of man's mind with the mind of God through the humble study of the works and ways of God; physical comfort and well-being, that is, those arrangements, provisions and observances which are most conducive to physical effectiveness for the duties of life and susceptibility to its enjoyments; material wealth, that is, the turning to the best account those immense stores which the forethought of the great Father has deposited in the earth for the satisfaction and solace of His children in this the babyhood of our being, and the wondrous productiveness of labour and the prerogative of art to embellish and ennoble this lowly life of man—in one word, *civilization*, that is, the making the life " that now is " as beautiful, orderly, graceful and enjoyable, as like the life " that is to come," as a schoolroom, a workshop, and a place of graves can possibly be made.

Isaiah saw that when the tree of life was planted in the world anew, its roots, striking deep into the mould, would make all the dead forces of nature feel " of the powers of the world to come :" " In that day shall the branch of the Lord be beautiful and glorious, and *the fruit of the earth* shall be excellent and comely." (Isaiah iv. 2.) Hence it behoves the Church of Christ to cultivate and manifest the most genial sympathy with the social and political well-being and advancement of our redeemed race. The sublime, sullen, almost savage, heavenly-mindedness which has led some saintly men to say in effect, " The world is coming to an end ! let it perish : we have a better country yonder," is not the true temper of a disciple of the Son of Man. God has not done with human history yet. The administration of the God-Man, through the agency of His Church, is not to leave His redeemed world in confusion, corruption, misery ; no, it is to advance towards unimaginable happiness. The whole planet is Christ's patrimony and His Church's demesne and dower, and under her faithful and loving cultivation it shall yet teem with the fairest fecundity of Eden.

Hence, one of the most legible and luminous marks of the true Church, one of the most legitimate tests of the genuineness of Church-claims is the visible effect of its action on society. If in those realms where an ecclesiastical corporation has most influence, society becomes corrupted to its core, an exaggerated externalism draping but not disguising the most noisome profligacy : if, under the auspices of " the Church," commerce be crippled and alternate syncope and spasm be the normal state of the community, assuredly that corporation lacks one essential sign of the true Church of Christ. Christ's Church must be the patroness of every humanizing movement, the nursing-mother of every pacific art, the prompter and pioneer of every philanthropic enterprise and the champion alike of liberty and law. It is hers to consecrate marriage, to teach the household virtues, to force away depopulating and debilitating vices. Like her benignant Lord, she must be ever " rejoicing in the habitable parts of the earth, and " her " delights " must be " with the sons of men." It is only in the Church that the true fraternal equality can be realized. She bids " the brother of low degree rejoice in that he is exalted, and the rich in that he is made low."

But in order to the accomplishment of this secondary, this mundane mission of the Church, it must always be kept secondary. To put her work of civilization before her work of conversion is to destroy both. The incidental blessings which a truly spiritual Church scatters along her path transcend the proudest trophies of a merely secular philanthropy; the shadow of her passing by works mighty miracles of healing.

Lastly, let us inquire, What is the Church of the Future, or What is the future of the Church?

Our text implies that the Church of the Apostolic age did not attain the highest or purest form which the Church is designed and destined to assume even in its mundane history. The Spirit speaks of the perfect Church as the future Church, of the future Church as the perfect Church: " *Till* we all come unto the unity of the faith and the knowledge "—the personal experience—" of the Son of God, unto a perfect man, unto the measure of the stature of the fulness of Christ." The perfection of the primitive Church was that of childhood, not that of maturity or manhood. This adult perfection is a consummation to be eagerly longed and confidently looked for, and strenuously, steadily aimed at by us all. This is the coming era of Church completeness. The certainty of its ultimate arrival, or rather of our ultimate arrival at it, is intimated in the Apostle's form of expression. It is not written *that* we all *may* come, but " *till* we all *come.*" The particle expressive of contingency usually attached to the subjunctive mood is here omitted. This blessed destiny is not so much looked at as future and final, as ever present to the mind of Christ, the great Grace-Giver, and therefore never to be absent from the mind of the Church as the goal towards which "we all" must heartily and hopefully strain. The attainment of "the measure of the stature of the fulness of Christ" is the object to which all the rich and varied intellectual, and spiritual endowments of the Church are to be directed and devoted: we all—from the highest to the lowest in gift and office. *Unto* the unity of the faith (as margin *is* not "in" as A.V.). For although the Object of faith is One from the beginning, and for ever, and the faith of all saints is the same living conviction, trust, surrender—"faith that worketh by love," yet the absolute oneness of the faith regarded as identity of view, seeing "eye to eye" is a point to be reached in the manhood of the Church.

It is a mistake to look back to the primitive Church as in every respect the normal Church, and a still grosser and more mischievous blunder to assume that the perfection of the Church is always to be a mere ideal, abstract, unhistoric, unreal perfection. The New Testament ideal of the Church is to be worked towards and ultimately attained. We must not make a pagod of antiquity, or seek the Church's perfection in the past. The Church, like the child Christ, must increase in *wisdom* and stature, and in favour with God and man.*

This consummation is to be arrived at through the kindly, fraternal action and interaction of the diverse and universally diffused gifts of grace. It will be the consummate oneness of perfectly harmonized, felicitously convergent modes of thought, varieties of taste, and correlated points of view. We *all*, multitudinous as we are, and diversely endowed,

* See on this point a noble passage in the Second Fernley Lecture, Pope's *Person of Christ*, p. 83.

shall reach an equilibrium of creed; for that "the unity of the faith" here presaged involves unity of doctrine is indicated by the following phrase, "every wind of doctrine, etc." *" To the unity of the knowledge of"*—*personal acquaintance with*—the Son of God. Experience is the all-reconciling expositor. *Of the Son of God.* The orthodoxy of experience is the deepest and the truest. The Divine Sonship of Christ is the central, culminating point of that orthodoxy. *The life* the believer *lives in the flesh, he lives by the faith of the Son of God.* His ambition is, "that I may know Him." Now ἐπίγνωσις signifies clear and assured knowledge founded on familiar acquaintance, so that it may be confidently said, *" Truly* our fellowship *is* with the Father and with His Son Jesus Christ." This knowledge follows on faith, and grows with its growth, and strengthens with its strength. Experimental knowledge is an advance upon faith.

To a perfect, full-grown man:—Here the ideal, the normal, the future unity of the Church is represented as so vital that it constitutes it a compact, symmetrical personality. It is through the maturity of individual faith and experience that the Church is to become a veritable unity, *a perfect* man. It is not written till each comes "to a perfect man," but "till *we all* come to a perfect man." However great, various, and, in other respects, developed an individual believer's graces may be, they are deplorably imperfect, unless consummated by a genuine catholicity.

To the measure of the stature of the fulness of Christ:—The Church in reaching its essential unity of faith and experience reaches its perfect manhood. " *Of* His *fulness* have *all we* received and *grace for grace."* *The measure of the stature of the fulness of Christ.*—What is this but the attainment by the Church, in the only possible way, in its individual members, of a completeness of Christian character—the maturity of those graces which we derive from Christ's own fulness, and which correspond with the features of His own character?

That—in order that—we be no longer children:—Here the mature manhood of the Church is plainly set forth as the mature manhood of its individual members.—" *Tossed about* " (like waves) *wavering, fluctuating, and carried around* to every point of the doctrinal compass—*by every wind of doctrine:* up and down, hither and thither; "*by*"—*in*—*the sleight of men*—in the cross currents of mere human cleverness, legerdemain of logic—κυβείᾳ—cheating dexterity of word-play, a designing manipulation of Scripture, *cunning craftiness,* and versatile expertness,—πανουργίᾳ—towards— πρὸς—*with a view* and tendency to the systematic artifice of Error—τὴν μεθοδείαν τῆσ πλάνης. Weakness of character and doctrinal vacillation result from arrest of spiritual growth, and a protracted childhood of experience. The unprogressive Christian becomes rather childish than childlike, and from an infantine *passion for novelty,* liable to all the inflated credulity of error and unbelief.

Grow into Him—like a living graft into the living vine, becoming constantly more and more vitally united with Him. Growth in grace is growth into Christ; until we become *to all His* " inward life restored," and " outwardly conformed to " Him, and thus reach " the measure of the stature of the fulness of Christ." Christ is here again represented as the source and centre of individual and associated Christian life, and therefore of thought, feeling, will, by virtue of His communicated life-force.

From Whom:—From *out of* Whom: spiritual growth is *from* Christ as its fountain, *into* Christ as its centre, *unto* Christ as its standard.

The whole body being fitly framed—joined together by mutual adjustment and interadaptation of all its component parts —by accurate juxtaposition, so as to form integral and closely related portions of a shapely and symmetrical body, well-proportioned in its anatomy, and thoroughly knit together.

"Till *we all* come to, etc." The goal of a perfect agreement in doctrine, a correspondent Christian experience, and a complete Christian character, is the goal of universal unity. To this trysting-tree of Church-union "we all" must enquire our way, with our "faces thitherward." The Divine ideal of the Church pourtrayed in Scripture—that of a vital and organic unity—is a realizable ideal. It is the Ground-plan and Elevation of God's great visible temple on earth, which will yet be built. Christ's own impetration in His High-Priestly Prayer, That they all may be one, that the world may believe that Thou hast sent Me," must yet be answered. It is only in a *holy, united Church* that the three first petitions of the Lord's Prayer can receive their fulfilment. Those petitions are, at the same time, precepts and prophecies. Our Lord, in teaching us what we should pray for, teaches us what we must aim at and expect. We are never commanded to ask for the impossible, or to sue for that which the sovereignty of God decrees shall never come to pass. The prayers which Christ Himself offered, and those which He taught His disciples, form the directory of His people's efforts, and the charter of His people's hopes, giving voice at once to the deepest and dearest counsels of God, and the truest and profoundest wants of man.

Although every local Christian community holds all the prerogatives of the Church—is, in fact, the Church-monad— the Congregationalist theory being to this extent Scriptural; yet the idea of the Church as a world-wide, visible, voluntary association is neither unscriptural nor Utopian. But it is not to be attained by anathematizing authority, or a centralization cemented with cursing and chicane. You cannot crush the members of Christ's body into a veritable, visible union by red-hot iron clamps, or by a system of monstrous make-believe. If the being animated with a common life, and imbued with common sympathies and antipathies, cannot bind believers together in devotedness to a common cause, then a bare external authority, claiming to lord it over charity itself, can only stiffen and deaden the body it pretends to unite. It is by living "joints" and sympathetic "bands" that the organic unity of the Church must be maintained. To resort to ungainly and humiliating surgical appliances to hold the body together is a confession of debility, distortion and disease.

As little can unity be attained by an indiscriminate inclusiveness, which would not only limit the Church's mission to urgent invitation, to the exclusion of discipline and oversight, but would stretch to cracking the stronds of the Gospel-net. It is to be attained by unswerving adherence to the foundation facts on which the Church is built, by invincible charity, mutual appreciation, deference, and teachableness, and by the ardent and untiring endeavour to keep, in any case, and at any cost of preconceptions and predilections, " the unity of the Spirit in the bond of peace."

The most effective hindrances to union are: First, that which is the root of all the rest, the divisive carnality which betrays a "tetchy and wayward infancy" of Christian experience. Second, the attempt to force on a factitious, fictitious, hollow, outside union, like that of the papacy. Third, the effort to include in a community held together by pecuniary endowments or historical traditions all who can be called Christians by degrading that venerable name into a vague conventionalism, making it cover all baptized persons who use Christ's name in their blasphemies, thus obliterating the distinction between the Church and the world, and making a so-called Church *broad* enough, by throwing the broad way into the narrow way. Third, The conspiracy to destroy that which, from the beginning, has been the rallying point of unity, by depriving the Church of the one common standard of appeal, the authority of Holy Writ, and by substituting for it a papacy of the pulpit and the press, a hierarchy of clever, self-sufficient men at liberty to prophesy out of their own hearts: thus transferring our allegiance from the Divine text to the human tongue. This, under colour of perfecting the freedom and comprehensiveness of the Church, would disband it altogether as a Society based upon revealed truth: a more effectual solvent of unity could not be invented. How can "we all come unto the unity of the faith," if there be no revealed truth as a stable, objective reality to which we may all converge? How can there be re-union without a rallying-point? To deprive us all of a common standard of appeal, under pretence of achieving a sudden manhood, is to doom the Church to perpetual childishness, to make us for evermore "children tossed to and fro, and carried about with every wind of doctrine." This is not to invest the Church with the *toga virilis* of assured faith, but to turn it out in the loose and "beggarly" tatters of thrice-turned, many patched guess-work. What safeguard have we against "the sleight of men and cunning craftiness," if the Bible be made the mere text-book of egotistic speculation, and thus be turned into the dice-box (κυβεία, Ver. 14) of dogmatizing doubt? How are we to make the "desired haven" of unity, certitude, experimental realization, Christian manliness, if we must be for ever the sport of this chopping, sickening sea of speculation, and this cyclone of conjecture; the gusts of dogmatic denial blowing from all points of the compass at once? Is the Christ-bearing ship never to outrow this lake-squall of "doubtful disputations?" Must the eternal verity on which the Church is built be always regarded as an open question?

Many dexterous writers and speakers assume that the Church is not built upon the rock of revealed fact, nor even on the sodden, shifting sand, but upon the wind-tossed waves; and that the normal condition of the Christian intellect is to be for ever adrift, and its manhood the state of "silly women . . . ever learning, and never able to come to the knowledge of the truth." (2 Tim. iii. 6, 7.) Nay, some are not content that the basis of a believer's faith and hope should be in a state of everlasting fluidity, but would vaporize it altogether into picturesque or portentous cloud. The "valiant for the truth upon the earth" must give place to

"Sophist madly vain of dubious lore,"

and "the trumpet" must only amuse and perplex the Lord's host with "an uncertain sound." Nay, no scientific hypothesis can be ventilated, however hasty and hazardous and audaciously substituting imagination for induction, but Church-officers must start up and warn the Church to loose its moorings and shift its anchorage; and eternal verity must be incontinently readjusted to the windy theories of the time. No sooner does a man who has acquired some specious sleight of pen pronounce one of "the true sayings of God," which he does not at the present personally affect, to be a "Hebraism" or "Semitic form of thought," than Christian theology must forthwith eliminate from its system the unpalatable truth. No sooner does some literary con-jurer bring forth upon the stage a brain-born Jesus, than officials of the Church will hail the phantom-Christ as if it were a new Advent. All this betrays an infantile instability for which there is no cure, but a steady growth in Christian knowledge and experience. The friends of unity must grasp firmly the banner of Christian faith and holy discipline, bearing this inscription: "Thy testimonies are very sure: holiness becometh Thine house, O Lord, for ever." (Ps. xciii. 5.)

Keen-witted unbelievers see clearly enough that to give up the faith is to give up the Church. Thus Mr. Morley writes, "Religious faith is the centre of existence to a Church that sincerely accepts it."

But in this anti-dogmatic age all who would be true to the Truth must avoid two errors: we must not perpetrate the mischievous folly of taking up precarious doctrinal positions, and proclaiming to friend and foe that if they be carried all is lost!* We must guard against theological panic. We must not proclaim some secondary tenet to be the very citedal of the faith. On the other hand, we must not hold ourselves bound to surrender at discretion the citadel of Divine truth to the obscene impieties of every Rabshakeh of rationalism or the grandiloquent menace of every Sennacherib of science, nor to belie our own consciousness and experience out of deference to the authority of men who will themselves acknowledge no authority but their own. Whilst we "contend earnestly for the faith once delivered," and "hold fast the form of sound words," the summaries and formularies of the faith

* On this point the warning of Dr. Weir is very weighty, and very timely: "Pious beliefs, how precious soever to those who entertain them; traditions, however venerable and beautiful and befitting; matters of religious observance and ecclesiastical comeliness, however reasonable and time honoured, must not be placed in a false position of unwarranted importance. Even the clothing in which vital dogma comes to us must not be mistaken for that which it expresses. Words familiar to the ear, and for that reason dear to the heart, must not be set before the truths which they express; but be made to wait upon them and minister to them, etc.; and if they be found to be no longer helpful but hindrances to that service, then they must be made to give way, lest the truths themselves should suffer injury and lose reputation."—*The Church and the Age*, Essay xi.

recorded in the New Testament, we must not grip with a spasmodic and stolid tenacity notions or expressions which do not bear the clear stamp of Inspiration, nor must we be swayed, right or left, by a seductive sentimentality, either to surrender one jot or tittle of that which the Spirit Himself has pronounced essential, or to let the theological "sword devour for ever" in defence of deductions however plausible or however pleasing to ourselves from texts which may, without any torturing, seem to express a truth, not quite so summarily decisive in favour of our own ecclesiastical theories, proclivities, and position.

The outward and visible re-uniting of the churches is to be effected, not by absorption but by alliance and gradual sound assimilation, mutual attraction and approximation, and the cordial coalescence of conscious affinity. Churches must be allowed to group themselves according to their tribal relationships, to combine in proportion to their combining power.*

Care must be taken not to crush on a premature external union. All unbelieving haste and unpractical impatience on this point must be studiously avoided. All we can do is, to take whatever steps may prepare the way for ultimate organic union. We must not suffer ourselves to be disheartened by failures resulting from over-eagerness. We must believe, hope, love, and speak "the truth in love,"

* The Congregationalist monad has proved itself capable of becoming a *dyad*. The congregations of Hare Court and Stamford Hill have coalesced, with a regular interchange of Ministers and Home-Mission dependencies, supplied statedly with Lay-preaching. Thus is formed a *bonâ fide* Congregational *Circuit*. And it works admirably. A similar Congregationalist Circuit has been formed at Yarmouth. If the principles of Congregationalism will admit of a *dyad*, why not a *triad* and a *tetrad*, and so on, in an indefinite series? Congregationalists find it necessary to combine for Missionary and Parliamentary action, why not for the support of the weaker churches and ill-salaried ministers?

and cultivate holiness and fellowship "*till* we all come, etc." "Nevertheless, whereto we have already attained, let us walk by the same rule, let us mind the same thing," saying each to the other, "If in anything ye be otherwise minded, God shall reveal even this unto you." (Philippians iii. 15, 16.) Whosoever professes faith in the Divine Redeemer, uncontradicted by his life, of him we "should say, Why persecute we him, seeing the root of the matter is found in" him. (Job xix. 28.)

"We all" must endeavour to bring our various Church-systems into as near a correspondence as possible with the Divine ideal presented in the New Testament; and that not in an unpractical, amateur, pedantic *doctrinaire*-spirit, or with a revolutionary readjustment of institutions to ideals, but patiently, lovingly, by setting "in order the things that are wanting." We must not be everlastingly starting new ecclesiastical companies, with a prospectus of perfection and a programme of finality, offering to Christendom the advantage of seeing a model-church in actual operation. We have seen that the Apostles left no programme of Church-organization: they had none: they left an ideal to be worked towards, and a working-plan to be adhered to, and a Church-organism shaped by the life that was in it, and overseers in charge. But whosoever undertakes to lay down an unimprovable form of Church-government takes upon himself a task which the Apostles never assumed. Thank God, we have in the New Testament the features of a pattern-church, but they are not rigid or fixed by measurement; they are the standing "fast in one spirit with one mind, striving together for the faith of the Gospel," "order and steadfastness in the faith of Christ," firm adherence to Gospel-truth, invincible unanimity, and an unbroken front towards the enemy. And the way to retain or to recover these is not an incessant, individual initiative, and restless re-arrangement of administration and public worship. Social, national, ecclesiastical perfection will not be reached by chronic disintegration and reconstruction. The likeliest and the quickest way of realising that world-convincing oneness of the Church for which Christ prayed is not by eager competition for the prize-medal for the best external constitution of the Church. In the actual state of things, imperfect as it is, patriotism is not at variance with philanthropy, and denominationalism is not at war with catholicity. Denominationalism and sectarianism are quite distinct ideas, as distinct as patriotism and misanthropy.* The wise course for a philanthropist is, not to join the " International," but to endeavour by all constitutional means to perfect the liberty, order, and progressive well-being of his " own people;" and if constitutional means be wanting, to emigrate: and the wise course for a true Catholic is to strive lawfully to perfect the vitality, efficiency, and unity of the Church of his education or conversion; unless he discovers some serious and irremediable deficiency in the means of edification, or immovable obstructions in his efforts for usefulness.†

Temporary denominational distinctions may subserve other purposes besides testing the charity, the good sense, and the good temper of the Church. If some church organizations

---

* It is very easy to be a sectarian Roman Catholic or Churchman, or to be a right Catholic Nonconformist. On the other hand, we must not fancy that bigotry can find no breathing-room, and that narrowness can find no sitting in secession-churches. If Judah has not yet ceased to "vex Ephraim," Ephraim has not yet ceased to "envy Judah."

† A gentleman in South Wales justified his leaving the Church in which he was educated and converted for another Christian community by declaring, " In my efforts to bring others to Christ, I was like a man trying to swim in a wire-net!"

are less accordant than some others with the finer faculties of our nature, they are, nevertheless, not altogether destitute of elements of nobleness and grace. Even if those fastidious keen-scented natures who are a sanitary necessity, though sometimes a discomfort, to the Church—since without them "where were the smelling?" (1 Cor. xii. 17)—should aggregate and segregate themselves into a distinct organ, it is far better to regard them as a section than a sect. Without "the smelling," what safeguard is there against subtle infection? But they *declare off* from the rest of the Christian Church. Well, what of that, if they have not lost the faith of Christ and life in Christ? If one member say to the rest, "I am not of the body, is it therefore not of the body?" (1 Cor. xii. 15.) In like manner the unchurching of Christian communities by good men (bad men are out of court), who have surrendered their better judgment to unscriptural Church-theories, does not touch the actual church-hood of those disowned communities, since it is utterly powerless to arrest or diminish the communication of life from the Head. "If the foot shall say to the hand, Thou art not of the body, is it therefore not of the body?"

We must not despair of or despise the outward unification of the Church, if it do not promise to take the shape which we think the best, or if it do not put the imperial crown upon the chiefs of our own church. With some writers, unity is but another word for absorption. Possibly Romanism and Anglicanism might acknowledge the apostolicity of the churches, if themselves might sit the one on Christ's right hand, the other on His left, in His kingdom. But the pretensions of certain churches, more correctly speaking aggregations of churches, to the exclusive title, privileges, and powers of the Church, and the audacious unchurching, the arrogant excommunicating of all other churches, notwithstanding the unquestionable signature, the signal, the acknowledged sanction of Christ Himself on their character and their labours, is obviously an insuperable barrier to union, so long as it is resolutely and most offensively thrust in the way. Whilst men will persist in denying membership in Christ's Church to those whose life in Christ and membership of Christ they dare not deny, for no other offence than their inability to embrace the dogma of Episcopal Succession, which is historically a mere ecclesiastical afterthought, and requires for its support the most arbitrary garbling and inconclusive handling of the Word of God—external union is effectually obstructed by the very parties, who regard *external* union as the principal thing. To make the dogma of Episcopal Succession, rather than the Godhead and Atonement of Christ, the only basis of Church union is to make the dogma of Episcopal Succession the foundation-truth of the Church.

We must also show a due consideration to the difficulties which the historical position of the various churches throw in the way of speedy external union. We must heartily join in all benevolent enterprises in which denominational co-operation would not be seriously obstructive.* The outward re-uniting of the Church is not hopeless. It behoves to be, and it begins to be.

Augustus Hare's superb description of the Rhinefalls † may well serve as an analogue of the re-union of the Church. "The cross-streams, which had been prancing along sideways, arching their necks like war-horses that hear the trumpet, broke from the main stream and forced their way into it. From the valley of thunder, where they encoun-

* See some fine spirited remarks on this point by Earl Nelson, Essay I., *The Church and the Age.*

† *Memorials of a Quiet Life:* a book, by the by, tending strongly towards re-union.

tered, rose a towering misty column, behind which the river unites unseen, as though unwilling that any should witness the awfully tender reconcilement." That "awfully tender reconcilement" of the long conflicting currents of Church-life is even now-being solemnized behind the mist of our encounters. What a yearning for unity pervades the churches! This very desire is, in its intensity, a presage and a pledge of its own fulfilment; only the Spirit of love could have inspired it. He is brooding, moving on the cloudy chaos. What a perceptible giving there is in the ice of exclusiveness. Its most chivalrous advocates now assume an apologetic tone. Many of the professed successors of Peter imitate him so far already as to stand in awe in the presence of the Spirit's work, in disregard of their own ecclesiastical preoccupations and pretensions. They have been driven by true religion and good sense, by the Spirit of God, into a position utterly untenable.

Another hopeful indication of our advance towards "the unity of the faith" is the growing up of a real science of Biblical interpretation, based on clear, sound, consistent and conclusive canons, before which sectarian, partisan and polemical exposition must gradually retire detected and abashed. From this will arise an all-sided, full-orbed theology. Christian theology will be constrained to "walk honestly as in the day," "not handling the word of God deceitfully." All-harmonizing truths will be discovered, "More of light and truth" will "break forth from" God's "Word." Unilateral systems of divinity will become obsolete. The auspicious synod of scholars of all denominations and all schools of thought now in session, for the purpose of a fresh study of the sacred text and of preparing a more accurate and consistent translation of the Scriptures, is mightily conducing to this end: and so are School Boards.

Another element of hopefulness is the fact that the extremes of theological teaching are connected by shades of opinion which melt into one another, so that any one familiar with the religious writers and preachers of the day could trace a continuous scale of theological thought from Newman to Kingsley, from Spurgeon to Liddon, from Manning to McNeile: whilst some men, like Julius Hare, Alford and Archbishop Trench, touch all points of Protestant divinity.

A further proof that gradual and ultimate coalescence is not to be summarily despaired of is seen in the reciprocal imitation and even exchange of tastes and mannerisms between the most opposite sections of the Church. Thus the usage of reading sermons gains upon Nonconformists whilst it loses ground in the Established Church; the former imitate the ecclesiastical architecture of the latter; the craving for a liturgical element amongst the one is contemporaneous with the demand for liturgical abridgment amongst the other; and Ritualism and Revivalism spring up side by side.*

But the sure basis of our hope is the power and the purpose of God. "Why should it be thought a thing incredible with you" that God should resuscitate and re-unite His Church? And the whole tone and tenor of our text implies that "we all" are not only to await, but also to advance this consummation by all believers so devoutly wished. It is not to be accomplished by a terrific Dispensational cata-

* "Where rolls the deep, there grew the tree ;
  O Earth, what changes thou hast seen !
  There, where the wide street roars, hath been
  The stillness of the central sea."

One might be tempted to parody the Laureate's fine lines,—

Where stretched the barn, now springs the spire ;
O *Church*, what changes thou hast seen !
There, where Revivals roar, hath been
The chillness of cathedral choir.

clysm, such as would imply that the Dispensation of the Spirit had been a failure on His own special domain— the Church; and that the expediency of Christ's bodily going away was simply the necessity of demonstrating the insufficiency of that "other Comforter" to the work of uniting and sanctifying the Church. "The zeal of the Lord of Hosts will perform this." Though we lose temper, patience, heart and hope, "He will not fail, nor be discouraged." He can conciliate the most opposite tendencies of truly Christian thought and taste; the delicate and graceful with the straight and strong. When He takes into His own hands His "staff Beauty," and His "other staff Bands," emblems of the broken "brotherhood between Israel and Judah" (Zech. xi. 7—14), "the stick for Judah" and "the stick of Ephraim," shall yet at His bidding become "one stick" (Ezekiel xxxvii. 16, 17). Then shall the truth be visible once more "Strength and beauty are in His sanctuary."

Those only need despair of the substantial union of the Church who despair of the substantive holiness of the Church. All the promises and prophecies of the ultimate union of the Church, as of its final triumph and universal extension, like Christ's High Priestly prayer, connect it with the sanctification of the Church (*e.g.*, Ezekiel xxxvii. 15—28.) What precise form the adult and re-united Church will take it is not for me to forecast. This, however, I will venture to say:—

A wide voluntary federation of churches, all holding the Head, yet of various forms of government, and with a varying theological terminology and varying modes of worship, bound together by their common faith in fundamental doctrines, a common inner life and a common outer life; their common hope of sanctity in this world and rest with Christ in the world to come, is surely a grander ideal, and would be a grander spectacle than a colossal, rigid, hollow, external union, of which the bond is one particular mode of ordination to the Ministry, and an arbitrary limitation of grace and salvation to the officiations of men so ordained; a union, moreover, requiring, and often only too glad to secure the secular arm—in other words, brute force—to carry it into effect.

The aggregate of churches thus voluntarily united by charity, rooted and grounded in love, and not in slavish subjection of reason and conscience to any human authority; with free intercommunion, no one of them claiming to be *the* Church exclusively, but each giving to all the rest and receiving from all the rest "the right hand of fellowship," —not alienated by "diversities of administration," not forfeiting the compact nationality of God's people by interesting provincialisms of theological expression and picturesque variety of usage; with varying modes and agencies of Christian benevolence: this, surely, is a veritable, visible, Holy Catholic Church. Of this grand Christian commonwealth the universal law is Holy Scripture, all peculiarities of administration being merely provincial bye-laws: and the *Te Deum* might form its grand national anthem. At any rate, when the Methodists sing, "The Holy Church throughout all the world doth acknowledge Thee;" a vast, magnificent whole rises up before our view. Verily, we think not only of all the countless churches of Methodism throughout the wide world, but of all the churches of the saints, by whatever name they pass among men; not omitting one misled Roman Catholic who is loyal to his Saviour, or one small, seclusive coterie of Plymouth-Brethren.

On the essential unity of the Church throughout all ages, and in heaven and earth, I have not space to enlarge; but all believing, loving members of the Church realize that

P

union. We feel our oneness with the Patriarchal Church. As "they without us cannot be made perfect," so we without them should be consciously incomplete. The struggles and triumphs of God's ancient people are our struggles and our triumphs. When "they went through the flood on foot; there did we rejoice in Him." (Ps. lxvi. 6.) Our identification with the future Church to the end of time is equally sensitive and entire. We can say of the last generation of believers, with that vivid sense of oneness which, as expressed by St. Paul, has been mistaken by a superficial criticism for Apostolic error, "Then we which are alive and remain shall be caught up together." (1 Thess. iv. 17.) Our oneness with the Church above we exultantly recognise in our elevating psalmody.

I cannot close without recalling the fact, that during the present year, the holy and catholic-minded man who founded this Lecture, and at whose suggestion the topic for the year was chosen, has been called up to the Church triumphant. With him "the Communion of Saints" was no dead dogma, but a substantial fact to be acted on and acted out, with appropriate sentiments to be cherished and practical duties to be discharged. It was a frequent and fervent utterance of his, "The Communion of Saints is the intercourse of God's people on earth, and their oneness with the Church in heaven." That intercourse with God's people on earth he systematically cultivated, especially by conscientious attendance at the weekly and quarterly gatherings for mutual edification and enlivenment. It was due to this habit, to a great extent, that the simplicity of his character and the depth of his spiritual-mindedness were unimpaired by the influx of wealth, and the charms of a wide and various reading. His oneness with the Church above is now no longer a matter of faith and feeling, but a consummated experience. His faith may we follow "considering the end of" his "conversation, Jesus Christ, the same yesterday, to-day, and for ever."

The connection of my subject with those of my revered predecessors in this lectureship is vital and indissoluble. We have seen that "the Holy Spirit" is the soul of the Church: Christ, in His adored Personality as the God-man is the Head of the Church: His Atonement is the foundation-fact on which His Church for ever rests. "Now unto Him that is able" not only to sanctify and reunite His Church in answer to the prayers which He has taught us by the lips of His Son, and to fulfil the word unto His servants on which He has "caused" us "to hope," but also "to do exceeding abundantly above all that we ask or think, according to the power that worketh in us, Unto Him be glory in the Church by Christ Jesus, throughout all ages, world without end. Amen." (Ephesians iii. 20, 21.)

SKETCH OF THE HISTORY OF CHRISTIAN FELLOWSHIP:

OR,

THE REALIZED COMMUNION OF SAINTS.

EVEN under the Old Testament, wherever there existed a sound kernel of vital godliness within the shell of the Mosaic ritual, there were confidential gatherings for the statement of religious experience. In Psalm cxi. 1, we find a marked distinction between "the assembly of the upright" and "the congregation."* Unhappily, this is nearly lost in the authorized version; but it is retained in the Prayer-Book version, and every other with which we are acquainted : "I will give thanks unto the Lord *secretly among the faithful*, and in the congregation." Hengstenberg also rightly translates, "in the *confidential* assembly of the upright and the congregation." Ab. Ezra and the Midrash Tillin, on this text, both recognise the contrast. The learned Buchanan, in his Latin version of the Psalms, likewise preserves the distinction : "*Sive inter fidos tractem secreta sodalis, seu sancti stipante caterva*,"—" whether I may discourse secrets among the faithful, as a privileged member of the society, or amidst the temple-throng." Keble renders, "I praise the Lord with heart entire : in *secret with the faithful*." Bonar, "The confidential meeting of the faithful." Merrick, " In *secret* with His saints *retired*, and midst fair Zion's crowded fane." Brady and Tate, " With *private friends* and in the throng." The idea of a confidential communication is implied in the Hebrew word. There is moreover a peculiar significance in

* See article by the Lecturer, in *Wesleyan Methodist Magazine* for January, 1867, on *The Pew*, etc.

the occurrence of the distinction *here*, as this is the opening verse of those eucharistic psalms, a portion of which constituted the "Hallel" of the Jews, sung at the Feast of the Passover, and by our blessed Lord at the institution of His Supper. Other indications of meetings for mutual edification amongst the spiritual members of the Jewish Church—meetings for close conference on the affairs of the soul, apart from the mere outward observers of Mosaic ritual and attendants at the temple-worship—must be recognised, unless we obliterate many passages of Old-Testament Scripture too well known to need citation here.

In short, it is impossible to collect and compare and connect the scattered evidences which we possess of the inner church-life of God's ancient people, so as to form a complete conception of it, without perceiving that *social* intercourse, for reciprocal instruction, confession and general edification, formed a vital element in the religious system of the Jews.

The services in the Jewish synagogues and places of prayer* were eminently social. Lightfoot has shown that the general supposition that the synagogues originated after the Babylonish captivity is a great mistake.†

All the peoples with whom Christianity first came into contact were familiar with voluntary religious societies, such as the θίασοι of the Greeks,‡ frequently alluded to by Greek writers. It is ascertained, from existing Greek inscriptions, that various religious brotherhoods flourished in Cyprus and the other islands of the Greek Archipelago, and as M. Carle Wischer thinks, were spread over Syria, Asia Minor and Egypt. "Such associations multiplied in an especial manner under the successors of Alexander, . . . the religious element becoming more and more apparent. The meetings were opened by prayer, and each society had religious officers—chaplains, as we should call them—often of both sexes. Banquets were held, to which all the members were admitted. *The only condition of admission was a moral one;* the

* Προσευχαί.

† Yet a shallow criticism, instead of taking Asaph's Psalm as evidence that synagogues existed before the Captivity (Psalm lxxiv. 8), coolly robs Asaph of its authorship.

‡ Smith's *Dictionary of Greek and Roman Antiquities*, Art. *Erani*.

candidate was to be holy and pious and good. . . . Freedmen and even slaves were admissible as members. The outward bond of union was that the members shared in the *sacrificial feast* of a particular divinity. Perhaps such customs throw a light upon the passages of St. Paul, where he speaks of men having fellowship with devils (or rather demons), of their being partakers of the table of demons. . . . Among the Romans, too, the sacrificial feast was the root of the associations known as *sodalitates*, which were held to create a relation almost as close as that of blood."*

What a large and vital element of Church-life the communion of saints, as realized in meetings for mutual edification and spiritual enlivenment, formed in the first four centuries of the Christian era, is plain from the frequent allusions to the Lovefeast in the writings of the Fathers, in the works of heathen assailants, and in the canons of Councils. Those allusions would be still more numerous and express, but for the fact of its intimate and organic connection with the Lord's Supper, the two connected means of grace being often included under the one word, *Eucharist*. Bingham has shown that, in the early centuries of our era, the Lovefeast sometimes preceded, and sometimes succeeded, the Supper of the Lord, but was almost invariably connected with it; but that at the close of the second century the Eucharist and the Lovefeast were distinct; yet closely connected services appears from the Canons of Hippolytus (*circ.* A.D. 200), used by the Æthiopian Christians; the Thirty-first Canon being, "That a deacon may dispense the Eucharist to the people with permission of the bishop or presbyter;" and the Twenty-fifth, "That deacons may pronounce the benediction and thanksgiving at the Lovefeast, etc." St. Clement, in his first epistle to the Corinthians (*circ.* A.D. 68), though not expressly mentioning the meetings for mutual edification, speaks with high approval of reciprocal admonition and exhortation as an established usage in the Church: "The exhortation and admonition which we exercise toward one another is good (in the sight of God), and exceedingly profitable, for it more closely unites us to the will of God." (Chap. lvi.) He also com-

* J. M. Ludlow on Gilds and Friendly Societies. *Contemporary Review*, March, 1873.

mends them highly for their mutual solicitude: "Ye were solicitous day and night for the whole brotherhood." (Chap. ii.)

Ignatius, in his epistle to the Smyrneans (*circ.* A.D. 107) makes the Lovefeast second in importance only to Baptism and the Lord's Supper; if he do not rather regard the Lovefeast as an essential part of the Eucharist: "Let that Eucharist be regarded as duly solemnized, which is either presided over by the bishop or by one to whom the bishop has allowed. . . . It is not lawful without the bishop (in person or by deputy) either to baptize or hold a Lovefeast." (Cap. viii.)

The Shepherd of St. Hermas, the Pilgrim's Progress of the early Church, regarded by those who were in the best position for forming a correct judgment as the production of the Hermas mentioned in the Epistle to the Romans, makes mutual instruction one of the primary Christian duties, involving the necessity of and constituting a powerful motive for earnest self-culture (Vision III. *Of the Building of the Church*, etc.): "My children, How will ye instruct the Elect of God ? Wherefore, instruct one another."

The earliest of the extant Christian Apologists, Justin Martyr, in his earliest work, *First Apology of Justin* (*circ.* A.D. 150), makes very prominent the close personal association and the mutual admonition, "We continually remind each other of these things, and we always keep together." (Chap. lxvii.)

Clement of Alexandria (Pæd. Bk. ii., Cap. i.; *circ.* A.D. 193) glowingly contrasts the Christian Lovefeasts with the heathen banquets. He indignantly rebukes "some who have the audacity to give, with unbridled tongues, the name of Lovefeasts to certain little supper-parties, fragrant with the strong steam of I know not what roots and soups, thus likening that good and salutary fruit of the Word, the sacred Lovefeast. . . . But the Lovefeast truly is heavenly food, a banquet of the reason" (τινίσ τολμῶσ, etc.). From the passage it is plain that the charm and value of the Lovefeast consisted in religious conversation—"the feast of reason and the flow of soul." Again (Bk. ii., Chap. iv.) he writes, "For if thou shall love the Lord thy God, and then thy neighbour, let the first kindly token of this, which truly is to Godward, be in thanksgiving and psalmody; but the second, which is towards one's neighbour, in seemly fellowship, 'Let the Word of the Lord dwell in you richly,' says the Apostle : so that He now also holds convivial intercourse with us.* For the Apostle again says, 'Teaching and admonishing one another in all wisdom, in psalms, etc.' This is our grateful merry-making :"—*ti γαρ*, etc. Clement also contrasts with the holy and spiritual convivialities of the Lovefeast, the licentious comings together of the Carpocratians (Sohm., Bk. iii.), and the vain-glorious socialities of other heretics (Bk. vii).

Athenagoras also (Legat, Cap. iii., A.D. 177) and Theophilus (*ad* Autolyc, Lib. iii., Cap. iv.) make distinct allusions to the Lovefeasts. Menucius Felix, at the close of the second, or the beginning of the third century, defending the Lovefeast against Pagan slanders, says, "Our festivities we season with sobriety and with pure converse :"—*Nos convivia, etc.* (Cap. 31).

The *Apostolic Constitutions*, mainly written towards the end of the third century (according to Krabbe, their most careful commentator), give detailed directions with regard to the conduct of the Lovefeast, as it is there termed, "an entertainment of love."

In the *Recognitions of Clement* (*circ.* A.D. 220), the right and duty of every disciple to be the distributary as well as the depository of Divine truth is emphatically asserted. Peter is represented as saying, "What so glorious as to prepare disciples for Christ, not who shall be silent, and shall be saved alone, but who shall speak what they have learned, and shall do good to others. I wish, indeed, that *all* who hear me—I wish, as I have said, all so to hear and to learn—that they may be able also to teach." (Chap. xvi., Clark's Translation.)

Tertullian, in the third century of our era, in his eloquent vindication of Christianity (*Apologeticus*, 39), describes the systematic social intercourse of the Christians as amongst their most prominent and beautiful characteristics. He writes : "I shall go on to exhibit the peculiarities of the Christian society, that, as I have refuted the evil charged against it, I may point out its positive good. We are a body knit together by a common reli-

* "Jesus, dear expected guest,
 Thou art bidden to the feast."
C. Wesley.

gious profession, by unity of discipline, and by the bond of a common hope. With the sacred words we nourish our faith, we animate our hope, we make our confidence more steadfast; and no less by inculcations of God's precepts, we confirm good habits. In the same place also exhortations are made, rebukes and sacred censures are administered. . . . You have the most notable example of judgment to come, when any one has sinned so grievously as to require his severance from us in prayer and the meeting and all sacred intercourse. . . . Our feast gives its reason in its very name. The Greeks call it Love."

And then follows his celebrated description of the Lovefeast:— "We so converse as those who know that the Lord hearkens to us. . . . Each one is encouraged to sing to God either in the words of Holy Scripture, or if he have the gift, the production of his own genius. . . . Prayer concludes as it began our feast, and thence we go home . . . as those who have been regaled at a supper of Wisdom and Discipline, rather than at a bodily banquet." "*Iter fabulantur, etc.*" Bingham justly terms this "a fine description of those holy banquets, where charity is the foundation, and prayer begins and ends the feast, and singing of hymns and religious discourses season the entertainment." (Orig. Eccl. xv. 8.)

Cyprian in his treatise on the Unity of the Church (*circ.* A.D. 252) makes the realization of that unity to consist in "mutual intercourse,"—"that so the love of the brotherhood may resemble that of the doves."

In the same century, Origen opens his grand vindication of Christianity against the attacks of Celsus, by a defence of the Lovefeasts which still formed such a prominent institution of the Church as to be the first object of assault by that keen enemy of the religion of love. Celsus accounts for the phenomenon of the delight which the Christians had in each other's society on the theory of a sort of anti-social freemasonry or conspiring communism. Origen recurs to the subject in the Sixth Book of the same Treatise (Chapter xxvii). That the Lovefeasts were privileged and confidential gatherings is apparent from the nature of the charges against them, namely, that they were clandestine associations constituting the Church a vast system of secret societies. The enemies of Christianity revenged themselves for exclusion from these carefully guarded Church-reunions by misinterpreting their privileged privacy as a cover to illegal and shameful practices.

Moreover, some system of classification of the various members of the Church, according to the various stages of their advancement in Christian knowledge and experience—and therefore surely some system of classes—would seem to be implied in the statement of Origen (Bk. iii., Chap. 52, 53) that Church-instruction was graduated, in accordance with the Apostolic practice alluded to in 1 Corinthians ii. 6; iii. 1, 2, quoted by Origen in stating the reason of the practice.

Dionysius of Alexandria (Bp. from A.D. 247—265) in his epistle to Fabius,* dwelling on the re-admission of the lapsed into the Church, writes—" They proved their sincerity, and brought them together again, and assembled with them, *and had fellowship with them in their prayers and at their feasts:*" which as Vales justly comments refers not to "public communion" but to "private fellowship."

In fact, as Bingham says, "*All* the Apologists rebut charges based upon the intimate, confidential social intercourse of the Christians." To which that great Christian archæologist adds: " However, although there were many who thus calumniated the Christian feasts by this variety of charges, yet there were some also who could discern the good effects of them, and the great influence they had, not only on their own members, but the heathen, as Tertullian notes,—Ap. Cap. 39. Nay Julian himself, though the bitterest enemy the Christians ever had, could not help bearing testimony to the usefulness of this practice, which he looked upon with an envious eye, as *that which* he imagined *chiefly to uphold* the Christian religion, and undermine the religion of the Gentiles. For thus, in one of his letters to the Gentile priests, he provokes them to the exercise of charity by the example of the Christians and their Feasts of Charity (Julian, Fragment. Epist., p. 555). ' These *begin first to work upon* honest-hearted Gentiles with their *Lovefeasts.*' This is a full vindication of them from all those aspersions which the former heathens had cast upon them, and *an ample testimony of their usefulness from the mouth of an*

* Given by Eusebius, Hist. Eccles, vi. 41, 42, 44.

adversary, who saw and envied *the progress which Christianity made in the world by means of these Feasts* of Charity, which *he was minded to introduce into his own way of heathen worship.*" (Bk. xv., Sect. 10.) Bingham also states generally that the Lovefeast "was the envy and admiration of the heathen." (*Ib.* Lect. 9.)

A direct reference to provision for the Lovefeast as an indispensable part of Church-arrangements is made by Athanasius in his Encyclical epistle (Sect. 4). "A large quantity" could scarcely have been stored for the mere celebration of the Eucharist apart from the Christian family-meal. The views of Athanasius, elsewhere expressed, are in full accordance with the spirit of the Lovefeast : *e. g.*, "The oneness of the body demands correspondence between the members and the effective sympathy of each to his fellow-ministers."

In the Fourth Century, Gregory Nazianzen, in his *Precepts to Virgins*, speaks of the Lovefeast with profound respect whilst warning against the use of "that decorous appellation" for fellowships of another kind (Song the Third) : the monks, taking advantage of a venerable primitive name, for the indulgence of passions unnaturally suppressed. (See the judicious comment on this passage, in Scholia Jacobi Bilii in B. Greorgii Nazianzeni Vitam.)

In the same century, Ephrem Syrus makes distinct allusion to a system of classification of Church-members corresponding with the Apostolic practice, mentioned in 1 Cor. ii. 6. He says in his quaint way, "The chief Shepherds offer deep things to the perfect ; and to the penitents, and to those that stand without the gates, they bring hay and barley." (Morris's *Select Works of Eph. Syr.*, p. 107).

St. Gregory the Great, towards the close of the Sixth Century, in commenting on Job vi. 25, "How forcible are right words!" administers the following fine rebuke to religious reticence and commendation of speaking the truth in love : "Whilst we avoid the mischiefs of the tongue, without caution, we are secretly involved in worse. For oftentimes while we are overmuch restrained in speech, we are subject to a mischievous degree of much talking in the heart, that the thoughts should be hot within, the more that the violent keeping of indiscreet silence confines them; and most often they let themselves take a wider range in proportion as they reckon themselves to be more secure, in that they are not seen by censors without. Whence the mind is sometimes lifted up by pride, and, as it were, regards as weak those persons which it hears engaged in talk. And when it keeps the mouth of the body shut it never knows to what degree it is laying itself open to evil by entertaining pride. For it keeps the tongue down, but it sets the heart up. . . . It censures all the world more freely to itself, in proportion as it does it at the same time more secretly. And, most frequently, over-silent people, when they meet with any wrongs, are driven into bitterer grief, the more they do not give utterance to all they are undergoing. For if the tongue declared with calmness the annoyance inflicted, grief would flow away from our consciousness. For closed wounds give more acute pain, in that when the corruption that ferments therein is discharged, the pain is laid open favourably for our recovery. And generally, whilst over-silent people fix their eyes on the faults of any, and yet hold the tongue in silence, they are, as it were, withholding the use of the salve after the wounds have been seen. For they become the more effectually the cause of death that they refused, by speaking, to cast out the poison which they might. And hence, if immoderate silence were not a thing to blame, the Prophet would never say, ' Woe is me, for I held my peace !' lest the tongue being bound up it be slack to render service : that strictness of silence being laid aside, by speaking such things as are meet, he may devote himself to answer the ends of usefulness : lest when it might speak to good purpose, it should keep itself in. Which the Psalmist considering, comprehended in a brief petition, ' Set a watch, O Lord, before my mouth, and a door of guard on my lips !' *For a door is opened* and shut. He prayeth not that a *bar* should be set on his lips, but a *door*. . . . A full fountain of thought abounds in the heart, but a disproportionate tongue, like a scanty channel confines it."*

The Council of Gangra[†] decrees (Canon XI. Beveredge's *Pandectæ Canonum*, t. ii. b. 17 F.) : " If any one despises the feast of charity which the faithful make, who for the honour of

* Oxford Translation. † A.D. 324.

the Lord call their brethren to them, and comes not to the invitation, because he contemns them, let him be *anathema*."

"These Lovefeasts," says Bingham, "as they were designed for the promotion of unity and charity (? and edification), were commonly held in the church, for the first three centuries."

But as Jewish or pagan notions of local sanctity began to gain ground the custom was discouraged. The Council of Laodicea * (an ominous but not unsuitable locality for such an enactment) banished them from the places of worship on this plea of local sanctity, forbidding any to eat or spread tables in the house of God (Canon xxviii., *Ib.*). The third Council of Carthage † forbade "the clergy to join in these Lovefeasts, if held in a church, and the people were *as much as might be* restrained from feasts of this kind,—" *Populi etiam ab hujusmodi conviviis*, quantum fieri potest, *prohibeantur*." But the custom was too inveterate to be rooted out at once, and therefore we find by St. Austin's answer to Faustus, that they were still kept in the Church (Bingham Bk. xv. 10).

Augustine (Cont. Faust. Lib. xx., C. 21) whilst admitting that occasional irregularities and improprieties occurred at the Lovefeasts, yet stoutly defends them, as notwithstanding these drawbacks, of very great utility.

Even so late as the year 692, the Council of Trullo did not attempt to suppress the Lovefeast, but simply reiterated the Canon of Laodicea, forbidding "on pain of excommunication" the holding them in the churches (Canon L. xxiv., L. xxvi; Beveredge's Pandectæ Can.). The Laodicean legislation had not availed to quench the fervent charity of the churches. It required three hundred and thirty years of sacerdotal rule to prepare the Church for the banishment from the sanctuary of that beautiful and blessed service which had originally been so vitally and organically connected with the Supper of the Lord. But by the close of the Seventh Century, the sanctity of places was more regarded than the sanctity of God's people, and that of the material temple rather than that of the spiritual. The occasional irregularities on the ground of which the Lovefeast was excluded from the place of worship were not nearly so grave as those which the Apostle

* A.D. 361. † A.D. 397.

corrected in the Church of Corinth, the worst being the permission of certain distinctions and indulgences to the wealthy, not so objectionable as a well-cushioned and well-curtained pew in a modern church or chapel.

The seceding bodies, orthodox or heretic, took with them the Lovefeast as an essential institution. The Audians, for example, the followers of Audius, a holy layman, "who lived about the beginning of the fourth century," and was excommunicated for reproving the clergy for "their gross immorality," "held meetings for common edification." (Neander, Ch. Hist., Vol. iv., p. 494.)

Saint Chrysostom describes the Lovefeast as an Apostolic institution coeval with the Christian Church, and still observed in his own day, as regularly as the sacramental communion, and in connection with it (Epist. Jud. xii.). He beautifully says, "The strong, if he be bound to the weak will support him and not suffer him to perish, and if again he be tied to the indolent, him he will rather rouse and animate. Brother helped by brother is a strong city." (On Prov. xviii. 19.)

In the anonymous *Discourse concerning False Prophets*, appended to the works of St. Chrysostom, but bearing distinct traces of later handling, the following sentence occurs: "Be horrified, and tremble exceedingly, ye who join with them (the false prophets) in the Lovefeast:"—φρίξατε, etc.

After the Lovefeast had been excluded from the places of worship, it rapidly declined. It is easy to see what a check these free mutual ministrations must have put upon sacerdotal usurpations, which reversed the order of Christ, making the *Jus Honorum* in the City of God to take precedence of the *Jus Civitatis*.* What a clear field the extinction of the meeting for reciprocal confession and admonition left for the Confessional, it is not difficult to realize.

To this catastrophe the hasty introduction into the Church of half-evangelized tribes strongly conduced, since uninstructed people, with whom baptism was made the substitute for conviction

* "In our heavenly commonwealth, the *Jus Civitatis* is a thousand times greater than the *Jus Honorum*, and he who most magnifies the solemnity of Baptism will be inclined to value most truly the far inferior solemnity of ordination."—Arnold, *Letter CCX.*

and experience, could scarcely be able to edify one another. Yet the Christian instinct of fellowship asserted itself in various ways. Whenever a new spiritual impulse stirred the stagnant Church, in modern parlance whenever revival set in, whenever a religion of experience rose up against a religion of externalism, the right and necessity of mutual ministration was perceived and acted on. Thus of the spiritual secessions in the Dark Ages, Neander says, "These could not fail to be struck with admiration at seeing uneducated, ignorant people . . . able to discourse with fluency on religious things, and to put to silence the regular ecclesiastics." (*Church History*, Vol. vi., p. 439.)

And not only amongst the various secessionists, but within the pale of the Roman communion, innumerable spiritual societies, brotherhoods and sisterhoods, were formed. Paschasius Radbert (*circ.* A.D. 839) gives a remarkable account of a singular anticipation of the Class-Meeting. Twelve hermits met once a week to narrate each other's experience, and to strengthen each other's "hands in God." (Horneck's *Happy Ascetic*, Chap. v.) Small circles of earnest Christians, lay or clerical, were formed in different localities. The instinctive yearning and the felt necessity for Christian fellowship and mutual support against worldly influences, especially within the Church, was the spiritual force which drew together such innumerable aggregations of earnest men and women in monasteries and convents, for the conjoint cultivation of the spiritual life, in the primitive and purest days of the various monastic orders. The absence of any provision in the regular ecclesiastical system, for the realized communion of saints drove the seekers for salvation into all kinds of eccentric and perilous expedients for the satisfaction of this profound want of the awakened soul. The flock of Christ, driven by the shepherds to the barren, misty heights of ceremonialism, were fain to strike out hither and thither—

> "Such track as tread the sheep
> Round slanting shoulder, and o'er rocky spur,
> To reach the rare sweet herbage."

Many who were not able or did not feel called to leave their homes attached themselves to monastic orders, as *fratres adscripti* or *conscripti*, thus gaining the privilege of joining the godly monks or nuns in their devotions. (Neander, Vol. vii., p. 320.) St. Francis of Assisi formed (A.D. 1221) a distinct order of these home-staying confraternities, under the name of *Fratres Tertiarii* or *Pœnitentiæ*. (*Ib.*, p. 372.) Earnest, successful lay preachers, such as Raymund Palmaris, born A.D. 1140 (Vol. viii., p. 8), an Italian artizan, formed their converts into religious societies under the guidance of their spiritual fathers. Detached fragments of miniature Methodism were to be found all over Western Christendom.

In the twelfth century arose the Beghards or the Beguines (Ullman, *Reformers before the Reformation*, Vol. i., p. 92; ii. 13, 15), "We recognise in them that strong inclination to social union, quickened by religion, which distinguished the twelfth century." (Neander, Vol. viii., p. 14.) Such again was the society formed by Keelin among the Slavonians (A.D. 1126, *Ib.*, Vol. vii., p. 45). Neander says of this: "A spiritual society of this sort being one of the wants of the time, belonging to that peculiar spirit of fraternization, with which the awakening religious life readily united itself, gave birth to many others, like those religious associations called the Apostolical."

Religious Societies of men and women were formed at Metz. "The members of them met the priests with arguments from the Bible to show they needed not allow themselves to be forbidden these private means of edification." (Neander, Vol. viii., p. 40.)

The origin of the great Waldensian church in a spiritual "society" founded by Peter Waldus is well known. Its vital principle is well described by Neander "a sober, practical, biblical element of the religion of the heart." (Vol. viii., p. 426.) It was a genuine Methodist movement.* "For the better inspection of morals . . . and for a communication of experience, each village belonging to these churches was provided with an Elder, or with two or three if it were large, whose office was to watch over a small number of brethren: and on the Sunday preceding the administration of the Sacrament notice was published in the church that the classes should meet in the houses of

---

* See on the point the *Methodist Magazine*, for 1805, p. 204.

their elders at the several appointed hours, the ensuing week. Accordingly, the minister proceeded from village to village, catechising the children and speaking with each communicant concerning his faith and experience." (Sutcliffe's *Mutual Communion*, p. 12.)

"Through the greater part of the Middle Ages we can trace a succession of *free, spiritual associations*, which were often oppressed and persecuted by the hierarchy, pertained rather to the life of the people than to the framework of the Church, exhibited more or less a regulated form . . . which all emanated from a fundamental endeavour after practical Christianity." (Ullman, *Reformers before the Reformation*, Vol. ii., p. 11.) The nicknames by which the hatred of the Church-world manifested the old hatred of him "that was after the flesh" to "him that was after the Spirit," involved like some subsequent nicknames (*e. g.*, Methodist) a "glorious infamy:" "Beghard" meaning *prayer-maker*, and Lollard *psalm-singer*. A large number of affiliated societies under the name of "Friends of God" spread over the Netherlands, Germany, and Switzerland. (Neander, Vol. ix., p. 520, etc.; Ullman, Vol. ii., p. 40, etc.) Many men of brilliant genius were members of this society. Archdeacon (now Archbishop) Manning truly wrote of these times: "Persons of a more devout temper, and more kindled with a love of the heavenly kingdom, drew into closer fellowships within the unity of the Church. There is nothing schismatical in a separation which both preserves all religious unity and makes those that live apart characteristically humble and charitable." (Sermons, Vol. ii., p. 279.)

One of the most remarkable of these spiritual societies was that of which Ullman (*Reformers before the Reformation*, Vol. ii., pp. 57—255)* gives an elaborate and most interesting account : "The Brethren of the Common Lot," or "Life," *Fratres vitæ communis*, of which fraternity Thomas à Kempis was a member, and in one of whose schools Erasmus received an influential part of his education. It was founded by Gerhard Groot, a Dutchman (born 1340, died 1384).

* See also Gieseler's *Ecclesiastical History*, Vol. v., p. 42, etc., and Wesley's *Ecclesiastical History*, Vol. iii., pp. 34, 35. Wesley says they "lived in the finest bonds of fraternal union."

"The grand object of the societies was the establishment, exemplification and spread of practical Christianity." (P. 71.) "As a whole it constituted an intimately connected, but free association, in which, along with a strict unity, sufficient room should, according to the Apostolic pattern, be allowed for the development of individual freedom. For the attainment of this end, the unity aimed at was founded, not so much upon outward statutes as upon an inward spirit; while the freedom accorded to the members was always under the restraint of love. . . . As continuance in the Society was an enduring act of free-will, whoever continued in it did so with his whole heart." (P. 88.) This Society "spread over vast countries" (p. 180) and "survived to the seventeenth century." (P. 172.) Its members "showed the liveliest zeal in the study of the Bible. . . . Their aim was to infuse life into the Church from the centre of an earnest and Christian piety of heart : . . . they showed great freshness and popularity in their labours as preachers : . . . they insisted on thorough conversion, efficacious repentance, and in opposition to the corrupt world formed a confederation." (P. 179.) They "were incessantly active in spreading their convictions . . . and in virtue of . . . earnestness and concentration . . . possessed high importance for the development of the future." (P. 183.) "The Brotherhood of the Common Lot was . . . pregnant of the future. It carried in its bosom various positive elements for the reconstruction and renovation of the Church, and although its tendency . . . disappeared at and with the Reformation, still in that event it prolonged itself on the grandest scale . . . Luther . . . acknowledges that they had faithfully kept the pure Word." (P. 184.)

Another notable way in which the conscious need of religious association manifested itself during the Middle Ages was the formation of religious Gilds for intertwined spiritual and social purposes :—For example, the Gild of Garlekhith, London, founded in the year 1375. The preamble of its rules describe it as "a fraternitie of good men and for amendment of her (their) lives, and of her (their) soules, and to noriche more love bytweene the brethren and sustren (sisters) of the bretherhede." (*Gilds and Friendly Societies, Contemp. Rev.*, March, 1873.) "All the brethren must be of good repute . . . there shall be wardens to collect the quarterage of the brethren and sisters, and to give account . . . there shall be quarterly meetings 'to speke touchynge the profit and ruyl (rule) of the forsaid bretherhede :' that each brother and sister shall, if able to do so, contribute somewhat by way of free gift ; that ill-behaved brethren shall be put out of the gild till they have mended their ways ; and that disputes among the brethren shall be referred to their wardens, whose award is to be obeyed under penalty of expulsion." (*Ib.* pp. 360, 361.) Then follow directions for mutual succour in distress.*

In fact, it was mainly by means of the communion of saints, variously realized according to the diversity of circumstances and temperaments, in voluntary spiritual associations, that living Christianity was preserved in the world by the blessed Spirit of God ; and the historical continuity of the Christian religion, of Christ's religion, may be much more satisfactorily sought in these blessed fellowships than in the concatenation of bishops of every grade of holiness and heathenishness from the loftiest sanctity to the lowest deep of worldliness and vice. Those brotherhoods which were not driven out of the ecclesiastical pale lent to the decrepit, scrofulous, and cancer-eaten Catholicism of the Middle Ages whatever lingering traces of the pristine loveliness of the Apostolic Church it could still present, so that after all

"Some beauty peeped through lattice of seared age."

In the sweet words of blessed Joseph Sutcliffe, "It must afford abundant satisfaction to every *converted* Protestant to see how beautifully the lily of piety flourished among the thorns of corrupted creeds and superstitious rituals. But, alas ! these sacred revivals were ever extinguished by the enormous mass of ecclesiastical corruptions." (*Mutual Communion*, p. 13.)

And as the societies were pregnant with the Reformation, so similar spiritual fellowships have deserved well of both insular and continental Protestantism, whilst Catholicism itself has still been rescued from utter rottenness by the like associations. A sensitive perusal of Froude's *History of England* will dissipate the absurd

* Another mode in which sympathetic religious enjoyment was sought in those dark days was by means of sacred dramas, passion-plays, etc.

and unscientific, though common and inveterate illusion, that the Reformation in England was merely or mainly the work of court-reformers, and a thing of kingcraft, statecraft, and clerical complaisance and episcopal facility. A sturdy nation like the English could not have passed through a sudden and critical religious change just to humour the abnormal amativeness of a popular king. The Vicar of Bray is not the true type of the English character. The goodly plant of Protestantism would not have sprung up so speedily if the soil of the Nation's heart and mind had not been "digged with the mattock" (Isaiah vii. 25) of Christian fellowship; if there had not grown up, under the smoke of our great towns, and in the seclusion of our rural parishes, small Scripture-searching societies, and little circles of local evangelism.

Yet it never occurred, even to the best and most sagacious men of the age, to make veritable fellowship a part of the Church-system. Even the learned and "judicious Hooker" can give no reason for the discontinuance of the Lovefeast in the Christian Church but their non-necessity: "Those feasts of charity which, being instituted by the Apostles, were retained in the Church long after, are not now thought anywhere needful." (*Eccl. Pol.,* *Preface,* Chap. iv. 4.) What change had taken place either in the spirit of Christianity or the constitution of human nature after the close of the seventh century of our era, so great as to render obsolete an institution of admittedly Apostolic origination, the erudite ecclesiastical jurist does not stop to explain. Yet his argument for the necessity of the separated ministry proves much more than he intended or imagined: "All things which are of God He hath by wonderful art and wisdom *soldered as it were together with the glue of mutual assistance,* appointing the lowest to receive from the nearest to themselves what the influence of the highest yieldeth. And therefore the Church, being the most absolute of all His works, was in reason to be also ordered with like harmony, that what He worketh might no less in grace than in nature be effected by hands and instruments duly subordinated unto the power of His own Spirit. A thing both needful for the humiliation of man which would not willingly be debtor to any but himself, and of no small effect to nourish that Divine love which now maketh *each embrace the other,* not as men, but as angels of God." (*Ib.* Bk. v., Chap. lxxvi. 9.) One would think that the direct deduction from this is the right and duty of reciprocal edification amongst all the members of the Church. His inference from this universal law of "mutual assistance," especially in the Church, is that we owe to the guides of our souls (namely, the separated ministry) "even as much as our souls are worth." And he forthwith strikes off into a rhetorical expatiation on the power of the ministry: "By blessing visible elements it maketh them invisible grace, etc."

But the feeling of the need of fellowship, the conviction of its essentiality to Church-life, and the yearning for it were not absent, even from the Church of England. Thus William Dell, Master of Caius College, Cambridge, in his remarkable sermon on the *Building, Beauty, etc., of the truly Christian Church*, preached in 1646, bears this clear testimony: "In the spiritual Building what one hath from the Spirit, it is for all. If thou hast the gift of utterance it is to build up me; if I have the spirit of prayer, it commends thee as carefully to God as myself; one watches over another as over his own soul, and if any be weak the strong support them; if any be doubtful, they that have the gift of knowledge direct them; if one be troubled, the rest mourn with him; if one be comforted, the rest rejoice with him; and they are all so linked together in the body of Christ, that the good and evil of one extends to all. *Where thou canst find such communion, there join thyself. Who would not willingly join himself to that people* where no man calls his grace his own, but all gifts are in common among all; every one having a share in the faith, hope, love, prayer, peace, joy, wisdom, strength of all, and all having a share in these gifts and graces that are in any one?" Dr. Thomas Fuller, too, in his own quaint, pithy style, expatiates on the advantages of Christian fellowship, illustrating his subject by the comparative ease with which one may join in a chorus rather than sing a solo, and by the fact that many a house can resist the wind, if one of a row of houses, which would soon fall with a crash, if it stood alone.

Mutual edification was one of the basal principles of Independency.

Baxter at Kidderminster held an experience-meeting "every

Thursday."* At Eckington, in Derbyshire, an attempt was made to revive the primitive Lovefeast, which was for a time successful. Holy Isaac Ambrose (died 1664) held weekly experience-meetings. In his *Media* he thus enforces the duty of Christian fellowship: "Christians must drive an open and free trade: they must teach one another the mysteries of godliness. They must tell their experience—their conflicts and comforts. As iron sharpeneth iron,—as rubbing of the hands maketh both warm,—and as live coals cause the rest to burn; so should the fruit of society be mutually sharpening, warming and influencing. Christians should also bewail their infirmities, darkness, want of love and unprofitableness one to another: to see whether others have been in the same case; what course they took and what remedy they procured. I fear, many perish through too much modesty and reserve. . . . Would Christians thus meet and exchange their thoughts they might encourage one another as the brethren did St. Paul. And have we not an express command for this duty of conference? 'Thus shall ye say every one to his neighbour . . . What hath the Lord answered? and, What hath He spoken?'" (Jeremiah xxiii. 35.)

Of the Moravian Brethren it is not necessary to speak, as their history is so well known. Their fellowships are distinctly traceable up to the time of Huss, and their own historians claim for them a still more venerable antiquity. *The Church of the United Brethren* was formed in 1620.

Within the Roman Catholic pale, the realization of the Communion of Saints was attempted by many earnest religious leaders during the sixteenth and seventeenth century. "Spiritual conferences" formed part of the system of the society of the Oratory of Divine Love sanctioned by Gregory XIII. in 1577; which enabled its members to stand against the scholarly infidelity and immorality of the time. Nicholas Pavillon the holy Apostolic Bishop of Alet (died 1677) formed throughout his large diocese, a regular system of fellowship and oversight, named "the Society of the Regents," hearing strong

---

* Orme's *Life and Times of Richard Baxter*, Vol. i., p. 145.

features of affinity with the Methodist Class-Meeting.* The famous societies of Port Royal have been made so familiar to English readers by able and attractive writers that to do more than just include them in our list would be superfluous. Of the "Religious Societies" formed about the year 1677, by Drs. Horneck and Woodward, and revived in the reign of William and Mary and widely spread in the principal towns of England and Ireland, the Rev. Luke Tyreman has given a full account in his *Life and Times of the Rev. Samuel Wesley, M.A.*†

The countless Societies of the "Pietists" in Germany next claim notice. The establishments of Franke at Halle are well known. John Frederic Lardin, Pastor of Blamount, in 1716, being the means of the conversion of many souls formed a veritable Class-Meeting in his own house. Roldanus, Pastor of Hienkerk, instituted a system of experience-meetings in private houses. Social unions for reciprocal edification spread over the land, such as Heinrich Stilling in his wanderings found to his soul's great good at Waldstadt and elswhere.

Of this class too was the Society in Holland to which Bunsen's sister belonged ; . . . of the character of whose members such a beautiful account is given in the Memoir of Bunsen. Such again was the Society at Berlin, of which the Baron von Kottwitz was the centre, whom Tholuck so finely describes in his dialogue of Guido and Julius.

Even in Scotland, where religious reticence might seem to be a part of the national character, the Lovefeast and the Fellowship Meeting have flourished with great vigour for considerable periods and over extensive districts. Sandemanianism, of which the Lovefeast is an essential institution, is of Scottish origin. Sandemanianism is one of the few forms of Church-life which preserve at the same time the social element of Christianity and an effective discipline. There was a certain nobleness in the disciplinary exclusion from this obscure society of the great Faraday, for accepting an invitation to dine with the Queen on a Sunday ; and

---

* See *Life of Nicholas Pavillon* and *Wesleyan Methodist Sixpenny Magazine* for October and November, 1869.

† See also *Account of the Religious Societies in London*, Chap. ii.

in Faraday's submission to the sentence, and humble awaiting restoration to membership and the preaching function, when the society thought his penitence satisfactory, and its own religious character sufficiently vindicated.*

The "Fellowship Meeting" was a popular and most beneficial institution amongst the Scotch Independents for sixty years after the introduction of Congregationalism into that country. It still survives in the north of Aberdeenshire. Many venerable Scotch Independents now living trace their conversion to these meetings, and speak of them with grateful fondness. The late Dr. Morrison, of Pimlico, in his Memoirs of his devoted brother, gives highly interesting details of these meetings, of which his sainted father was a great promoter, and to which people would gather from the distance of eighteen or twenty miles.

On the other hand, to what an extent, the very conception of *fellowship* has died down in the Church of England is indicated in Dr. Hook's *Church Dictionary*, a by no means unfair or partisan book. The following is the whole of his article on Fellowship: "*Fellowship.* An establishment in one of the colleges of an university, or in one of the few colleges not belonging to universities, with a share of its revenue."

Yet sporadic attempts to form stated gatherings for reciprocal edification in the Established Church have come within the writer's knowledge in different parts of the country, as at Hull and at Ironbridge, near Fletcher's Madeley.

The way in which fellowship follows revival, "the associated study of salvation," a resuscitated interest in Scripture has received beautiful illustration in our own time in the Reformation now proceeding in Mexico. " During the American war with Mexico, many copies of the Spanish Bible of Alphonso found their way into the homes of the Mexicans; and from this handful of corn there now waves a harvest beautiful as the heights of Lebanon. The people *gathered first in little knots* to read, with marvellous interest, the life of the Son of God. Then they met in private houses, and then in halls hired for their congregation. They sang the hymns of their own lyric poets, made their own ritual,

* For a description of the Sandemanian Lovefeast, see *Unorthodox London*.

and called men from among themselves to preach the Word and to administer to them the Sacraments. . . . The religious reform diffused itself until it reached some forty towns and villages, and had many societies. . . . Here God has prepared the Spaniard and the Mexican for carrying the Word of Life all down the vast continent which stretches away below, and filled with people who speak the Castilian and the Indian tongues." (Bp. J. C. Keener, D.D., in *Nashville Sunday School Advocate*, March, 1873.)

Mutual edification has from the beginning been an important ingredient in the services of the Society of Friends, in fact, part of their system. A beautiful description of the mode in which the silent meeting becomes a speaking meeting, under the afflatus of the Spirit, is given in Mr. Bayward Taylor's fine new poem. (*Lars*, pp. 76—80.) An earnest effort has been made within the last few years by intelligent and devoted members of the Society to organize a regular system of experience-meetings, as a breakwater against the encroachments of Socinianism, vagueness of doctrine and secularity, and as a quickening and binding force. This subject has been freely ventilated in the periodicals of the Society, and many tentative meetings have been inaugurated. The movement, as might be expected, progresses slowly.

There is an incessant recognition in theory of the essentiality of fellowship, even where the realization of it seems utterly unthought of. Thus Brown, of Wamphray, says: "All the members of the Church are bound to keep holy fellowship, *both* in Divine worship and in the *performance of such spiritual offices as tend to promote mutual edification*." And having said this, he forthwith proceeds with his arguments, as if he had never said, or heard anything about "mutual edification:" "But since all the members of the Church cannot in actual fact meet together *for God's worship*, particular churches, less or greater, are instituted as convenience may require."

The want of some systematic provision for mutual edification is deplored by earnest clergymen and Nonconformist ministers, such as Canon Gregory and the Rev. Newman Hall. The incumbent of a populous parish in a large town confessed with solemn tenderness to a Wesleyan Minister: " I am utterly at a loss for some such appliance as your Class-Meeting. I do my best to awaken sinners and build up believers, but I have no means even of proximately ascertaining the amount of my success."

Canon Gregory complains that in the Church of England the poor are "the mere recipients of charity." What an indignity to Christ's poor to make them the mere "belly for meats!"

On the origination of Methodism in spiritual re-unions; of Wesley's experience-meeting in Georgia; of his own obligations to antecedent religious societies; of the providential formation of "The United Societies;" and of the nature and importance of the Class-Meeting, it is not necessary to dwell. All this has been well and often told.*

It may be desirable, however, to correct certain current misapprehensions as to the Class-Meeting. It is objected that the Methodists have no right to insist upon *meeting in class* as a *sinè qua non* of membership: Christ and His Apostles did not demand *meeting in class*, therefore Methodism has no right to require it. With all due deference, we must submit that this objection arises from a superficial view of the case. What Methodism insists on is veritable *fellowship* and effective oversight,—*bonâ fide* fellowship, as an institution; the fulfilment of the repeated Apostolic injunctions to that effect, and the imitation of the primitive Church in this practice—effective oversight, the *watching for souls*, "as those that must give account." Now this, if done efficiently and systematically at all must be done by some definite arrangement or other; and the Class-Meeting is admittedly the best way which has yet been discovered. Those who in earnest sincerity object to the insistence on the Class-Meeting must rest their objection on one of two grounds: Either that mutual edification is not an indispensable part of Church-life, or that the Class-Meeting is not the best, the most effectual, and to the objectors personally, the least distasteful arrangement. If they take the former ground, their quarrel is with the New Testament and the first seven centuries—the ante-Popish centuries—of the Christian Church; and with Methodism only for carrying out, as it best may, the requirements of the New Testament, and recovering a vital and strangely neglected element of original Christianity. If they say, it is not mutual edification

* See especially Christopher's *Class-Meetings*. For an account of the religious fellowships in Norway, see *The Oxonian in Norway*; with those of Sweden Dr. G. Scott has happily made us familiar.

and confession that we demur to, but the Class-Meetings; then they are bound to propose some mode of mutual edification more effective than the Class-Meeting, or, at least as effective, whilst less distasteful to themselves. Surely no reflective person will venture to say, " The Class-Meeting is not exactly like the fellowship-meetings of the Apostolic Church, therefore we are free from the obligation to obey the express and reiterated injunctions of God's Word, with regard to spiritual oversight and reciprocal edification." " The Sacrament," *as now administered*, differs in the details of the solemnity from the primitive Supper of the Lord quite as much as the Methodist Class-Meeting, Fellowship-Meeting, and Lovefeast differ in details from the Agapæ and other social gatherings of original Christianity. But no sensible man holds himself excused from attendance at the Lord's Supper, because a large liturgical element has been introduced at the expense of the early free, social element, and the posture of reception changed. So long as the one essential part of the Lord's institution is retained—the conjoint participation of the symbols of His blessed body and blood—and no forbidden or unwarrantable usage introduced, no right-minded, right-hearted person would make a variation in the mode of communicating a pretext for disregarding Christ's appeal, " Do this in remembrance of Me," or refuse to join where "The kneeling hamlet drains The chalice of the grapes of God." If it be said, We admit that reciprocal edification and the regular spiritual oversight of each individual member of the Church are essential parts of the Apostolic Church-system, but we have an insufferable aversion to the Class-Meeting: the answer to that is, on our part, We have no fanatical devotion to the Class-Meeting. The moment some more effective, or as effective and more attractive mode of fellowship is discovered, the Class-Meeting will be superseded. Ours is simply the Horatian position: " If you know anything fitter than these, frankly communicate it; if not, make the best of them along with me." * The mode of fellowship is not " sacred from revision," but, I hope, the fact of fellowship is.

To admit that reciprocal edification and confession, and direct

---

* *Si quid novisti rectius istis, etc.*

personal and spiritual oversight are essential to a Church-system formed on the model or in the spirit of the New Testament, and yet, either on the one hand to demand an abandonment of that New Testament platform as a concession to one's individual antipathies; or, on the other, admitting it in theory to repudiate it in practice, neither accepting that which is provided nor suggesting anything better is, to speak mildly, childish and unreasonable, and not very respectful to Apostolic precept and precedent.

If it were absurd and wrong to say, I admit the duty of attendance at the Lord's Supper, but the present modes of celebration are neither in exact accordance with primitive usage nor with my own personal predilections, therefore I am under no obligation to "Do this in remembrance of" Christ! or to say, I confess that public worship is a sacred duty, but the existing modes of solemnizing it are nowhere enjoined in Scripture and are far from harmonizing with my own tastes, therefore I decline public worship altogether! then what is it but a frivolous excuse to say, "I cannot obliterate from Scripture the injunctions to mutual edification and confession, and the requirement of submission to spiritual oversight; but your arrangements for carrying out the one and the other are neither prescribed in Holy writ nor in accordance with my own likings, therefore my responsibility in the matter is at an end!"

But it is urged—The very beauty and utility of the Class-Meeting is its voluntariness. Clearly: but the beauty and utility of attendance at the Table of the Lord is its voluntariness; the beauty and utility of membership is its voluntariness; and the beauty and the value of love to God and man is spontaneousness. Does this impair the obligation of attendance at the Lord's Table; of Church-membership; of love to God and man? or make insistence on them all unwarrantable?

The elimination from the Communion of the primitive social element makes the difficulty of harmonizing this antipathy to fellowship still greater and graver now we have not so much as the "holy kiss," * or a significant clasp of the hand. But to suppose that Christian fellowship is realized and Church-obligations discharged by the due reception of "the Sacrament" and by money

* This were repugnant to modern English usages and feelings.

contributions, is a superstition which Protestant teachers ought not to be parties to. Is there no danger of making the cup of the Lord a mere sleeping draught to an uneasy conscience ?

The practical peril and perplexity of this demand to be excused from reciprocal edification and direct spiritual oversight are vastly aggravated by the fact that those who challenge exemption are the very parties who most urgently need them and who should be the very last to object to them, namely, the better conditioned and the more educated classes: the very persons who most require shelter and strengthening against worldly influences, and are bound to accept gratefully all the helps the Church can offer for promoting the growth of the spiritual life. The successful merchant, the thorough business-man, the devotee of a learned profession, the man of science, the undergraduate or Fellow of a College, the man of literary tastes and habitudes, the accomplished young lady—all these have souls as precious and in a Christian course as arduous as have colliers, ploughmen, fishermen. The lowering and delusive action of surrounding worldliness and unbelief is in them peculiarly subtle, stealthy, all-pervading. If the Class-Meeting were but a dyke for reclaiming one hour a week from the secular sea, surely it should be thankfully accepted. The more strongly the world clutches us through the hours, the more imperative is our need to shake it off at times and hold Communion with the living Church. What professional man, what man of science, what student does not know, or if he know not, does not prove, that highly intellectual habits have a tendency to blunt the spiritual susceptibilities and to film over the eye of faith, and, as a sunken shaft dries up by percolation a living stream, make to dwindle the clear current of celestial joy. May not this very distaste for fellowship itself be an alarming symptom of its special need ?

But it is said, All this is out of date; Methodism is no longer a congeries of "United Societies;" it is a Church. I confess myself at a loss to perceive the antithesis. What was the Church at the beginning but a congeries of united societies. The Church, to the end of time, must be a Society including a multitude of local societies.

Yes, but. *Methodism is no longer a Society within a church.* Palpably; and why try to make it so again ? It is, at present, a

Church on the New Testament model, namely, an aggregation of societies vitally united and in possession of "the Sacraments," and an ordained ministry. Is it the grand *desideratum* of the day to make Methodism perform for itself the service which the Established church performed in the last century, namely, furnishing to an earnest, loving Fellowship the background of an easy-going decorous Churchism ? That will be the inevitable result if the demands alluded to be conceded ; that, and a kindred mischief, the forming within nominal Methodism a caste of Communicants who declare off from that which is acknowledged on all hands to be the very marrow of Methodism. These belonging almost exclusively to the "respectable" order of society, the *respectable* thing will be to neglect fellowship.

What then is to be done ? I venture to submit a few suggestions : First, admit no one to the Table of the Lord, who will not by submitting to direct spiritual oversight, allow the minister who administers the Sacrament to him to *take account* of his soul, as "those that must give account." A complaisant throwing open of "the Communion" to all respectable comers is at variance with the vital principles of Methodism, and of Apostolic Christianity. Second : admit to the Table all baptized, well-conducted professors who will be amenable to direct personal spiritual oversight. If they will not be persuaded as yet to avail themselves of our meetings for fellowship, meet them on their own ground, and draw them as close as you can. Try a Bible-class, where the shrinking and fastidious may be gradually drawn to fellowship. Induce a few confidential friends to meet together : make arrangements for a quarterly inquiry into the spiritual state of each communicant who does not meet in Class. For this purpose let an exact list of all such be preserved in the Circuit-book. All that communicants who do not meet in Class would then lack, besides that great lack which they inflict upon themselves, and the being included in the annual statistics of the Society, would be the eligibility for certain offices in a church of which the internal structure is organized *fellowship* and the Class-Meetings the vascular tissue of the body. Recognition they would have— the highest possible—admission to the Table of the Lord. Registration they would have—in the Circuit-book. To demand eligibility for certain offices and reporting in the Minutes of Conference is to demand, in favour of exceptional cases, a structural revolution in Methodism, involving an abandonment of one of its essential principles, the obligatoriness of reciprocal edification.

Let everything be done that can be done short of this to meet individual idiosyncracies, at whatever cost of patience and of toil. Let the Class-Meeting itself be more compliant and elastic, less conventionally formulated in the mode of its conductings. Let a motherly tenderness and leniency be manifested to the respectable shortcomings of the good, but let no one be allowed to think that no other point of contact between members of the same church is necessary but those of the pew, the pulpit, the parlour, and the Communion rail. Let the *duty* of mutual edification be persuasively pressed home on every communicant.

I am bound to record my thoughtful conviction that the year which should witness the sacrifice of the Society-structure of our church in favour of sounding statistics and of officials who are strangers to the deeper fellowship of our church, would indicate to future Church-historians the chronological point where the great tidal flow of revival began to recede. The experience of our American churches does not invite us to this risky revolution. It was on this very point that Wesley himself re-affirmed the axiom "the half is better than the whole," half a million of truly united Methodists is better than a million of but half-united adherents. Granted, that we may have to endure some practical embarrassment and some argumentative difficulty (though the latter has been much exaggerated), yet better this than the evils already indicated.

> "Never let the world break in;
> Fix a mighty gulf between;"

Rather than *that*,

> "Keep us little and unknown,
> Prized and loved by God alone."

But the greater numerical loss and sacrifice of public prestige would be entailed by the cessation of our witness for the *obligatoriness* of Christian fellowship. "A dispensation is committed to" us. If we desert the experiment so successfully carried out for a century and a quarter of a church built on the Apostolic Plan and Elevation ; then "deliverance" from the disorganized condition into which the Church had sunk during the Dark and Middle Ages "will come from some other quarter," Methodism will lose the glory of demonstrating the practicability of the Apostolical ideal.

I will only add that it is a thoughtless aspersion to charge Methodism with setting up unscriptural terms of communion. If it did, it would be a schism. But Methodism never has made the Class-Meeting the only mode of access to the Table of the Lord.

ORIGIN OF THE "HIGH CHURCH" AND "BROAD CHURCH" THEORIES.

DURING the first two centuries of its history the Christian Church never thought of itself otherwise than as "A Holy Catholic Church which is the Communion of Saints."* Beautifully does one of the earliest Fathers, Irenæus, state the primitive Church principles: "Our faith which is . . . always, by the Spirit of God, renewing its youth, as if it were some precious deposit in an excellent vessel, causes the vessel itself to renew its youth also. For this gift of God has been entrusted to the Church . . . in order that all the members receiving it may be vivified, and the communion with Christ has been distributed throughout it, that is, the Holy Spirit, and the means of confirming our faith. . . . For where the Church is there is the Spirit of God ; and where the Spirit of God is, there is the Church." (*Against Heresy*, Bk. iii., Chap. 29. Clarke's Translation). So also Tertullian, " Where one or two are is the Church, and the Church is Christ." (*De Pœnit*, 10.)

* Hagenbach, Vol. i., p. 185.

The relation of the Church to the World is finely stated in the anonymous epistle to Diognetus, one of the very earliest literary productions of Christianity.* "What the soul is to the body, that are Christians in the world. The soul is dispersed through all the members of the body, yet is not of the body; and Christians are scattered through all the cities of the world. The soul dwells in the body, yet is not of the body; and Christians dwell in the world, yet are not of the world. The invisible soul is guarded by the visible body, and Christians are known indeed to be in the world, but their godliness remains invisible. The flesh hates the soul and wars against it—though itself suffering no injury—because it is prevented from enjoying pleasures; the world also hates the Christians, though in nowise injured because they abjure pleasures. The soul loves the flesh that hates it . . . Christians likewise love those that hate them. The soul is imprisoned in the body, yet keeps together that very body; and Christians are confined in the world as in a prison, and yet they are the preservers of the world. . . . God has assigned this illustrious position, which it were unlawful for them to forsake." (Clarke's Translation.)

This Divine idea of the Church is nobly stated by Origen in the Bk. vi. of his treatise against Celsus, Chap. xlviii. :—"The Holy Scriptures declare the body of Christ, animated by the Son of God, to be the whole Church of God, and the members of this body—considered as a whole—to consist of those who are believers; since, as a soul vivifies and moves the body, which of itself has not the natural power of motion like a living being, so the Word, arousing and moving the whole body, the Church, to befitting action, awakens, moreover, *each individual member* belonging to the Church, so that they do nothing apart from the Word." And still more strikingly in Chap. lxxix. : "If any desires to see many bodies filled with a Divine Spirit, similar to the one Christ, ministering to the salvation of men everywhere, let him take note of those who teach the Gospel of Jesus in all lands in soundness of doctrine and uprightness of life and who are themselves termed

* By some attributed to Apollos. Certainly it is the work of "*an eloquent man mighty in the Scriptures*" and evidently written when Christianity was yet a " new thing " in the world.

'Christs' by the Holy Scriptures, in the passage, 'Touch not mine anointed (τῶν χριστῶν μου) and do my prophets no harm.' . . . Owing to Him, there are many Christs in the world, who, like Him, have 'loved righteousness and hated iniquity,' and therefore God, the God of Christ, anointed them also 'with the oil of gladness.' But inasmuch as He loved righteousness and hated iniquity above His 'partners' (τοὺς μετόχους αὐτοῦ), He also obtained the first-fruits of his anointing, and if we must so term it, the entire unction of the oil of gladness; while they who were his partners" shared also in his unction, *in proportion to their individual capacity*.

But by degrees, alas! first the sentiment, then the habit of thought, next, the processes, and last of all the dogmas of ecclesiasticism began to develop in the Church; until the idea of the Church, which soon came practically to mean the clergy, thrust itself in between the individual believer and his living Head, and became a huge idol, an image of jealousy in the temple of the Lord. The clergy began to regard and to proclaim the Church, namely, themselves, as the sole consignees of Divine grace. Thus the doctrine of Baptism was completely changed. St. Paul and St. James attributed regeneration to faith in the *Word*. The former thanked God that he had baptized so few amongst the Corinthians, and yet claims to be their spiritual father, inasmuch as he had "begotten them through the Gospel." In the Acts of the Apostles, it is the believing, Christ-invoking candidate who washes away his own sins in Baptism. Thus Ananias says to Saul,—"Arise and be baptized, and *wash away thy* sins, calling on the name of the Lord." But by and by the faith of the baptized and the force of the truth confessed are thrown quite into the background, and the *Church*, by its clerical officiations, *regenerates* the neophyte by baptism, and rests on this its claim of Maternity.

Africa, not Italy, is the native land of this swarthy error—the High-Church theory. Carthage, not Rome, was its birthplace. It was the bold, imperious genius of St. Cyprian which first precipitated and crystallized into cold, hard, definite dogma the sacerdotal sentiment which had been floating, or held in solution, in the imaginations of the clergy. He had conceived some vague unscriptural notions about the efficacy of baptism. According to his theory, it conferred regenerating grace, but not the Holy Spirit! so that the birth of water was not contemporaneous with the birth of the Spirit, much less virtually identical with it, and yet the water of baptism, or rather the *Church* which administered the baptism, or more definitely still the officiating clergyman, and *not the Holy Spirit* was the real regenerating power. But according to his gospel, the Church (namely, of course, the clergy) had also literally in its *hands* the Holy Spirit. Whatever might be left for Him to accomplish after the Church had by baptism regenerated the soul He was shut up to do by means of the Church, *i. e.*, the clergy. The famous Novatian disturbance gave occasion for the propounding of his system. Novatianism was an exaggerated form of Puritanism.* Its adherents chose the name of Puritans —Cathari. It bore some resemblance to Plymouth-Brethrenism. Its leading tenet was the non-readmission of backsliders within the pale of the Church; in other words, the incompetence of the Church to condone gross sin, even on the repentance and reformation of the offender. This was a terrible heresy, directly contrary to the spirit and letter of the New Testament. It also shaped itself into formal schism. These unevangelical rigorists chose their party leader as their bishop, repudiating the authority of the bishop duly elected by the Church; thus setting up a rival communion and an anti-bishop and starting *de novo* a fresh and antagonistic episcopal succession. This was a real and definitive secession, a disruption of the *outward* unity of the Church. It was as decisive a dismemberment of the *external* oneness of the Church as the secession of the southern States of America was a dissolution of the original confederation. Moreover, in this instance, the dissidents were the exclusionists. They were not expelled, but went out deliberately and defiantly. They unchurched all whom they had left behind. They denied the validity of the baptism of the main body of the Church, re-baptizing all who came over to them from the ancient Communion. What was to be done? Unfortunately, Cyprian stepped forward, a man of lofty charac-

* If indeed the Catholic champions are to be trusted. But it were just as fair to learn the doctrines of the Novatians from Cyprian and Optatus as those of Protestants from the Papists.

ter, and venerable though very juvenile saintliness, and fervid and impetuous fancy, converted after he had passed the meridian of life. His eloquence was like that of his great master, Tertullian, rushing like a lava-flood. His genius was of the true North African type, befitting " the land of the cypress and myrtle :

'Where the rage of the vulture, the voice of the turtle
Now melts—and now maddens—.'"

His Letter to Donatus is one of the richest gems of Christian correspondence.

The Church as a visible and unbroken unity filled his imagination, and was the ruling passion of his heart. The fierceness with which he denounced the schismatics gushed out of his tender love and reverence for the Church as a glorious and symmetric whole. This is illustrated by the following beautiful passage in his Treatise on the *Unity of the Church :*

" The Holy Spirit came as a dove, a gentle and joyous creature, with no bitterness of gall, no fierceness of bite, no violence of rending claws, loving human houses, associating within one home ; nurturing their young together ; when they fly abroad, hanging in their flight side by side ; leading their life in *mutual intercourse* ; giving in concord the kiss of peace with the bill ; in every way fulfilling the law of unanimity. This is the singleness of heart that ought to be in the Church ; this is the habit of love that must be attained." *

But, alas ! the bearing of Cyprian himself was much more like that of the eagle than that of the dove. In his zeal for external unity, he forgot the longanimity, and the all-bearing, all-enduring hopefulness of true charity.

A rhetorician by profession until his ordination and swiftly following elevation to the episcopate, which occurred when he was about forty-eight years of age, only two years after his conversion from heathenism ; a master of his art, his rhetorical facility was very far in excess of his reasoning faculty. In fact, his polemical writings are a rich repertory of almost every form of false logic. His reasoning is rotatory, and kindles and flashes

* *De Unitate*, 8.

with the swiftness of its revolution on its own axis. If magnificent invective, majestic fulmination, downright dogmatism, and relentless denunciation, could heal the hurt of Zion, Cyprian's eloquence would have been the balm of Gilead; but, alas! he has but one "simple" for dislocation, and that is corrosive sublimate. All that the Separatists retain, their unchallengeable orthodoxy on the fundamentals of the faith; the admitted purity and benevolence of their lives, their heroic constancy under heathen persecution, all this is nothing—worse than nothing—to him. In his theology, the visible external holding together of the Church is the foundation-truth of Christianity. That being disturbed for a day, he thought all else is worthless. A Novatianist's faith in Christ; his baptism in the name of the Trinity; his Christian obedience unto death availed him nothing. All this was, in Cyprian's view, far more than neutralized by connection with an irregularly constituted Christian community. Hence he retaliated the sectarianism of the sectaries, giving it the flattery of his servile imitation, insisting on the re-baptization of all who, having been baptized by them, sought admission into the older Church order. The direct faith of the baptized persons in the Son of God and the blessed Trinity went for worse than nothing; their confession of Christ was blasphemy, however loyally maintained in life and death; a Novatianist's heart-belief was not "unto righteousness;" his *confession* of Christ was not "unto salvation." The force of the truth itself was nothing, if the baptism were administered by one irregularly ordained. Thus faith, confession, the truth, Christ and the blessed Trinity were, by "the insolence of office," thrust into the background; and the regularity of episcopal succession was made the one grand guarantee of grace and salvation. This, of course, made the Church and that rigidly limited to a succession inaugurated in one particular form, the direct object of faith and source of salvation; and Christ and the Spirit of God accessible only through a certain order of men.

And where does the Father of High Churchism place the root and centre of Church unity? In our Lord's declaration to Peter, "I will give unto thee the keys, etc.;" and in the subsequent commission to him, "Feed my sheep." At the same time, he admits that this was a bare and barren, a merely nominal primacy, temporary, and terminating before our Lord's ascension. He confesses that, "to all the Apostles Christ gives an equal power;" and "certainly the rest of the Apostles also were, as was Peter, endowed with a like partnership, both of honour and power." (*De Unitate, etc.*, 4.)

But in the fact that the words of authorization were spoken to Peter individually, before they were addressed to the eleven Apostles collectively, Cyprian thinks he sees not only some mystic symbol, but also some sacred origination of Church unity. He says, "A beginning was made from unity, that the Church may be set forth as one;" as if the one Christ were not a better centre of unity than the one Peter!

On the theory, then, of this recently evangelized rhetorician the oneness of the Church is not constituted by its one Head, the oneness of its faith, and the oneness of its life—the indwelling Spirit; but by the fact that the Apostolic authority was announced to *one* of the twelve—Peter individually,—before it was announced to the whole body, Peter included. This play upon the word *one* is, to treat it gently, much more like the arithmetical mysticism of Jacob Behmen, than the massive reasoning of St. Paul, to whom it never occurred to write, There is one Peter. On such a vague and puerile proposition did the Apostle of High Churchism base his system. His contention amounts to this: *No one can be saved who is not in the Church! no one is in the Church who has not received baptism through the regular succession of the episcopate.* How so? Make that appear. *Our Lord gave Apostolic authority to a single individual—Peter—before he gave it to the whole eleven alike—Peter included! Ergo :*—to reduce Cyprian's logic to anything like form is to reduce it to the absurd.

In proof of the oneness of the Church as a body, Cyprian conclusively quotes St. Paul: "There is one body, etc.;" but it did not occur to him that nothing can be essential to the oneness of the body, which was not in existence at the time when St. Paul made that affirmation. In what did the oneness of the widely-scattered Christian societies in Europe, Asia, and Africa consist at the date of the Epistle to the Corinthians (about A.D. 62), when there were no bishops as distinct from presbyters.

For the vital and effective unity of the primitive Church, Cyprian and his party would have substituted the temporary and merely symbolical primacy of Peter,—for which in his view and that of his following, there was no correspondent primacy in the post-Pentecostal Church, inasmuch as he and they, indignantly repelled the idea that anything greater than a bishop could possibly sit beneath the roof of the temple of God, or that the essential dignity of a *bishop* left room between earth and heaven for *any one* bishop to be higher than *every one* bishop.

Cyprian did not perceive what a plausible pretext his practical dogma—that the real, permanent unity of the Church had its root in an ephemeral and typical primacy of Peter—gave to the assumption of a perpetual primacy on the part of some one bishop as a visible centre and symbol of the unity of the Church. On the contrary, he and the bishops of his school, at the Seventh Council of Carthage, over which he presided, indignantly protested against the assumption of a tone by the Bishop of Rome which might seem to imply that he or any bishop could claim the slightest superiority over any one of his brother bishops. Cyprian, in his opening speech, with evident reference to what he felt to be an assumption of something like authority in the letter of Stephen, Bishop of Rome, says, "Neither does any of us set himself up to be a bishop of bishops, nor by tyrannical terror does any compel his colleague to the necessity of obedience, since every bishop has his own proper right of judgment, and can no more be judged by another than he can judge another."* But the use which papistic writers made of Cyprian's Treatise on the Unity of the Church (utterly at variance with the opinions of Cyprian elsewhere expressed) shows what a convenient basis the theory of Cyprian laid for the assumption by some one see of authority over all other sees. Cyprian's doctrine is, that the whole of the episcopal authority inheres in every individual bishop. "The episcopate is one; a whole, of which each part is held by each bishop. The Church also is one." (*De Unitate*, 4.) To make his analogical reasoning harmonious, he should have added: *and each part of the Church—the entire Churchship—is held by each one member of the Church for the whole.* But that would not suit his purpose.

* Clarke's *Translation.*

To what a terrible extent the theory of Cyprian obtrudes the abstract personification of the Church,—made concrete by episcopal claims, between believers and their Lord,—and makes the spouse "to usurp authority" over her Divine Head, is apparent from such passages as this : "As the sun has many rays, yet but one light; and the tree many branches, but one strength fixed in the deep-struck root; and as from one source flow many streams . . . yet the unity is still preserved in the spring itself. Part a ray of the sun from its body, its unity does not brook a division of light, break a branch from the tree,—once broken, it cannot bud again; cut off the stream from its fountain, and being cut off it dries up."—True, but who, or what is "the sun," the "tree," "the fountain ?" *Christ ?* Not according to Cyprian and his school. Hear him out : "Thus the *Church*, irradiated *with* the light of the Lord, sheds forth *her* rays over the whole world. *Her* fruitfulness. . . . *She* broadly stretches forth, yet is there one fountain-head; one source . . . by *her spirit we are animated.*" * Thus is the Divine *He* eclipsed by the human *She*.

Cyprian's mind was of that class which can see no difficulty in the hypothesis which it has first conceived, and then espoused. He writes : "No need for lengthened comment or arguments. It is easy to furnish proof to faith. A short summary of the truth is enough." He quotes one saying of Christ, and takes no heed of its counterpart : "He that is not with Me is against Me; and he that gathereth not with Me scattereth." This clearly decides in Cyprian's hermeneutics, that whoever administers or receives baptism otherwise than within the regular episcopal succession is "against Christ," "an adversary," "Antichrist."

It would be idle to attempt an analysis of a performance which is not connectedly argumentative, and even as a rhetorical production is amorphous and invertebrate. It would be wrong to say that a hollow, factitious, and delusive uniformity is, in Cyprian's view, infinitely better than an irregular vitality; inasmuch as he refuses to admit that Christian vitality can be irregular, or that ecclesiastical uniformity might possibly be hollow and factitious. His whole treatise,—if that may be called

* *De Unitate*, 5. *Ibid*, 4.

a treatise which is, in fact, a flaming polemical pamphlet,—is but a laboured, specious, roundabout way of asseverating that the vital continuity of the Church consists in the unbroken line of its episcopacy. The root-idea, or, more correctly speaking, the central fallacy of Cyprian's theory is the audaciously unscriptural assumption that the chief factor in human salvation is episcopal officiation in the direct line. He supports this strange thesis by passionate overstatement and resolute onesidedness. With deliberate recklessness he splits Christ's teaching into halves, grasps one half, and implicitly denounces the other half as heresy. He is a controversial Cyclops, who lays about him with his rhetorical club, regardless of all rules of fair fighting. To secure a front place for the extremal concatenation of sacerdotal ministrations, he hustles into the far background the heart-faith and mouth-confession of the penitent believer, his personal calling upon the name of the Lord, the action of truth on the intelligence, conscience, and will of man; God's "own will" begetting the new nature "by the word of truth." According to his theory, saving grace is rigidly confined to the one channel of ecclesiastical legitimism. Faith, if dissociated from the single lineage of bishops, is unbelief; loyalty to Christ, even to the death, Christian benevolence and integrity, are vices of the deadliest and most diabolical kind. Not only the human intellect and conscience, but Christ and the Holy Spirit are made to play a very subordinate part in the work of salvation compared with that of the Church, namely, *the priestly order.* Doubtless, the impetus of controversy sent him further than at first he meant to go, and he would have shrunk from the application of his principles which was unflinchingly made by his disciples in after-ages. Papistical writers subsequently fortified his polemical positions; his earth-works, rashly thrown up in the heat of controversy; and counted them as amongst the permanent bulwarks of Zion: even as they hardened into the dogma of Transubstantiation the rhetorical phrases of impassioned Church oratory.

Besides, it is but just to remember that Cyprian was the inventor of the *High Church* theory of Christianity only in the sense in which other men may truly be said to have founded systems: he did but condense and precipitate the poison of priestism, which was floating in the atmosphere of the Church of his time. He had not to coin the dialect of sacerdotalism; it was ready to his hand. But he gave new force to old phrases. He was the mouthpiece and the genius of a large party amongst the bishops.

Neander gives a very just statement of the case: "He, (Cyprian,) acted as the representative of the episcopal system, the struggle of which against the presbyterian system had gained strength during the whole progress of the Church. The contentions of the Presbyterian parties amongst one another might have become utterly prejudicial to discipline and order in the Church. The victory of the episcopal system especially promoted unity, order and quiet in the churches; *but then*, it was prejudicial to the free development of habits of life befitting the Church; and the formation of a priesthood, which is quite foreign to the Gospel economy, was not a little furthered by it." He subjoins the following weighty reflections: "The more a Church answers its proper destination and corresponds to its true model, the more must it be shown in the *mutual relations of all its members; that all taught, led, and filled by the One; all drawing from the same fountain and mutually imparting as equal members of the same body, stand in reciprocal relation, as we find it was, in the early churches.*" (Rose's Translation.)

Again, Cyprian did not create, though he did very much to aggravate the confusion between the Jewish and the Christian economy. His master, Tertullian, had already called the bishop—*High-Priest,—Summus Sacerdos*,—without perceiving that this was to pronounce the watch-word of a Korahite revolt of priests against the One High Priest. The terms *ordo, plebs, etc.*, order, laity, clergy, clerics, thoughtlessly used at first, "naturally tended to introduce unevangelic relations." (Neander, *Church History, Ib.*) *Thoughtlessly* introduced, for Tertullian himself would have utterly repudiated the ideas which inevitably attach to such expressions. This is plain from the well-known passage in his work *De Baptismo*.* He says there "Laymen have the right to administer the sacraments, and to teach in the churches, for that

* Written *before* he became a Montanist.

which all equally receive, all may equally give; unless you make the word *disciple* a synonyme for bishops, presbyters, or deacons. The Lord's Word ought not to be hidden from any, wherefore Baptism, which is equally derived from God, may be administered by all. But the most holy Apostle has said, 'All things are lawful unto me, all things are not expedient.' Let it suffice to make use of these ¦rights where place, time, or person demands it."

Cyprian's theory leaves the Church at the mercy of the bishops, allowing no remedy for universal episcopal corruption or heresy. According to it, should the whole body of the bishops apostatize, not only would the unity of the Church be irretrievably lost, but the stream of salvation would be cut off from the city of God. Supposing all the bishops should lapse like Fortunatus, Basilides, and Martial (Cyprian's *Epistles*, lxiii., lxvii.)—what then ? For in his view, to communicate with a lapsed or heretical bishop was to share his doom: and a lapsed bishop on repentance could not reclaim his office. It is true that Cyprian's unfailing inconsistency does not desert him here. When Florentius Pupianus wrote to him with reference to some rumours to Cyprian's disadvantage, he takes the lofty ground of Episcopal impeccability. To believe it possible that a bishop should go wrong, is to impeach the omniscience of God! It is, in fact, atheism and audacious insurgency against Christ. "*This is not to believe* in God, this is to *stand forth as a rebel against Christ and His Gospel!* .... you think that God's priests are ordained in His Church without His knowledge ! For to believe that they who are ordained are unworthy and unchaste, what else is it than to believe that His priests are not appointed by God, nor through God ?" (*Epistle* lxviii. ; Clarke's Translation).

It is but fair to remember in extenuation of Cyprian's doctrinal extravaganzas that he was made a bishop when in years, but "a babe in Christ," only two years after his conversion from heathenism, and, as his writings prove, whilst yet in the petulant infancy of his Christian growth. He was the spoilt child of popularity, being elevated to the presbytery, and then incontinently to the episcopate in utter disregard of " the Apostolic" injuctions "Lay hands suddenly on no man."—" Not a novice, lest being lifted up he fall into pride." But the presbytery of Carthage were driven to this gross irregularity, by the urgency of the popular hero-worship. Alas! this extenuation will not hold good for the multitude of grave divines who have adopted his crude hypothesis.

According to Cyprian and his school, the Church is utterly incompetent, in any emergency whatsoever to provide itself with a new line of superior officers. The regular succession of bishops once lost, the stream of salvation is "like water spilt upon the ground which cannot be gathered up again." In his view the damnableness of Novatianism consisted in its infringement of the sacramental monopoly of the legitimately ordained. The Novatian presbyters were "rivals of the priests:"—this was the gravamen of their crime. He exclaims, "Does he think that he has Christ who acts in opposition to Christ's priests!" (Sect. 17.) For a Judaizing sacerdotalism is the natural parent of an unevangelic exclusiveness.

Yet let us not forget that Novatian's disruption of the external and visible unity of the Church was a terrible thing, and that its terribleness was much more apparent to believers in the third century of the Christian era than it is to us, who, alas, have become familiarized with the piteous spectacle of the dislocated members of the body of Christ!

This was a crucial trial for the wisdom and the charity of the contemporary Church-leaders. And it proved too much for both the wisdom and the charity of Cyprian, who rushed to the front as the champion and expounder of the unity of the Church. He could not discern the difference between dislocation and mortification or amputation; between a disjointed member of the body and a dead member. A false Church-theory, even when practically carried out by disturbing, impeding, pain-inflicting irregularities, was not of such a deadly potency as to neutralize a living faith in the living Redeemer. Novatian, with all his crotchets, perversities, and provocations, still *held* the *Head*, preached the Gospel, and led a harmless and exemplary Christian life, his schism excepted. True, he had unjustifiably withdrawn from the external communion of the Church, and set up a church in accordance with his own ideal. But neither his false theory nor his practical divarication could countervail the man's faith in Christ, loyalty to

Christ, and life in Christ. So long as the twisted, loosened limb retains the life of the body, it is still of the body. A wrongheaded Church-theory, even when asserted by action, cannot neutralize a faith in the fundamentals of the Christian religion.

Cyprian and his following, as Augustine afterwards, though in a milder tone, in his contest with the Donatists,—justified their want of charity towards the schismatics, by pointing to the uncharitableness which was at the root of the schism. They retaliated, in effect, the impeachment.—You may have as much faith, as much benevolence, as much zeal, as many and as heroic martyrs as we have, but the root of your schism is uncharitableness; and faith, benevolence, martyrdom "without charity," profit nothing. But they lost sight of two facts:—that external communion with the main body of the Church without charity, profits as *little* as uncharitable faith, liberality, martyrdom; uncharitable conformity is as worthless as uncharitable nonconformity, and that if the want of *perfect* charity vitiates faith, benevolence, confession of Christ, even unto death, then the virtues and services of many of the boldest champions of unity were as nugatory as those of the separatist confessors. It never occurred to Cyprian and his party that by retaliating Novatian's excommunication they were doing their best to complete and perpetuate the schism. They should have set an example to their erring brethren of the charity which "beareth all things, hopeth all things, endureth all things." They should have persisted in regarding the Novatian schism, not as a definitive disruption, but as a temporary occupation of the Sacred Mount, the Aventine, and the Esquiline. But the hot-headed, high-minded Cyprian was not fitted to play the part of a Christian Menenius Agrippa. He should have seen that in the case of the earnest but misguided Novatians, the life of the Church had for a season retired into its root, and should have hoped for its speedy return. It was the inflaming splinter of uncharitableness in his own eye which would not let him "see clearly to take out the mote from" his brother Novatian's eye. Hence his arrogant browbeating. He challenges the sectarians to try the issue, and then forthwith refuses to acknowledge them as belligerents, but hunts them down with rhetorical hue and cry, like outlaws, traitors, or mad dogs, or, to use his own words, "antichrists," "adversaries of Christ." He (as St. Augustine afterwards) pronounces the separatists as totally destitute of charity, and regards them as beyond the pale of charity in one of its essential and cardinal functions—leniency, and generosity of construction, and "rejoicing in the truth," which was, in the main, still held by them. Had a brotherly tone been assumed towards Novatian and his partisans; had they been credited with what they signally possessed—"a zeal for God, but not according to knowledge;" if whilst exposing with the most earnest fidelity the unscripturalness and arbitrariness of Novatian's distinctive dogma, and the mischievousness of his divisive action, the Church-leaders had still recognised in him a noble-natured, richly endowed, saintly,—though withal wrong-headed, misled and misleading Christian brother,—in all human and divine probability the fracture would have, to use a surgical phrase, been *healed by the first intention*. But the barbarous surgery of the ecclesiastical physicians of the time, "helped forward the affliction." The Novatian schism, though initiated by Novatian was consummated by the Catholics, who, by defending the right in a wrong spirit and on wrong grounds, constituted themselves a faction, and profaned catholicity itself into a party badge. Mutual uncharitableness amongst men who held with an equally loyal tenacity to the foundation facts of Christianity completed the mutual estrangement and mutual repulsion; and "question fierce" called forth "stern reply." Reciprocal unfairness and unbrotherliness changed a family feud into a civil conflict until

"...... The mortal jar,
The havock of the border war,"
Could "never, never, be forgot."

The lofty Christian sentiments, the axioms of common sense and charity afterwards enunciated so clearly by St. Augustine—though, strangely enough, he was incapable of giving his principles a fair application—never came within the ken of the impetuous bishop of Carthage : "If he who recedes from unity is willing still to act as he did whilst yet in unity, in that which he still receives, *and teaches he still remains united:*" *Si ergo*, etc. (*De Baptismo*, Bk. i., Chap. i., Sec. 2).

In truth, the spiritual affinity between the two antagonists, Cyprian and Novatian was as marked as that between the brothers Boanerges. They were both *sons of thunder*. Neither of them *knew what spirit he was of*. Novatian "rejecting the repentance of his brother" (anonymous contemporary treatise *Against Novatian*): Cyprian rejecting the Christian virtues, services, and sufferings of his brother. Both were actuated by an impassioned zeal for the glory and security of the Church. This was the propulsion which carried both the one and the other through all their perilous gyrations. Both were exceeding jealous for what Cyprian calls "evangelical vigour." They were both honest men, of fine fibre.

They were both able writers, Novatian excelling as a reasoner and an expositor, Cyprian as a rhetorician and an advocate; the connectedness and continuity of the former, in his treatises concerning the *Trinity* and *On the Jewish Meats*, contrasting very strongly with the looseness and inconsequence of Cyprian's on *The Unity of the Church*. On the other hand, Cyprian sometimes carries Novatian's false doctrinal positions by heavy exegetical artillery, and at the point of the logical bayonet. (See especially Epistle lv., Oxford Edition, 25, 26, etc.) They were both eloquent men, but Novatian was the *mightier in the Scriptures*, having a less fanciful and arbitrary exegesis. Cyprian's genius was the more brilliant, yet Novatian was capable of splendid bursts of enthusiastic oratory. Witness his magnificent apostrophe to the weirdly concocted Christ of third century rationalism,—"A Christ feigned and coloured up,"[*]—which might be as fitly addressed to any one of the imaginary Christs of the Nineteenth Century rationalism: "*Who* art thou ? *Whence* are thou ? *By whom* art thou sent ? *Why such* as thou art ? Or how hast thou been able to come ? . . . Why dost thou strive to take me away from the Lord ? . . . What shall I gain from thee ? . . . What testimony of the prophetic word hast thou ? Or what substantial good can I promise myself from thee, when I see that thou hast come in a phantasm ?"

Novatian was not without a strong sentiment of brotherly love to which appeal might have been made. He writes, "He (the Holy

---

[*] Novatian *Concerning the Trinity*, Chap. x. 2.

Spirit) links by love, binds together affection, keeps down sects, orders the rule of truth, overcomes heretics ;" and the genuine Christian element which his too self-reliant austerity perverted into an unevangelical purism is indicated by the added words,— " turns out the wicked, guards the Gospel." (Novatian, *Concerning the Trinity*, Chapter xxix.)* Both were enrolled in " the noble army of martyrs."†

Yet a strong infusion of the essential virus of heresy, an egotistic rationalism, infected the spiritual constitution of each. An attempt to make church-discipline more stringent, and church-exclusiveness more rigid than Christ and His Spirit had made, drew Novatian into grievous heresy and schism : an attempt to consolidate the external unity of the Church, and to glorify the officiations of its ministers misled Cyprian into a heresy much more perilous, more insidiously poisonous because more seductive and likely to spread.

Novatian's heresy was comparatively local and ephemeral; within two hundred years it had dwindled away. But the poison-plant of Cyprian's sacerdotalism struck its roots deep into the heart of the Church, and at this very day its pestiferous branches cast a blighting shadow over more than the half of Christendom. His *words do* still *eat as does a cancer.*

Novatian was solicitous for the moral and spiritual utility and beauty of the Church, but he forgot that the restoration of backsliders is one great function of its utility, one signal proof of its spirituality, and that gentleness to the fallen is one prominent feature of its divine beauty. If Novatian's scheme obliged him to ignore a vast portion of Holy Writ, Cyprian's theory compelled him not only to disregard one whole hemisphere of truth, but also to add to and amend the oracles of God. His system audaciously tampers with the sayings of Christ. The Master announces, " He that believeth and is baptized shall be saved, and he that *believeth not* shall be damned." No, in effect, says Cyprian, " He that believeth and is baptized shall be saved,

* Again he writes, " All the body, joined together by links and inwoven and grown together by mutual members in the bond of charity, increaseth to God."—*On the Jewish Meats.*
† Socrates, Hist. Eccl., Lib. iv., Chap. 28.

and he that is not baptized or is baptized apart from the main body of the Church, shall be damned." " One Lord, one faith, one baptism," saith the Spirit. Cyprian's theory virtually interpolates " one episcopate."

Both Cyprian and Novatian were daring and defiant innovators. The former admits that the usage which he strove to introduce was totally at variance with the immemorial custom of the Church. He could produce no precedent in its favour but that of his predecessor, Agrippinus. Yet this champion of antiquity and uniformity defends his novelties by maxims which might serve as the watchwords of reform, if not of revolution to the end of time. He exclaims, "In vain do some, who are beaten by reason oppose long custom, as though custom were superior to truth, or that were not to be followed in spiritual things which has been revealed by the Holy Spirit as the better way." (Epist. lxxii., Sect. 11, Oxford Edition.) This is an argument worthy of George Fox, and contains a distinct doctrine of development. See also his other famous axiom : " Nor ought custom which has crept in among some, to prevent the truth from prevailing and conquering : for custom without truth is the antiquity of error." (Ep. lxxviii. 9.)

He writes, epistle lxvii., to the clergy and people abiding in Spain concerning Basilides and Martial, bishops :—" Nor let the people flatter themselves that they can be free from the contagion of sin, while communicating with a priest who is a sinner, and yielding their consent to the unjust and unlawful episcopacy of their overseer, when the Divine reproof by Hosea, the Prophet, threatens, and says, 'Their sacrifices shall be as the bread of mourning ; all that eat thereof shall be polluted, teaching manifestly, and showing that all are absolutely bound to the sin who have been contaminated by the sacrifice of a profane and unrighteous priest.' . . . On which account a people obedient to the Lord's precepts, and fearing God, ought to separate themselves from a sinful prelate . . . especially when they themselves have the power, either of choosing worthy priests or of rejecting unworthy ones."—Clarke's Translation.

Cyprian was not altogether inaccessible to moderate and charitable sentiment. He admits that " the hesitating anxiety of a mind undecided in the fear of God is not to be blamed."

(Epist. lv., Oxford Edition.) Moreover he sometimes announces principles which, if rightly applied, would have cut up his ecclesiasticism by the roots. "It behoves a bishop not only to teach but also to learn; because he also teaches better who daily increases and advances by learning better; which very thing, moreover, the same Apostle Paul teaches, when he admonishes, that 'if anything better be revealed, to one sitting by, the first should hold his peace.' *But there is a brief way for religious and simple minds, both to put away error, and to find and to elicit truth. For if we return to the head and source of divine tradition, human error ceases: and having seen the reason of the heavenly sacraments, whatever lay hid in obscurity, under the gloom and cloud of darkness, is opened into the light of truth. If a channel supplying water, which formerly flowed plentifully and freely, suddenly fail, do we not go to the fountain, that there the reason of the failure be ascertained, whether from the drying up of the springs the water has failed at the fountain-head, or whether, flowing thence free and full, it has failed in the midst of its course: that so, if it has been caused by the fault of an interrupted or leaky channel, that the constant stream does not flow uninterruptedly and continuously, then the channel being repaired and strengthened, the water collected may be supplied for the use and drink of the city, with the same fertility with which it issues from the spring:* and this it pleases the priests of God to do now, if they would keep the divine precepts, *that if in any respect the truth have wavered and vacillated we should return to our Lord and origin, the evangelical and Apostolical tradition.*" (Ep. lxxiii., Sec. 10.)

And, again, let us call to mind the enormity of Novatian's irregularities. His action was a violation of all constitutional order in the Church, on utterly insufficient grounds. He did endeavour, in the name of an unscriptural ecclesiastical purism, as Cyprian says, "to break asunder the structure of the ecclesiastical body." Moreover, Cyprian was on one point logically right as against the majority of the bishops, in maintaining that to concede to the separatists the validity of their baptism was to concede to them a vital connection with the Church, notwithstanding their external severance. And it must be confessed that not only Romanists and Anglicans but also Presbyterians and Independents, as Sir Harry Vane accused the representatives of those bodies in his own time, have fallen into the error of Cyprian, "preferring the Church in name, show, and outward order," to the truth and life of Christianity.

In Cyprian's view truth derives all its value from "ecclesiastical unity," that is to say, its connection with the regular line of bishops: "Know that, in the first place, we ought not to be inquisitive as to what he teaches, so long as he teaches *out of the pale.*" (Epist. lx.) His mode of evading the force of St. Paul's noble declaration:—"Some, indeed, preach Christ even of envy and strife. . . . What then? notwithstanding, every way, whether in pretence or in truth, Christ is preached; and I therein do rejoice, yea, and will rejoice;" is very characteristic of the logic and the hermeneutics of himself and his school. He dismisses it with the observation that Paul is "not speaking of heretics and their baptism," but of some that "entertained malice and dissension." As if a great Apostolic principle were only applicable to the occasion which called for its utterance, and as if "malice and dissension" were not the very virus of schism! But the real gravamen of Novatian's irregularity in Cyprian's view, as compared with that of men who perverted the Gospel into a means of adding affliction to the Apostle's bonds, is indicated by the comparison drawn by the eager bishop: "It is one thing for those who are within the Church to speak in the name of Christ, another thing for those who are without, acting against the Church, to baptize in the name of Christ." (Epist. lxxiii. 12.) As if it were not at least as competent to an Apostle to unchurch malicious dissentients, who still preached Christ, as to a bishop to unchurch a wrongheaded dissentient who still preaches Christ. But to preach Christ in rancorous dissent was a very venial fault, according to Cyprian, compared with baptizing in misguided dissent; for on Cyprian's principles what comparison can there be between the importance of preaching Christ and baptizing?

Cyprian's syllogism, on which Popish High-Church principles (so-called) are based is very simple: There is no salvation outside the Church; but such and such an organization and succession is the Church—that and no other: Therefore, there is no salvation outside such and such an organization and succession: — a bare and bold assumption, without any scriptural basis whatsoever, but directly contradictory to the teaching of Christ and His Apostles. But the fundamental errors of High-Church principles is that the individual believer does not obtain salvation—pardon and renewal—directly from Christ, and does not *hold* directly on Christ, but can only approach Christ at first, and abide in Christ continually through clerical ministrations, and consequently that the Church confers salvation in such wise that, without clerical officiation, salvation is impossible. The Church, namely, the priesthood, was made an effectual barrier against immediate contact between the individual believer and his Saviour, as prohibitory to Christ as to the believer.

It would be grossly unjust to Cyprian to suppose that he deliberately faced all the logical consequences of his positions. Logical laxity was one of his most inveterate mental habitudes : he would have felt no difficulty whatever in repudiating the most inevitable deductions from his premises. The two ingredients which he infused into the discussion of Church principles were those which, of all others, ought to have been resolutely excluded—precipitancy and dictatorialness. He never realized the obvious applications of his dogma which were made by the usurping priesthood in after times. The true problem of Church-government never presented itself to his mind—the combination of collective force with individual freedom in the highest possible degree. Hence, with serene unconsciousness, he sowed the seed which afterwards ripened into Popery. Instead of basing the Church upon a rock, he based it upon a figment—the exclusive priestly functions and rights of the Christian ministry, and the limitation of grace and selection to their manual and labial officiations. The practical mischievousness of his writings on Church principles it is scarcely possible to exaggerate. Not only did smaller men follow his lead, and treat his writings as he treated the Scriptures, with an egotistic ecclecticism, picking out what they liked, and ignoring what they did not like ; but far greater men than himself— St. Augustine, for example—quoted his dogmas as classical and even as authoritative.

But nothing could be more condemnatory of the tone and temper of Cyprian and his contemporary party and subsequent copyists towards the earnest separatists of his day, than his own lofty notions of the motherhood of the Church. How unlike a grave and tender mother, to disown and pursue with a maternal malediction, because of a mistaken jealousy for the sanctity of the homestead and the purity of the hearth !

This eager application of the lancet and the knife was not the likeliest way to facilitate "the revulsion of the extravasated blood into its proper channels."* Thus this noble-natured, hero-hearted man did the Christianity he loved the enormous disservice of distinctly articulating that evil doctrine of hierarchical mastership in the Church, which has acted like an uncouth spell. He also promulgated the kindred dogma that irregularity of episcopal succession is a worse evil than episcopal mercilessness and rapacity. His rigidly symmetrical theorizing and his impetuous humour equally incapacitated him for smoothing out the tangle. He is the slave of selected metaphors and unilateral maxims, and only half-sees, when he sees at all, scriptural illustrations and axioms.

But, although to a terrible extent, fictitious, Judaistic, and even Pagan notions of the clergy, and the Sacraments, and consequently of the Church had fastened themselves on the "minds of the leading Church officials, yet to some there was still open vision." This appears from a truly monumental though much overlooked work, a counterblast to Cyprian's Treatise *De Unitate*, an anonymous contemporary treatise *On Rebaptism*. Whilst paying due deference to the talents of Cyprian, the author puts his finger firmly on the weak points of the style and temperament of that picturesque polemic. He describes him as "gifted with the arrogance of heretics . . . renowned, amongst those who are most similar and agreeable to himself as having corrected the errors and vices of all the churches." With admirable thoroughness and precision he investigates the Scripture doctrine of Baptism. He demonstrates from the Gospels and Epistles that Baptism is not essential to salvation in the same sense that repentance and faith are : that the *contingency* of missing Baptism "cannot take away salvation from a believing and penitent man."

Cyprian's adherents in the Seventh Council of Carthage re-echoed

* Stillingfleet's *Irenicum*.

his outspoken sacerdotalism. The bishop of Tuberto, said :—"Water sanctified in the Church *by the prayer of the priest* washes away sin." This baptism is called, not *Christ's* baptism, but "the Church's baptism;" and "ecclesiastical baptism," not *Christian* baptism.

Cyprian's Church theory was further manipulated by Optatus. He distinguishes, however, between the ornaments and dowry of the Church "*ornamenta*" and "*dotes*," and her holy members and vitals, *sancta membra ac viscera.* The former he makes the throne of Peter. These are, (1), the episcopate, in the person of every bishop; (2), the Holy Spirit (*Spiritus Sanctus*), Who is made merely a part of the *trousseau* of the Bride of Christ; (3), baptism (*fons*); (4), the seal on the fountain. So the members and vitals of the Church are not the believers, but the sacraments and the names of the Trinity.

Then came the great champion of the High-Church, Broad-Church theory, Augustine. The whole of Augustine's writings against the Donatists, who formed the great secession of his time, amount to a cool and clever, but not the less unconscious begging of the main question in dispute. He was to the full extent as one-sided as they.

His theory as set forth in his controversial writings and in his didactic treatise, or rather, discursive Epic, "The City of God," divides mankind into three sections : 1. *The real Church* composed of the numerical aggregate of the elect, whether at present within the visible Church or without it, whether for the time being Catholic, heathen, or heretic; 2. *The visible Church*, according to his nomenclature "the framework of unity," consisting, in its vast majority, of reprobates, foredoomed from eternity to everlasting perdition; 3. The rest of mankind, who are neither elect nor "within the outward framework of unity." What conceivable satisfaction could there be to Christ Himself or Augustine, in a Kingdom emphatically "of this world," a nominal earthly empire of Christ, embracing a comparatively few loyal subjects, and countless multitudes of pretended adherents utterly disloyal in heart, and myriads of them open rebels in life? and yet this had for the imagination of Augustine an irresistible charm.

The truth is—that he shaped his theory according to the actual state of "the outward framework," and those whom it enclosed at the time of his conversion. This is plain from his argument that Noah's ark was a type and prophecy of the Church. He urges that the correspondence between the tenants of the ark and the members of the Church, of his own day, as comprising "clean and unclean," is so palpable as to afford a key to the spiritual meaning of the whole structure.

Thus Christ's rule, even in His Church, was to be a *rule in the midst of His enemies;* and the Church, as an institution, was to be, in the main, not the representation of Christianity, but a gross and ghastly misrepresentation. The numeric majority of her children where yet in bondage to corruption and condemnation; the children not of God, but of the devil. The Church, as a visible, recognisable institution, was not to represent the real Church, the body of Christ, but to belie it. So widely apart was Augustine's notion of the Church, as an institution, from that of the Acts and the Epistles.

According to the New Testament, the Church was to correspond to the sincere individual Christian, being, as yet, imperfect, but striving after perfection; for a time the battle field of the Flesh and the Spirit, but in *its main characteristics* presenting a beautiful and striking contrast to society outside its pale. Augustine's exaggerated distinction, antithesis, contrast, between the real Church and the visible; the Church as a spiritual fact, and the Church as an institution of which the History might be written, is itself in contrast with the ideas of the Apostles and St. Luke. He is angry with the spiritual insight of the Donatists, which can see Christ in the prophecies of the Old Testament, but cannot recognise in Christ's rule of the nations with a rod of iron, a forepicturing of His administration of His Church, or in His grant of the heathen for His inheritance an authoritative pronouncement that baptized heathenism was to be the principal constituent of society in the City of God (*De Correctione Donatistarum*,) Chap. i. 3). "Jerusalem from above is" no longer "free," but the vast majority of her children are in bondage. Of what use is her fecundity if as to the majority of her children she "gendereth to bondage ?" Instead of *endeavouring to keep the unity of the Spirit in the bond of peace,* even when outward union was for a time dissevered, he would maintain the union of "the framework" in the chain of brute force welded by the secular power (*Ib.*, *passim*). The reverentially rejoicing service which Kings and Judges are required to pay to the Son, is in Augustine's view the forcing unwilling subjects into the banqueting-hall of Christ, without appetite or Wedding garment, and compelling men to come in at the point of the sword. Nebuchadnezzar is the pattern for Christian rulers : " Why," he exclaims, " may not the Church by main force compel her lost children to return ?"—*Cur ergo non coget Ecclesia, etc.* (*Ib.* Chap. vi. 23.) His picture of the good Shepherd bringing back *the lost* sheep is not as carrying it on His shoulder rejoicing, but driving it back to the fold " by the terrifying crack or even the smart of the whip.* (*Ib.*) He exults that "men were forced into the Catholic communion by the laws of former emperors :"—*Per priorum Imperatorum, etc.* The Apostolic readiness to revenge all disobedience by " weapons—not carnal " may be understood without absurdity,—*non absurde intelligetur,* as justifying the use of carnal weapons by the *Civil authorities* to enforce a hollow outward union a "feigned reconciliation." (*Ib.*, Chap. vii. 24, 25—30.) This he pleasantly terms " a sort of medicinal molestation."† So the tender mercies of " Mother Church " are cruel. He justifies the application of brute force to the Donatists by reasoning which implies that the transference of a person from the Donatist to the Catholic Communion would be his rescue from eternal death.

Augustine justly states the matter in dispute : " The question between us is, Where is the Church ?" And his own very diffuse answer to the question amouts to this : *The Church is co-extensive with all the evangelized nations.* Catholic unity is the unity of all nations, 'the unity of the whole world.'" (*Answer to Petilian,* Bk. ii., Chap. lxxiii. 104 ; lxxviii. 174 ; xcvii. 221, 222, *et passim.*) He distinctly implied that external unity was of greater importance to the Church Catholic, than unity of faith and life, than doctrinal or ethical purity. " Dissension and division make you heretics ; but peace and unity make Catholics." (*Ibid,*

---

* *Flagellorum terroribus, vel etiam doloribus.*

† *Quædam Medicinalis Molestia.*

Chap. xcv. 219.) "*Dissensio, etc.*" He pronounces all seceders accursed, irrespective of their faith or unbelief, holiness or licentiousness. (*Ibid*, Chap. xcvii. 221.) He deduced his doctrine of promiscuous inclusiveness within an external unity from our Lord's declaration, "Ye shall be witnesses unto Me . . . unto the uttermost parts of the earth.;" and charged the Donatists with giving Christ the lie, because they could not see that this involved the right of men of abandoned lives to membership in the fellowship of the saints. It was quite natural and consistent that one who thought "the framework of unity" of infinitely greater importance to the Catholic Church than holiness of life, should advocate compulsory uniformity, rivetted by the point of the sword. And yet this being within "framework" for which he is so jealous, is not to be "within the framework of the Church, which grows through connection and contact between members—the members of Christ . . . for that Church is founded on a rock."* The Catholic Church of Augustine, then, is built mainly on the sand, and only touches the rock at certain points; yet he (not needlessly) disclaims the wish "that ecclesiastical discipline should be neglected, and that anyone should be allowed to do exactly whatever he may wish." *Neque hoc, etc.* (*Ibid*, Bk. iii., Chap. iv. 5.) What that discipline was he does not explain, but it plainly did not include expulsion from the Church for gross and incorrigible immorality, since he denounces everything of the kind, and regards the tenancy of office in the Church by openly and habitually wicked persons as essential to the very idea and ground-plan of the Catholic Church ; otherwise there would be no meaning in the injunction to provide room in the ark for unclean beasts, as well as clean. But he unfortunately reversed the numerical proportions of the clean and unclean in Christ's Church, taking the clean by couples and the unclean by sevens : moreover, he did not provide separate dens for the beasts of prey, stalls and cribs for the peaceful and the serviceable.

Augustine also commits that most mischievous error of implicitly substituting "the framework of unity" for God, in his argument

* *Cont. Lit. Petiliani*, Bk. ii., Chap. cviii. 247. *Ipsi autem non sunt, etc.*

from Scripture. Thus, as a reason why a person converted to God by the preaching of a Donatist should by no means join the Donatist community, but at once betake himself to the, "according-to-the-whole-world Church;" he urges, "Neither is he that planteth anything . . . but God," not perceiving that his *argument* identifies "the framework" with God, or substitutes it for God; otherwise what could such an acute dialectician see in his own argument? You were converted under a Donatist preacher; but God alone is the efficient cause of conversion: *Therefore* (one would think), God works with Donatist preachers. But the Augustinian syllogism is: You were converted to God by a Donatist preacher: But God alone converts: *Therefore*, join the Catholic Church. How so? Thus:—

A converted man is bound to connect himself, not with the instrumental, but the efficient cause of His conversion:

But God, and not the Donatist preacher was the efficient cause of your conversion:

Therefore, join the Catholic Church. Do you see it now? No, I have not yet found the Catholic Church, either in your major or your minor premiss. How, then, does it get into your conclusion? Well, try again:

It is your duty to join that which is the efficient cause of your conversion:

But it is your duty to join the Catholic Church. Therefore, the Catholic Church is the efficient cause of your conversion.

Again, he incessantly calls this "framework of unity," "the unity of Christ;" although he has avouched over and over again that it is no such thing, but that the unity of Christ is the unity of life in Christ. In his *City of God*, he sometimes represents the outward Church as the body of Christ, and membership in it as membership of Christ's body.

But forthwith he changes his front, and confounds "the framework" with the real living body, *e.g.*, "The man who is cut off from *the body of Christ*, who is righteous, can in nowise retain the spirit of righteousness, even if he retain the form of membership which he receives when in the body. Let them, therefore, come into the framework of the body."

He incessantly writes, as if charity and conformity were one and the same thing, and makes the external union identical with the "unity of the Spirit." "Deservedly you must perish, unless you come over to Catholic unity." (*De Correct.*, Donatist, Chap. x. 43 : *Merito si in unitatem, etc.*) How so, if we believe in Christ and live christianly ? "*Because all this without charity profiteth nothing.*" In vain .he sought to take out the splinter of sectarianism from the eye of his opponents, whilst himself blinded with the beam of bigotry.

Donatism, like Novatianism, in its principles, viewed apart from the occasion of the secession, was a vehement reaction against the shameful connivance at profligacy of life amongst members of the Church. (See especially Milman's *History of Christianity*, Vol. ii., p. 298, edition 1867.) The Catholics, instead of admitting and endeavouring to reform the disgraceful laxity of church discipline, defended it by a resolutely one-sided interpretation of Scripture. In this case, as in the Novatian controversy, and so often since, the sacerdotal party was the party of indiscriminate inclusion — High-Church and Broad-Church were identical. The idealistic Donatist-theory of a Church absolutely perfect in all its members was as unscriptural as that of Augustine, that the tolerance of notoriously wicked livers in the Church is its normal and ideal condition, as set forth in type, prophecy, and parable.

Augustine, we have seen, does not advocate the absolute abandonment of Church discipline. He even intimates *excommunication** as one of its functions. But for what crime he would permit excommunication it is difficult to conceive. He urgently postpones the purity of the Church to the peace of the Church. His rule amounts to this: Make the Church as pure as you can, without violating "the peace of unity."† He would still allow any number of unmistakable goats to be, not only in the pasture, but also in the fold, rather than make a disturbance in turning them out.

Archbishop Trench says, "Augustine affirmed the *identity* of the Church now existing with the final and glorious Church ; but he denied that the two were co-extensive." (*Parables*, p. 85.)

---

* *Ad. Don., post Coll.* v.   † *Ib. Salva unitatis pace.*

But Augustine's theory of the Church was by no means so sound and coherent as it looks in the hands of his erudite expositor. The Archbishop says : " He did not affirm two Churches, but two conditions of one and the same Church." The fact is, Augustine repeatedly distinguishes, not only between the existing Church and the final and glorious Church, but between the existing Catholic Church and the existing real Church ; though he often confounds the one with the other. He alternately distinguishes and confounds them according to the exigences of his argument, or the set of the current of his rhetoric, or distinguishes and confounds them in the self-same passage. Thus (*De Baptismo*, Lib. vii., li. 99) : " Some there are in the house of God, after a manner of speaking, so as not to be of the very fabric of the house *which* is said to be built upon a rock, *which* is called the one dove, *which* is the beauteous bride without spot or wrinkle, and a garden enclosed, a fountain sealed, a well of living water, a paradise of pomegranates ; *which* house also received the keys, and the power of binding and loosing." Here he distinctly claims for the real body of Christ, the spiritual Church, all " the glorious things spoken " in Scripture of the " City of God ;" to the exclusion of those whose connection with the Church is superficial, unreal, and merely nominal, or as if *by courtesy*, " in a manner." And this clearly involves a distinction between the true, the holy Church and the Catholic Church, "the Church diffused throughout all the world."

Trench rightly states the practical bearing of Augustine's teaching both as to its matter and its motive. " He would retain in the Church *open* offenders who *from their numbers* could not, without greater evils ensuing be expelled." (Parables, p. 85.) Where does Christ, or where do His Apostles, make the "numbers" of "open offenders" a reason why they should be retained in His Church ? This is palpably to prefer numbers to sanctity, and the empty boast of bigness to the real glory and commanding influence of holiness. Did the *fewness* of " the names in Sardis, which" had " not defiled their garments" exculpate, in the flaming eyes of the Head of the Church, the negligence of the too facile angel ?

The fact is, that Augustine adjusted his theory to the actual condition of the Catholic Church of his time. Discipline had been so neglected that the moral decency of the Church could only be recovered at a numerical sacrifice, too humbling for an imagination elated with the reversal of the relative position of Christianity and Paganism from a statistical point of view. The temple of God had already, to an appalling extent, been polluted with Augean filth; and Augustine found it easier to wield the herculean club of polemical interpretation than to turn the stream of holy discipline through the contaminated Church. And so the visible purity of the Church was immolated at the shrine of its numerical greatness.

The larger the "numbers of open offenders," surely the more urgent the need for the vindication of the moral strictness of the Church. This adjustment of the Church-theory to a degenerate and disorderly condition of the Church, Trench euphemistically describes as "the bringing out into her own clear consciousness that which hitherto she had implicitly possessed, yet had not worked out into a perfect distinctness even for herself." (*Ib.*, p. 89.) In plain English, no one before Augustine had dared to claim for *open* wickedness vested rights in the Church of Christ.

Thus "the Catholic Church" diverted her indignation from "open" wickedness in her adherents to spend it all on right-believing and well-living Nonconformity. Trench himself lets out the secret of Augustine's theory and his own: "Long custom had too much reconciled to the mournful spectacle." (*Ib.*, p. 94.) "Without greater evils ensuing!" What evils greater than centuries of corruption? Yet, after putting forth Augustine's interpretation as the doctrine of the Church, Trench allows "the exercise in the meantime of godly discipline, and where that has become necessary, absolute exclusion from Church fellowship." (P. 99.) But what has become of *godly discipline*, when "open offenders," by virtue of their "numbers," and a new version of the Parable of the Tares, are not only permitted a place in the Church, but have their tenancy defended as the normal and Christ-decreed condition of His Church? And what renders "absolute exclusion necessary," if open offending do not?

Then, again, Augustine changes his front. In defence of the

validity of the ministrations of ungodly men, he puts forth the noblest evangelical maxims :

" Why do you not allow that Christ is always the Head of the Christian, that the Christian always plants his root in Christ. Whether a man receive the sacrament from a faithful or a faithless Minister, his whole hope is in Christ." "Christ is always the Origin of the regenerate and the Head of the Church." "My Origin is Christ; my Root is Christ; my Head is Christ." "The seed of which I am born again is the Word of God." Again, "The believer is not justified by the man by whom he is baptized, but by Him of Whom it is written, 'To him that believeth on Him that justifieth the ungodly, etc.,'" (*Cont. lit. Petilian*, Lit. iii., Cap. xxxvii. 42.) "For purifying and justifying he (the Minister) is nothing ; seeing that this is not accomplished . . . . except by Him of Whom it was said, 'Purifying their hearts by faith.'"

Sometimes he sharply distinguishes between the true Church and the external ; *e. g.*, to the question, "Are not they in the Church who are on the rock ; and they who are not on the rock, not in the Church ?" He regards our Lord's saying in Matt. vii. 24, as decisive. Salvation by external Church membership was utterly alien from the creed, and the convictions of Augustine. And yet whilst making his loose exposition of the Parables of the Tares and the Draw-net the law of Church discipline, he would have people driven to the Lord's Supper at the point of the secular sword.

The difference in his view between a worldly Churchman and a heretic was that the former was in "secret," the latter in "open separation :" *Sive occultis, sive apertis.* (*Ib.*, Lib. v., Cap. xxvii. 38.) He testifies that "the unrighteous so long as he is unrighteous, cannot have the salvation of which baptism is the sacrament." Yet he did not shrink from avowing, on the authority of Cyprian, that undisguised Anti-Christs may be retained as accredited members of the Church.

Augustine's notion of extra-conditional or pre-conditional election tended still further to complicate his theory of the Church. He includes in the Church elect heretics and heathens who are not yet converted. *Multi etiam quidem, etc.* (*De Bap.*, Lib. v., Cap. xxvii. 38.) It is in this sense that he pronounces the judgment which I have heard a pious Ultramontanist apply to pious Protestants as contrasted with ungodly Roman Catholics. "Many who seem to be without (the Church) are within, and many who seem to be within are without:" *Multi qui foris, etc.* (*Ib.*)

In his notion, the oneness of the baptism consisted in the sameness of the formula, and the external element—water,—and of the inexplicable something—not saving grace—which was inseparably connected with the formula accompanied by the application of water. This something was, he maintained, dormant or deadly in the schismatic, but "began to profit to salvation"—*incipit prodesse*, etc.—on his entering "the Catholic Church." (*Ib.*, Lib. v., Cap. xxviii.) Thus his idea of the *opus operatum*, in some respects corresponds, in others contrasts, with the "High-Church" fancy. Along with the Roman Catholic and the Romanizing Anglican, he believed in what Neander styles "a mystico theurgic" element in Baptism. It had *some* necessary effect on heretics and worldly churchmen alike, but no beneficial effect on either. He expressly and repeatedly restricts the power of forgiving sins to "the good children,"—*bonis filiis* (*Ib.*, Lib. vi., Cap. i, *et passim*), whilst the goodness or badness of the officiation had no effect whatever on the communication of the indefinable deposit conveyed by baptism. Yet he hesitated to regard baptism as a mere spell, like "the word which split Eildon hills in three,"—or a sort of Christian fetish. He awaits "the declaration of God's judgment through the medium of some revelation" to determine whether baptism be valid "if done as a farce, or a comedy, or a jest." In his vocabulary the "validity" of baptism implied much more than its due authorization, and was by no means limited to members of the main body of the Church.

But the Donatists were not content with Augustine's vague, indefinable, nobody-knows what baptismal grace. They sensibly assumed that in Christianity everything is real and realizable; that the baptizer and the baptized should be able to state plainly what the advantage of his baptism is, and not be reduced to reply as Augustine, in effect, does: "Really, I cannot tell you, but it *must* be something, otherwise Christ would not have ordained the rite."

Whether the palm of unyieldingness and uncharitableness

belonged to Cyprian and Augustine, on the one side, or to the Novatians and Donatists on the other, it were hard to determine. It was an agony of one-sidedness and immoderateness : and although the "Catholics" being the majority, and having secured the championship of the civil power, remained in possession of the field, they did not owe their victory to truer methods of Biblical interpretation or to charity and good-temper. It should also be remembered that the "Catholics" had the telling of the story, the working of the telegraph wires of history. Wesley's caveat applies strongly to the case of the Novatians and the Donatists : "No branch of Ecclesiastical History is so difficult, on account of the injurious treatment that has been shown to the heads of religious sects, and the unfair representations which have been given of their tenets. (*Ecclesiastical History, Introduction*, p. 13.) " I have sometimes doubted whether both Novatian and his doctrine have not been greatly misrepresented, whether he was not himself one of the holiest men who lived in that century." (*Ib.*, Vol. i., p. 145.) As to the state of the Church in Cyprian's time, he writes : " The main body of Christians went as far in all ungodliness and unrighteousness as the heathens themselves." (*Ib.*, p. 130.)

To what an extent a passionate tenderness for the external union of the Church may blind an acute and generous intellect appears from the fact that Augustine could not see that orthodox seceders may yet be members of Christ's body, whilst he was capable of enunciating such truly Catholic sentiments as some already quoted, and the following : "Nor, nevertheless, does that which is perverse in them nullify all things which are right, but rather it is reduced to nothing by them ; even as in the man of good hope and trusty faith, who nevertheless is but a man, if in anything he be otherwise minded, what he sees aright is not thereby neutralized, until God reveal that also to him in which he is otherwise minded."—*Sicut in ipso homine, etc.* (*De Bap.*, Lib. vi., Cap. xxv. 47.)

Yet the more orthodox the seceders were, the holier, the more devoted to Christ, so much the worse he made them out to be. How so ? asks Petilian. " By their fruits ye shall know them," replies Augustine. (Cont. Lib. Pet. Lib. ii., Cap. lxxiii. 164.) The interlocutions between him and Petilian amount to this :—

T

Augustine: I assure you that these sweet, blooming bramble-berries, which I admit would be grapes of the finest quality, worthy of the chelic of the Heavenly King, if they only grew within the Catholic enclosure, are not grapes at all, but poisonous brambles, inasmuch as they grow outside.

Petilian: *Catholic* enclosure! I thought "Catholic" was a word of the widest inclusiveness. Your assumption of the word "Catholic," as a term of exclusion to distinguish yourselves from thousands of believers whom you do not deny to be as good *Christians* as yourselves, besides being an arrogant assumption, is a flat contradiction in terms. By limiting the Church to your own party, you constitute yourselves a schism. What does *Catholic* mean, if not καθ' ὅλον, *according to the whole?*

Augustine: I know as well as you do that Catholic means *according to the whole:* that is, the *whole* of the *Catholics*. But you are not Catholic.

Petilian: Am I to understand then that, if the branches of the true vine "run over the wall," they forthwith become brambles?

Augustine: Clearly.

Petilian: Make that appear.

Augustine: "By their fruits ye shall know them!"

Petilian: I always took that saying of our Lord to mean that the fruit determines the classification of the tree; that a vine is recognisable as a grape-producing tree.

Augustine: Just the opposite. Grapes that grow outside the vineyard are bramble-berries. Our Lord Himself determined that, when He said "a tree is known by its fruits."

Petilian: But to my poor apprehension you reverse the Master's decision and assert that fruits and tree are known by the ground on which they grow.

Augustine: "I should not be able to find any means of refuting you, unless I should either laugh at you as joking, or grieve over you as mad; . . . and since I do not think you to be in a merry mood—you see the alternative."* (*Cont. Lit. Pet.* ii., xxxviii. 91.)

The indictment against this great and holy man, Augustine,—the most vigorous and eager intellect of his age, is very heavy.

---

* *Non invenirem, etc.* (See also Cap. lxxiii. 163.)

He set the evil example of adjusting the theory of the Church to its actual condition, instead of striving lawfully to recover its primitive discipline and rehabilitate its moral order. He formulated into dogma the pitiful excuses by which negligent Church-overseers had attempted to palliate their unfaithfulness. Thus custom was made to consecrate corruption, until the subtle curse of Timon of Athens fastened on the City of God, and its

> "Degrees, observances, customs, and laws,"
> *Declined " to their confounding contraries."*

The Church ceased to be a

> " Mother severe of infinite delights,"

and became a doting and relentless beldame, humouring the naughtiness of those of her children who flattered and adored her, and pursuing with remorseless vengeance those who testified against her vices, and would not be party to her crimes.

And the process by which Augustine defended Church abuses was scarcely less depraving to the Church than the defence itself, namely, an adroit manipulation of Scripture, and an unequal "handling" of "the Word of God :" an ungentle treatment of parable and prophecy, the resolute or reckless protrusion of some passages and suppression of others.

Many tap-roots of the Upas-tree of the Papacy spread widely in the writings of this eloquent and earnest man. He did not venture to apply to baptism, apart from repentance, faith, and confession, the passages of Holy Writ which refer to baptism connected with repentance, faith, and confession; but he so far travelled out of the record as to teach that some undefinable infusion was conveyed to the baptized infant, by virtue of the pronounced formula and the applied water, without which regeneration and salvation were impossible. Of course, his disciples would not stop short here. They very naturally wished to be able to tell parents what this mystic communication to their children really was—hence the various theories of Baptismal Regeneration. Thus Augustine's great scholar, Hooker, makes it to be "that infused Divine virtue of the Holy Ghost which giveth to the powers of the soul their *first disposition* towards *future* newness of life,"*—thus making baptismal grace an infusion conveying an impulsion and giving a new bias, but not "newness of life." And each ecclesiastical theorist has his own hypothesis as to what this is of which no trace is discernable, either in the consciousness or the character of the recipient, being received unconsciously and antecedently to the development of character. But the root of the heresy is the attributing, without Scripture warrant, *something* or other to the *opus operatum*, independent of the repentance, faith, and confession of the recipient.

Augustine took equal liberties with the Lord's Supper. He stopped far short, indeed, of teaching, even by implication, that the Sacraments would compensate or condone the want of holiness of heart and life; but he degraded the Lord's Table by urging the civil magistrate to drive people to it at the point of the sword, and by giving the negative to St. Paul's appeal: "Is it not the *communion* of the body . . . the blood of Christ?" He denied that conjoint participating in the Lord's Supper implies fellowship, communion, or concord at all, on the strength of the assumption that Judas was present at its institution. Augustine held that the Sacrament was of no more benefit to the worldly professor than it was to Judas, on the supposition that he ever partook of it: on the contrary, it aggravated his damnation; and yet he would have him compelled to take it, that is, compelled to aggravate his damnation, under whatever penalties the Civil magistrate could be induced to bring to bear upon him. The presence of the worldly professor he admitted to be of no service to the Church, but of vast disservice and disgrace; excepting that it swelled the numbers of the Church, as Judas made up the Apostolic compliment of twelve. He did not assign to the Lord's Supper, as to baptism, any mystico-theurgic element. He maintained that there was no salvation away from the main body of the Church, and no salvation in connection with the main body without faith and holiness. But if, in baptism, some infusion takes place by virtue of the formula, and the application of water, irrespective of the consciousness and character of the recipient, why not in the other Sacrament? If membership in the main body of the Church is to be enforced by the most formidable penalties temporal and

* *Ec. Pol.* v., lx. 2.

spiritual, then surely it must have some intrinsic value; not merely to aggravate the damnation of those who join out of sheer deference to civil and ecclesiastical authority and power. Thus Augustine prepared the way for the dogma of salvation by sacraments and by priestly officiations.

Again, his theory, by its denial of salvation to sincere and devoted believers in Christ who were associated with some other than the original line of bishops, and by claiming for those who were connected with that line exclusively the title of the Church, traced the outline of the High-Church hypothesis, which links all the powers and privileges of the Church to the unbroken line of bishops; whilst, by "preaching the Church" where the Apostles preached Christ as the direct and only object of faith, the trust of the soul, if not formally transferred from Christ to the Church, was effectually arrested by the obtrusion of the Church between the soul and its Saviour.

But Augustine's writings have still more effectively built up the Broad-Church theory, and have mightily conduced to the perilous confusion between the Church as a privileged spiritual society on the one hand, and a more or less evangelized community on the other, of whom the great mass are still in heart and practice, "alienated from the life of God." In the coolest manner he deprives of all significance those Apostolical appeals, descriptions, directions and remonstrances which have no force whatever but in the fact that the Church, *as an institution*, is the intimate association of the faithful in separation from the worldly; and he yet claims for his promiscuous aggregation the right to be the custodian of salvation. In order to save the sanctity of the Church, he denied that the "Catholic Church" was the real body of Christ, and then, that he might deny salvation to the secessionists, he demanded for that which was not the body of Christ, on the ground of a hypothetical holiness, all the exclusive rights and royalties of the real Bride.

Because the Church, as yet, is not "without spot or wrinkle or any such thing," and yet is Christ's Betrothed, being in process of cleansing "with the washing of water by the Word," Augustine represents unsightly and offensive ulceration, premature corrugation and every such thing as, if not the normal, yet the foredoomed condition of the visible Church; and in some way essential to its visibility.

The fact that the parable of the Draw-net instructs "fishers of men," that the urgency and freeness of the Gospel invitation and summons are not to be checked by fear lest some should pervert the grace of God to their own destruction, or the frivolous and worldly should get entangled in the meshes of evangelistic appliances, we are surely not to assume that the meshes of the Church-net must be so wide apart as to leave the fish at liberty to swim in and out at pleasure, and to belong to the two contrasted societies of the Church and the world at the same time? But Augustine's theory amounts to that.

Cyprian, Optatus and Augustine made no distinction between town and territory in the Christian commonwealth, between the city of God, and its unenclosed suburbs. Doubtless, there is in Broad-Churchism, as in High-Churchism, an element of truth. In some systems of theology the relations between nature and grace have been unskilfully and unscripturally stated. There is an evangelical side of Broad-Churchism. A country, the immense majority of whose population are baptized, and Christian by profession, must have some special relationship to God corresponding to their enlightment and consequent responsibilities. Hence the Wesley's* and Cowper throw around our country theocratic associations not very unlike those which Keble connects with the Established Church. The saying which Shakespeare puts into the mouth of the Bishop of Carlisle is not without solemn force and tender significance:

> " O, forfend it, God,
> That, in a *Christian climate*, souls refined
> Should show so heinous, black, obscene a deed."
>
> *Richard II.*, Act IV., Scene 1.

But the application of the term Catholic or Churchman to every baptized person who owns the authority of the lineal episcopal Church, to which Augustine lent the prestige of his genius and piety, has resulted in the most monstrous absurdities. Voltaire, whilst known to be the head of a great conspiracy for the destruction of Christianity, and whilst attacking Christ Himself with the

* Hymns 82, 298, 546.

most rancorous fanaticism, is still none the less a Catholic, and as such receives the Sacrament. This fundamental absurdity throws the whole Church system *off the perpendicular*. Archbishop Whitgift, during the Elizabethan reconstruction of the English Establishment, laughs to scorn the demand for a restoration to the people of a voice in the election of their spiritual overseers; on the ground that so many "atheists" as well as other misbelievers and mislivers are members of the Church!

If the corporation which claims for itself exclusively the title of the Catholic Church were indeed Christ's veritable representative on earth, no wonder that the world does not believe.

Augustine, like his master, Cyprian, seemed incapable of putting a charitable construction on the acts of the seceders. And yet the "Catholic" party could not be more zealous for the glory of the Church than they. But the "Catholics" placed the glory mainly in numerical greatness and external union, the Novatianists and Donatists in its purity and the vital connection between the visible and the invisible Church; which the Catholic usage (and theory, adapted to that usage) was grievously weakening and endangering. And when the inevitable crisis came, and a stand was made against a policy which could not but come to that which it did come, that appalling corruption of the Church, the Papacy, Augustine set himself to defend, as best he might, the melancholy *status quo*, fancying a hollow state-enforced external union to be of greater value than the unity of the Spirit.

And this heterogenous accumulation of individuals of all sorts of character and course of life was declared to be the medium of salvation, not so much in the sense of a witness, a helper, an example and a guide, as the dispenser of mysteries and the consignee of grace; and was urged to persecute opponents.*

It is superfluous to add that the writings of St. Augustine abound in passages bearing a directly opposite aspect to the at once vague and narrow dogmas on which so much false Church theory

* "If we are willing to speak and perceive the truth, that is unjust persecution which the schismatics inflict on the Church of Christ, and that is just which the Church of Christ inflicts on the schismatics, and, moreover, the Church persecutes out of affection, the enemies out of rage." *Si ergo enim, etc.* (*De Corr. Donat.*, Cap. iii. 11.)

has been built.* The antidote often grows side by side with the poison. If his readers would take the one along with the other his teaching would be at least innocuous. What Keble says of certain passages in the Works of Hooker applies with equal force to Augustine and to all Protestant writers who have fashioned their Church-theories on his model. "If they are expressly or virtually contradicted by other passages of the same author, the utmost (? legitimate) effect of such contradiction must be to neutralize him in this controversy and make him unfit to be quoted on either side." (Pref. to Hooker's Works, p. lxxii.) Happy would it be if that were agreed to on all sides, and the Word of God be thus allowed an impartial hearing.†

No theologian has had so much influence as St. Augustine, especially in the construction of Church theories. His consummate dialectic skill; his daring, yet often tender, imaginativeness, and his lofty character and triumphant championship of some doctrines of Revelation, as well as the trouble-saving peace in-our-time convenience of his theory, readily account for this. Hence an authority has been thrust upon him not unlike that claimed by the Church of Rome, to be the decisive interpreter of Scripture; contradictory pronouncements, in the one case as in the other, being adopted or rejected as the emergency demands. Augustine's theory was espoused and acted on by Gregory the Great; he maintained that "the ungodly are the largest number in the Church." (Bk. xxxvi. 76.) He made the Church (not Christ) "the door." (Bk. v. 46.) He held that there was no salvation out of the visible—namely, his own section of, the Church. He admits, however, that "Holy Church, like Job, says some things right, and some things foolish."

Augutine conceded the name *Christians* to those believers whom he would neither include within the Church, nor allow salvation.

* *E.g.*, he admits that separation without schism is not inconceivable. "The sacrilege of schism most clearly hangs over them, *if they had not cause for separation.*"—*Apertissimum eminet, etc.* (*De Baptismo*, Lib. v., Chap. i. 1.)

† Augustine also followed the lead of Cyprian in degrading Christian controversy by the arts of the retained rhetorician. When hard pressed by an opponent or puzzled by an inquirer, he did not scruple to cover his retreat by a grim pleasantly or a gruff personality.

They are "anyhow Christians"—*quoquomodo Christiani*. (*De Cir. Die.*, xvii. 51.)

But in sound Scriptural conceptions of the Church he was far behind St. Chrysostom. Take, for example, St. Chrysostom's comments on "There is one body, one Spirit." "The body is not disjoined from the Spirit, for then would it not be a body. If there be one Head, then there is one body. To live without the head is impossible. The Church is nothing else but a house built of the souls of men. One body—one by *sympathy*."

At the Reformation, the great theological leaders adopted in the main the doctrinal system of St. Augustine, including his theory of the Church, adapted to the necessities of their own position.* Hence Calvin set up his miniature Theocracy at Geneva, enforcing on its population, by severe civil pains and penalties, strictness of living and accuracy of creed, assuming the identity of the Church and the State ; in one respect improving on his master, compelling baptized people to put on " Gospel-like behaviour" as well as to take the Supper of the Lord.

In England also the ablest writers on the Church borrowed Augustine's platform, with all its incongruities, which even Hooker did not reconcile or avoid. In fact, he extended that platform to fit the then-existing condition of England. He pronounces : " If by *external profession* they be Christians, then are they of the visible Church of Christ . . . and yea, although they be impious idolaters, wicked heretics, persons excommunicable, yea, and cast out for notorious improbity. Such withal we deny not to be the

---

* But the Reformers stoutly maintained that the perpetuity and continuity of the Church consists in the perpetuity and continuity of the confession of Christ in the world and the ministry of salvation. That it depends on the succession of bishops—they never imagined. The Marian martyrs derided the notion of salvation by sacraments ; the Elizabethan leaders, even Archbishop Whitgift, did not contend for the Divine right of Episcopacy. To Jewell, Reynolds, and Grindall, High-Church notions were utterly repugnant. Anglican High-Churchism was at first a mere polemical redoubt thrown up, to confront the Cartwright—Travers—dogma of the Divine right of Presbyterianism, by Bancroft and Bilson. (*The Perpetual Government of Christ's Church*, 1593-4), and shaped and fortified by Laud, Hammond, Leslie, etc.

imps and limbs of Satan." (*Ec. Pol.*, Bk. iii. 7.) Yet this same Church is ".a supernatural (?*preternatural*) society." If we ask whence he derives his notion of the Church, his reply is, " Church is a name which *art* hath devised thereby to sever and distinguish that society of men which professeth the true religion from the rest which profess it not." He also embraced Augustine's rule of compulsory attendance at the Table of the Lord ; and when it is urged that unwilling recipients, taking the Communion unworthily, eat and drink damnation, his reply savours strongly of the cynicism of the answer given by the Sanhedrin to Judas. " What is that to us ?" *

Field, too, in his great work *Of the Church*, although his starting point is distinctly Scriptural and evangelical, yet soon begins to build upon the basis of Augustine. His differentiation of the Church from all other societies is in perfect accordance with Holy Writ. "It is the work of grace and the heavenly calling that give being to the Church, and make it a different society from all other companies of men in the world." (Bk. i. 6.) To escape the confusions of his Gamaliel, he has a hypothesis of " degrees " of Church membership. He seems to have regarded the visibility of the Church as something like that of a revolving light, now brilliant, now hidden. (*Ib.*, 10.) He was far from thinking that Christ has left His Church at the mercy of the bishops. " Though, all others falling from the faith, the truth of God should continue only in some few of the Laity, yet the promise of Christ concerning the perpetuity of His Church might still be verified." (*Ib.*) Yet unhappily his own light also revolves ; he does not see steadily, but only intermittently, that the continuous visibility of the Church is its continued adherence to and experience of the fundamental facts of Christianity, and the perpetuity of Christian worship, teaching, ministerial oversight and corporate fellowship.

Ever and anon, when one thinks he has clean escaped, he gets entangled again in Augustine's net. In one passage he declares that the openly wicked are not of the Church ; in another he writes as if the wicked and the good were two distinct and diverse classes in the Church. He alternately disclaims the wicked and includes them, under some vague phrase, such as "in

---

* See *Ec. Pol.*, Bk. v. 8.

respect of the whole considered generally." (*Ib.*, 11.) Similarly, he affirms that "none of the privileges which Christ hath bestowed on His Church belong to the Church generally considered," that is, the Church as including openly wicked people; and yet he seems to imply that the office and work of the ministry, the dispensing of the word and sacraments, belongs to openly wicked clergymen if they be regularly inducted.

He happily diverges however from Augustine and Cyprian, by regarding orthodox separatists as still parts of the Church, "in respect of the profession of the whole saving truth of God, all outward acts of religion and Divine worship, power of order and holy Sacraments." (*Ib.*, 13.) Yet on this point, too, his concession is retractile, and his argument rotatory. One asks : Are openly wicked professors on the one hand ; and orthodox and Christianly living separatists on the other, members of the Church, or are they not ? His answer with regard to both amounts to this : In one sense they are, in another sense they are not. One asks next : Whether of the two senses is the one to be practically acted upon ? Are they to be recognised as members of the Church, or are they not ? Of orthodox separatists his answer really comes to this : They are either, neither, and both. They are in and out of the Church, more or less. As to the openly wicked, his answer is, in substance this : If things were as they ought to be, they would not be recognised : but then to turn so many out is too terrible to think of! One naturally asks in reply : Is it not more terrible to keep them in ?

In effect, he falls back on Agustine's policy : The openly wicked are to be expelled when they are not too numerous to be conveniently got rid of. And so, practically, they are left in the Church, and the "in some sort" of his premises is not to be found in his conclusion. But like his great predecessors on the same track, his self-refutation is complete.

The Scotch Kirk took its theology and Church principles from Augustine, as edited by Calvin, yet most jealously guarding the Headship of Christ. The pitiable perplexity into which its noblest minds were thrown by the incompatibility of their spiritual New Testament views of the Church with their hypothesis of a promiscuous Church-State is strikingly described by Dr. Walker, in his *Scottish Theology.*

All the confused and conflicting systems of Erastianism and Broad-Churchism, identifying the Church with the State, have grown out of the unauthorized doctrine of an indiscriminately inclusive Church; from Calvin's stern theocracy, compelling unregenerate professors to live as if they were regenerate, to "assume" Christian virtue, if they "have it not," and its imitations in Scotland and puritan America; to the Bunsen*-Arnold theory, which makes the coast-line the boundary of the English Church, and insists upon regarding a profligate or infidel Prime-Minister as a Church official, (He certainly exercises a lofty Church function in the appointment of the bishops); and the German programme, which makes the Church a department of the State, a cheap moral police.

I confess that the latest theory, that of Rothe, startling as it looks, seems to me the legitimate deduction from the assumption of the identity of a professedly Christian nation with the Church, —when viewed in the light of history. His suggestion is that, assuming the Church and the State, in "a Christian country" to be the same—the distinction being merely verbal, and altogether unreal, delusive, and embarrassing—the sensible and practical course would surely be to allow it to become obsolete, by simply merging Church into State, or State into Church. But seeing that no nation in its senses would again entrust its interests to a hierarchy wielding the powers of the State, the alternative is, to let this superfluous institution, the Church, evanish, like a ghost that scents the morning air. *Precisely:* if the distinction between the Church and the world be at an end, since the world is not at an end, either in the theological or the secular sense, then let the Church depart in peace.

Yet the ideal of Calvin, Hooker, Bunsen, Arnold, and other great men,—a Christianized State—will ultimately be realized, but not on their principles, nor on their plan. "The kingdoms of this world" shall yet "become the kingdoms of our God and of His Christ;" not by a system of *lying for God*, but by *conversions*.

But how sadly all these man-made hypotheses delay the consummation and protract the Church's warfare, it is easy to perceive.

---

* Bunsen, however, strove to correct the inherent evils of his hypothesis by giving vitality to the *congregation,—gemeinde.*

The influence of Augustine's teaching on ecclesiastical writers is still great.

It would scarcely be respectful to close this Essay without referring to the recent work of Dean Goulburn, entitled *The Holy Catholic Church*. It is unnecessary to say that this work contains much that is sound, scriptural, and truly Catholic and Apostolical in doctrine ; not unworthy of its author, one of the best preachers of the day, and a devotional writer, whose works are read with avidity and profit by many Nonconformists, at least, by many Methodists. But, alas ! a fond devotion to an arbitrary hypothesis betrays him into the most hazardous positions and the rudest self-contradictions. He lays much stress on the etymology of the word *Ecclesia*, but in his Church system forthwith leaves out the *ec*, and argues as if the word were simply *'clesia*. He pronounces it "certain" that the word "means, according to its etymology, a body *called out*" (p. 4) ; but in his subsequent reasoning, lets drop the *out*. He repudiates the phrase, " The invisible Church," affirming, " There is properly no such thing. The Church of Holy Scripture, whether under the Old or New Dispensation, is always a visible thing." (P. 2.) And yet he makes the visible Church to be the Draw-net before any discrimination takes place, and apart from the " vessels." This promiscuous assemblage of good and bad, then, is Christ's body, the fulness of Him that filleth all in all, " the bride of Christ !" He perceives that the Church is " a living organism ;" and yet insists that it is a corporation whose continuous existence depends upon a particular mode of inducting its principal officers ; that, in fact, the Church is left at the mercy of those officers, namely, the bishops : if they go wrong, all is lost. Had Nero been aware of this, and put to death all the bishops, the Church would have been extinct, the "living organism" would have become a defunct corporation. (Was it, then, the instinct of self-preservation, which kept the Church silent as to this terribly vulnerable point of its organism during the earlier ages of its history ?) He refers to " the charter of incorporation." He justly says, " the first thing which we have to look for is, the charter of the Church's foundation. Where do we find it ? Answer, in the following words, taken from

St. Matthew xviii. 19, 20 : 'Again I say unto you, That if two of you shall agree on earth as touching anything that they shall ask, it shall be done for them of My Father which is in heaven. For where two or three are gathered together in My name, there am I in the midst of them.'" (P. 124.) But not a word occurs there to intimate that the life of the Church is bound up in the unbroken line of its bishops. Its perpetuity, its invincible tenacity of life, its exhaustless recuperative energy is, in "the Charter of Incorporation," indissolubly connected with the presence of Christ. "Wherever two or three are gathered together in" His "Name."

Dean Goulburn, in fact, re-edits the old "fable" of Apostolical Succession. The cause between the Church of Christ and the lineal bishops is, in substance, this : Did Christ recall the privileges and powers which He at first guaranteed to His Church collectively, and its little local gatherings of "two or three" (Matt. xviii. 17—20), and vest them in the Apostles alone ? and, if so, on the demise of the Apostles, did those privileges and powers revert to the Church as a body, or were they conveyed by the Apostles to the bishops ; on such wise that, failing the line of bishops, the Church determines, and apart from that line the Church can have no existence ? Dean Goulburn decides for the bishops, but endeavours to soften the hardship to the Church by regarding the bishops as the representatives of the Church. He illustrates this by the House of Commons, but evidently does not think that the fact of the people having no longer, as at first, a voice in the election of their bishops, destroys the representative character of the latter. The grounds on which he rests this decision are as precarious as they are slender. He founds episcopal claims mainly on the ambiguous and misleading translation and inaccurate punctuation of a part of Acts ii. 42, which the A. V. renders, "They continued steadfastly in the Apostles' doctrine and fellowship." Now the accurate rendering of this passage is, as we have seen (Lecture p. 77), "They continued steadfastly in the doctrine of the Apostles, and in fellowship :" " of the Apostles " intervenes between doctrine and fellowship. By transposing " of the Apostles," altering the form of the genitive and omitting the comma, a different aspect is given to the text. In the Greek it is no more the Apostles' fellowship, than the Apostles' breaking of bread, or the Apostles' prayers.* And yet the worthy Dean makes this misrendering the very sheet anchor of his Church-theory, reiterating it unweariedly and inculcating it in his Catechism as the grand Key text of his system. (P. 40, *et passim*.) On p. 40, and subsequently, he makes fellowship as distinct from doctrine, synonymous with "the Christian Church;" thus classing the Christian Church amongst items of observance : breaking of bread and prayers.

The conclusion to which the Dean's principles conduct him are most admonitory ; namely, that the Church, to whose Mission of " Presenting, Exhibiting, and Defending the Truth," he devotes a chapter, may become so divorced from the Truth that God's people shall be reduced to the dilemma of forsaking either the one or the other: that this was in effect, the condition of affairs on the Continent at the Reformation ; England being saved from the terrible alternative by the fact that " the great majority of the existing Bishops and Clergy came round to the principles of the Reformation." (P. 42.) Hence Continental and Scottish Protestantism, as well as English Nonconformity is Churchless. The Dean quotes with grateful approprobation a royal epigram which puts the point with exquisite neatness. " The late King of Prussia is said to have observed that in Rome you see a Church without Christianity ; in the sects Christianity without a Church ; but that in England an attempt was made to maintain both— Christianity and the Church together. We are thankful for such a testimony." (P. 48.)

The Dean maintains that, "whatever may be alleged in favour of certain separatists at the Reformation, nothing can justify a refusal in this country to join the Church of England." (Pp. 43, 44.) But what does all this amount to, except that as to *all that, without which the Church can have no continuous existence*, the Church

---

* The enumeration of the eminent expositors who see that "fellowship" in the text has no special reference to the Apostles and is incapable of the meaning which Dean Goulburn assigns to it, would be almost endless. Suffice it to name, Bengel, Baumgarten, Neander, Lange, Whitby, Wordsworth, William Arthur, Alford, Barnes, Mosheim, Olshausen, Meyer.

of Rome and the Church of England are so much alike that you cannot distinguish the one from the other. What is this "one thing needful," which the Churches of Rome and of England have, and Scotch, and Continental, and American Protestants and English Nonconformist have not? "The bishops, who alone could confer holy orders, and thus continue the Apostles' fellowship." (P. 42.)

And what is *essential* to the making of a Bishop? Nothing but a regular mode of induction. St. Paul makes the whole value and validity of the succession to consist in the identity of the truths transmitted, and the fidelity and teaching power of the men entrusted with the transmission. "The same commit thou to faithful men, who shall be able to teach others." (2 Tim. ii. 2.) Dean Goulburn, on the contrary, admitting that the succession, without which, on his theory, there can be no Church, has comprised innumerable men most unfaithful and incompetent, who transmitted something very different from the Apostolic doctrine, yet maintains this does not in the slightest degree affect the validity and value of the episcopal succession; thus making non-essential, though, of course, desirable, the very elements on which alone the Holy Spirit insists.

I much regret that I have not left myself space for further examination of the Dean's hypotheses. I can only express wonder and regret that a doctrine so divisive and distancing, and involving consequences so appalling, should be founded upon such a flimsy basis; indeed, mainly on merely subjective inferences, such as "I am utterly at a loss to see" (p. 18); and our Lord "must have known" . . . to all which the sufficient answer is, "Who hath directed the Spirit of the Lord, or being His counsellor hath taught Him?" (Isaiah xl. 13.) We appeal to "the Charter of Incorporation."

ERRATUM.

P. 109, line 23, for "latter" read "lesser."

www.ingramcontent.com/pod-product-compliance
Lightning Source LLC
Chambersburg PA
CBHW031328230426
43670CB00006B/271